The History of Building Regulation in London

with an account of the

District Surveyors' Association

HENRY FITZALWINE KNIGHT,
Noble by Birth; a Free Brother of the Drapers Company and the first
LORD MAYOR of LONDON.
From an Original Painting at Drapers Hall. Grignion Sculp.

THE HISTORY OF BUILDING REGULATION IN LONDON 1189-1972

with an account of the District Surveyors' Association

by C.C. Knowles A.M.I.C.E.,
(District Surveyor from 1925 to 1955)

and

P.H. Pitt, C.Eng., F.I.Struct.E., A.R.I.C.S.
(District Surveyor)

Architectural Press, London

ISBN 0 85139 281 4

This edition first published 1972

*Set in Great Britain by Scarbutts Ltd. and printed by H. E. Warne Ltd.
London and St. Austell*

CONTENTS

I. The development of London and the first building regulations . . . . Page 3

II. London under the Tudors, 1485–1603. The first efforts to restrict the erection of new buildings. . . . . Page 12

III. London under the Stuarts and Commonwealth, 1603–1659. Restrictions on the erection of new buildings continued, and the birth of the London Building Acts. . . . . Page 18

IV. London under the Restoration. Charles II, 1650–1685. The great fire of London and the first comprehensive Building Act . . . . Page 26

V. Building Enactments, 1700–1774 . . . . Page 37

VI. The Administration of the Building enactments in 1774. Appointment of statutory surveyors. . . . . Page 44

VII. The nineteenth century. The early years, 1800–1837. The chimney sweepers' Acts. Paving Acts. . . . . Page 55

VIII. The opening years of Queen Victoria's reign, 1844. The first Building Act for whole of London. The District Surveyors' Association is founded . . . . . Page 60

IX. A public execution. Proposed new Building Acts. The City and Dangerous Structures. District Surveyors and underground rooms. Years 1850–1856 . . . . . Page 67

X. 1856–1876. Office of Superintending Architect created. Additional authority conferred on District Surveyors. Metropolis Local Management Act, 1855 Page 73

XI. Amendment Acts and Bylaws, 1878–1886. Dangerous structures. Commissioners of Sewers. The passing of some notable surveyors. . . . . Page 82

XII. 1888–1895. The London County Council replaces the Metropolitan Board of Works. The Tribunal of Appeal is constituted. The Association add the Building Act of 1894. . . . . Page 86

XIII. 1895–1900. The last of the Victorians. The London Building Act, 1984. The Borough Councils are formed. . . . . Page 93

XIV. The twentieth century. New Building Enactments. The London County Council and District Surveyors. Years 1900–1915. Page 97

XV. The First World War. The bombing of London, 1915–1919. The reinforced concrete regulations. Years 1915–1920 . . . . Page 101

XVI. London after the First World War. Great building activity. Districts re-arranged and made coterminous with borough boundaries. Town Planning develops. Years 1920–1930. . . . . Page 103

XVIII. New methods in building. District Surveyors become officials of the London County Council. Scientific basis for new Building Bylaws. The Acts of 1930, 1935, and the London Building Act (Amendment) Act, 1939. Years 1930–1940 . . . . . Page 107

XVIII. The Second World War . . . . Page 118

Addendum 1. Rebuilding after the war. Changes in districts. Articles of the Association revised. The Town and Country Planning Act, 1947. Years 1947–1954. Page 133

Addendum 2. London transformed. Years 1954–1970. . . . . Page 139

Appendix. . . . . Page 150

Index . . . . Page 159

ILLUSTRATIONS

facing page

1. Frontispiece

2. London in the fourteenth century 8

3. London and its environs in the sixteenth century 12

4. Engraving from a contemporary painting of the Great Fire at Ludgate in the City wall 28

5. Wall thicknesses and room heights – 1667 Act 32

6. Proclamation of 1667 33

7. A variety of buildings at the Bank in the time of George III 40

8a.
8b. Contrasts in the London of 1820 54

9. The fire brigade in 1820 78

10. Nineteenth century houses showing parapets at party walls 96

11. Graph of London's population, building operations and fees 97

12. London by night in the Blitz 122

13. The morning after 123

14. St. Paul's-among-the-office-blocks 133

15. The County of London showing Metropolitan Boroughs 132

16. Greater London and the London Boroughs 133

INTRODUCTION

London is renowned and venerated for many things and among which the most evident is perhaps its historical associations as recorded by that heterogeneous collection of buildings in the construction of which so many colourful personalities have taken a hand and to a few of whom a passing reference is made in the following pages. Londoners should remember that the Kings of England, particularly the Stuarts, frequently exercised their prerogatives, often with little results, in an effort to improve the building and restrict the congestion of habitations in their capital. Further the nobles of the land, who became the fortunate possessors of landed estates contiguous to the City, often developed these areas on town planning lines and they thus conferred, by the laying out of many green squares, lasting benefits on the citizens of the growing township. These open spaces are our jealously guarded inheritance today.

Of the government of London during the last century something has been said on the work of the Metropolitan Board of Works and of the amendments to the Building Acts which they secured. On this foundation the London County Council and the Greater London Council have built the present Acts and Bylaws. These building statutes have been framed and controlled always by a central authority, invested with powers to vary certain provisions, and this undivided authority has served the best interests of the community, for uniformity of practice has resulted throughout the Metropolis. Whereas had these Acts and their interpretation been left to the various whims, fancies, and prejudices of small local bodies, confusion must have followed.

Appointed by the above central authorities and earlier by the Lord Mayor and Justices and subject to the rules of the Acts came the "folk in the field" the District Surveyors, who have watched over the tremendous growth of the Metropolis since their office was confiemed definitely by the Building Act of 1774. The fact that the Building Laws for London have been administered faithfully for so many years by a small group of Surveyors whose actions and judgments were so independent and subject to so little control and that they were able, through this long period, to maintain their position is indeed remarkable. The office of District Surveyor has been justified by the passage of time and by the integrity of the men, as a body, appointed to the office.

The contribution made by the District Surveyors towards the development of London is recorded, to some extent, in the following narrative. They have worked continually to obtain better and more comprehensive building law and at all times they have accepted and advocated proved new methods of construction as the science of building progressed and different materials became available. For the purpose of pooling experience, securing uniformity of practice in the administration of the Acts and advancing sound principles of construction the District Surveyors' Association was founded in 1845, following the passing of the first Building Act in 1844 covering the whole of the Metropolis; although meetings of the Surveyors had taken place for many years prior to that date.

Many of the earlier Victorian Surveyors left the scenes of their labours with a reasonable certainty that a son would carry on the tradition and profession of his father and would moreover succeed to the vacant district. The assurance that their work would thus continue must have provided them with a source of great consolation but it tended to make the office a very close profession indeed. The coming of the London County Council and the restriction on private practice of those appointed to the office broadened out the issue and opened up the position to a new type of entrant. The change which occurred in 1940, by which all future District Surveyors would be officials of the Council, can be regarded as the outcome of an age in which individual effort is losing its significance and members of the community are becoming either units in great concerns or items in officialdom.

Of the routine work of the District Surveyors little has been said. The combination of a legal mind with a complete knowledge of the mechanics of construction is not found in many persons. Moreover his work, involving as it does the climbing of ladders, scaling roofs to examine chimney stacks and creeping into cellars to inspect foundations is not everybody's fancy. "A soldier's day consists of twenty-four hours on duty" and to some lesser extent this applies to the District Surveyor for he may be rung up at any hour of the night or day and informed that a collapse has occured and asked what he is going to do about it. His statutory work certainly tends to produce an argumentative state of mind which is very evident at meetings of the Association. On the other side few men, once appointed, wish to leave the office and the amazing variety and complexity of the questions which arise in connection with buildings and the law thereon provide a fascinating attraction difficult to relinquish when once experienced. In this respect and as an example of the interest and devotion to the work of those Surveyors now dead the words of Arthur Crow are typical: "That in retiring after thirty years of official life he could say that he had enjoyed it all and some of his best enjoyment had been in the witness box fighting on behalf of the London Building Acts."

CHAPTER I

The development of London and the first building regulations

The beginning of London is lost in the mists of history. The early Britons knew the locality as a vast marshy waste watered by a tidal river, but when and how the first community came to settle on the higher ground north of that river in the vicinity of the present Ludgate Hill is not known with certainty. Caesar makes no reference to a settlement and no records exist of any village or town before the Claudian conquest in the first century. The historian Tacitus mentions London in his 'Annals' with a description of the events for the year 61 A.D., by which time a centre of commerce was in existence – developed probably in conjunction with a Roman encampment. In this year, 61 A.D., the Inceni under Boadicea or Boudicca sacked and burnt the township killing most of the inhabitants. The epic struggle of Boadicea with the Roman invader, who had due reason to dread this redoubtable Queen with her chariots and hordes of wild tribesmen, is duly recorded in our history, but it is doubtful if many Londoners today passing her statue by Westminster Bridge realise that this early champion of English liberty probably caused the first great fire of London.

The City that arose on the ashes became of much importance as its Roman name Augusta signified. It was also known as Lundinium Augusta, but finally the old Celtic name of London prevailed. In due course the town developed into a stronghold in the Roman defences of the country, for the southern approaches were protected by the Thames, while a semi-circular wall over three miles in length covered the flanks and formed a barrier against attacks from the north. A wooden bridge over the river, in about the same position as the present London Bridge, connected the city by roads leading through forests to the south coast. These highways, over which the Roman legions marched, remain with us today. The bridge was reconstructed in stone between 1176 and 1209 and it remained the only permanent crossing from the city to the south bank of the Thames until 1729. The City of Westminster, which also arose under the Romans, served as a further defence to the western approaches to London.

The Romans ruled Britain for about 400 years and when their legions departed in 410 A.D. the Celtic population was left defenceless. The Teutonic tribes and Anglo-Saxons swept over the country from east to west plundering and destroying all they could of the Roman civilisation. Possibly London remained in ruins for well over a century. The people lived on the land and trade with the outer world practically ceased. Sometime in the sixth century, probably towards the end, London revived and the Anglo-Saxons came into possession. Sir Laurence Gomme, Clerk to the London County Council (1900-1914) held that London continued with an independent Roman community which maintained Roman customs and laws and that the institutions were changed to those of an English city by the strong hand of King Alfred the Great (871-901). This great king delivered London from the Danes and under his directions the Roman walls were repaired and strengthened for he realised the strategic importance of the city. The Anglo-Saxon Chronicle records for the year 886 – 'King Alfred occupied London, and all the English race submitted to him which was free from the thraldom of the Danish men, and then he entrusted the town to the keeping of 'Ethelred aldorman'. The citizens subsequently repelled many attacks by the Danes and they accepted a Danish monarchy only when the remainder of the country had been forced to do so.

London had never been the capital of the country for the Anglo-Saxon kings were crowned at Kingston (King-stone) and elsewhere, and they maintained their authority from the City of Winchester – the centre for the kingdom of Wessex. The Danish King Canute (1016-1035) is reputed to have brought the seat of government to London, but he was buried at Winchester, which appears to have been his capital.

Events over the five hundred years of Saxon and Danish rule point to the existence of an organisation of some power and centralisation in London. The citizens were summoned by the ringing of the great bell of St. Paul's, to attend three chief folkmoots during the year. The name of the new sheriff was announced at the Michaelmas meeting and at the others arrangements were made for keeping the watch. It was the sheriff Ansgar, a very great Londoner indeed, who led the city's contingent at the battle of Hastings and who, although grievously wounded, subsequently discussed terms of surrender with William the Conqueror.

When William invaded England he found two cities of importance, the royal city of Winchester and the commercial city of London. Winchester surrendered without resistance but once again the citizens of London, with their defences, the river and walls, proved too much for the attacker. William withdrew[1] after destroying the suburb of 'Sudvirki' which, as its present name Southwark denotes, constituted a line of earthworks or fortifications to the southern entrance to London Bridge. A deputation from the city subsequently waited upon William at Berkhamstead and acknowledged him as their king; London had not been conquered but its leaders had recognised in William a skilful and strong king; a matter of great importance in those days. London had approved of the king and this right of approval in some measure still obtains. William was crowned at Westminster on Christmas Day, 1066, and thus ended the last successful invasion of England. The division of the kingdom among the nobles who fought in William's army followed and royal officers were appointed sheriffs, to see that the taxes were paid.

The first complete survey of England followed – the Doomsday Book, giving details of all landed property in the kingdom, the acreage, persons, cattle and the value of everything of moment on the land, even to fish ponds. London and Winchester were not included in this record. William continued the tax instituted by the Danes termed 'Danegeld' and some indication of the relative value of London and Westminster at that time can be gained from the tax each paid. The assessment for Middlesex amounted to 853½ hides, for London 1,200 hides and for Westminster 118 hides. Middlesex paid £85. 0. 6d., London £120 and Westminster at the same rate £11. 16. 0d.

William confirmed the rights of the citizens of London in a charter but at the same time he commenced the building of the Tower, on ground outside the city's jurisdiction, as a threatening reminder of the powers of the crown. He built 2 more major fortifications – Baynards Castle which remained an army headquarters until 1307 and Montfichet Tower on the bank of the Fleet river. In the reign of Stephen the citizens are said to have purchased the right to elect their own Sheriff, but this right was denied by the Plantagenet kings, Henry II and Richard I. Charters were not granted without payment and in fact these state documents were issued with a view to emphasising the authority of the king and they also served as a sideline in raising money for the crown.

The combined rule of the Romans, Saxons and Danes covered a period of well over one thousand years and nothing now remains in London, above ground level, of the buildings

---

1. William turned Westward through Surrey, Hants, and Berks., crossing the Thames at Wallingford wasting and subduing the lands – until he came to Berkhamstead in Herts.

they erected. The many beaufiful inlaid pavements discovered in the nineteenth century at depths of from twelve to fifteen feet below the present levels of some fifty city streets provide evidence of a Roman London graced with artistic and handsome structures. Further foundations of extensive buildings of Roman origin have come to light by excavations conducted on sites cleared after the second world war bombing.[1] The Saxons accepted Christianity and two churches of special significance were built in the early part of the seventh century. St. Paul's in the City, which may have replaced a Roman temple to Diana, and St. Peter's at Westminster. The latter church was incorporated with the Abbey built (1049-1066) by the great King Edward the Confessor (1042-1066). He was buried there in the first week of 1066. The site is now covered by Westminster Abbey.

The Normans (1066-1154) followed the Romans in the use of the semi-circular arch and notable examples of their skill in building remain today in churches and cathedrals situated in various parts of the country. London under their rule became a city of beauty and renown; evidence of which can still be seen in the following buildings: the Tower Chapel, the Round Church of the Temple and the choir of St. Bartholomew, Smithfield. The people, however, at the conclusion of the Norman line with Stephen in 1154 were living in timber or mud shacks covered with roofs of straw or stubble.

Sir Laurence Gomme in his book 'The Making of London' refers to – 'the grip of the Plantagenets' and states, 'the Plantagenet work was a great work, albeit done roughly and perhaps brutally at moments. Men were killed with little regard to the sentiment of human life; executed for crimes they were hastily assumed to have committed, killed in the streets without warning, butchered without mercy or consideration and yet one must recognise that Plantagenet times, reading through the evidence as a whole, were good times for London – necessary for its evolution from a city with claims to independence to a city with claims to recognition as a constitutional unit of a well-founded and well-organised state'.

Two events which ultimately had far-reaching results on the development of the state were the signing of the Magna Charta in the year 1215 and the commencement of the British Constitution in 1265. London can claim to have had a considerable hand in both of these achievements, for the citizens sided with the Barons and King John granted the charter on finding himself deserted and shut out of London. The first Parliament assembled in the reign of King Henry III when, driven by the extravagance of this king, the city revolted and took up arms with Simon de Montfort. King Henry was defeated at the battle of Lewes and brought a prisoner to London. The Parliament that resulted consisted of two commoners from each town and two knights from each shire, but subsequently the knights drew away from the commoners and created the House of Lords.

Great strides were also made in local government. The people of London were certainly ready on all occasions to take advantage of the turbulent times and to obtain control, wherever possible, of their own affairs. The state, through the granting of charters by successive kings, had encroached seriously on the municipal rights of the citizens, but a change was now coming. In the absence of King Richard I, away on crusades, a concession, in return for assistance, was obtained from his brother John in the year 1191, by which the city received permission to hold a Commune. London as a corporate body dates from 1191 and the first Mayor appeared in 1193, but certain old documents give the date of his appointment as 1189 – the year King Richard I was crowned. The right to elect their own Mayor was granted to the city by King John in 1215 (May 8th). Henry Fitz-Ailwyn was the first Mayor of London and he held the office to the end of his life, about five and twenty years. The population of London is stated to have been about 40,000 in the reign of King

1. A notable example was the discovery of the remains of the Roman Temple of Mithras on a site west of the Mansion House. Being in the way of a new building (Bucklersbury House) the remains were moved to their present position next to Queen Victoria Street.

Richard I (1189–1199) and there were terrible tumults in the city.

The Mayor assumed control over the Wardmotes, Magistrates, Bailiffs, Officers and Servants and although the office became suppressed in times of trouble particularly in the reign of Edward I, when he dispensed with the mayoralty for eleven years, the necessity for a leader could not be denied. The chief citizens would elect and support their Mayor and he would uphold the customs of the city and speak for the people. Under Edward III the Mayor became one of the Judges of Oyer and Terminer for the trials of criminals at Newgate. The building regulations that are generally recognised as being the first of any consequence are directly associated with Henry Fitz-Ailwyn and they were known as:

Fitz-Ailwyn's Assize of Buildings of Allaying Contentions as to Assizes of Buildings.

"In the year of our Lord 1189, in the first year, namely, of the reign of the illustrious King Richard, Henry Fitz-Ailwyn being then Mayor, it was by the more discreet men of the city thus provided and ordained for the allaying of the contentions that at times arise between neighbours in the city touching boundaries made, or to be made, between their lands and other things; to the end that, according to the provisions then made and ordained, such contentions might be allayed".

The said provision and ordinance is called an 'Assize'. Twelve men were elected in full hustings; and they were sworn to attend faithfully to carry out the same, at the summons of the Mayor. Hustings is known as the oldest Court on record in the city and at one time it constituted the sole Court. The word, apparently, comes from Hus-thing, a cause pleaded in a house and not in the open air. The following matters were dealt with in the Assize:

Party Walls

In order to provide a party wall between the properties of two neighbours each was required – 'to give one foot and a half of his land on which they shall build at their joint costs a stone wall three feet in thickness and sixteen feet in height'. Arches used as 'Almeria or aumbries', cupboards or larders, could be formed provided they were one foot only in depth (the party wall at the back between the cupboards would be one foot in thickness). A neighbour (adjoining owner) who could not afford to build his portion of the wall 'ought to give unto him who so desires to build by the Assize three feet of his land.' The building owner should then build the wall upon that land at his own cost. The adjoining owner, who gave the land, could then have one half of the wall and place his timber joists and roof thereon.

Many other clauses were contained in the Assize – obstruction to view from a window, but this could not be objected to unless – 'some writing could be produced by the objector showing his right to the light.' Probably the boards – 'Ancient Lights' – came from this old regulation requiring evidence of right. The carrying off of water and the fixing of corbels (joists in walls) and the construction of pits for receiving water, clean or foul, in the vicinity of an adjoining owner's land were all dealt with.

A neighbour could object to a building in course of erection adjoining his ground and impede or stop the work. The building owner could then demand the Assize. The Mayor and his twelve men would then attend, on an appointed day, and after hearing the case of complaint, answer to settle the matter. The award they issued could be enforced by the Sheriff at the sole cost of the person offending.

Paragraph 15 contained a reference to the old type of building in the city – 'that in ancient times the greater part of the city was built of wood and the houses were covered with straw or stubble and the like.' It also refers to the fire which took place in the first year of King Stephen's reign (1136) when 'by reason of a fire that broke out at London Bridge the church of St. Paul's was burnt and from which spot the conflagration extended destroying houses and buildings as far as the church of St. Clements Danes.' The next paragraph continues – 'after this fire many of the citizens built stone houses covered with thick tiles to protect against the fury of the flames and to avoid a similar peril.'

In the year 1087 or 1088 St. Paul's Cathedral was destroyed completely by a devastating conflagration which swept away most of the city. The fire mentioned above in 1136 occurred during the rebuilding of St. Paul's and the extent of the damage thereto is not definitely known. Of the cathedral existing prior to 1087 no records remain. Other fires in earlier years had caused great damage and the original wooden church of St. Paul's appears to have been consumed thereby in 961 A.D. Memories of these terrible fires must have provided the moving motive for Fitz-Ailwyn's Assize and this effort should receive credit for setting up a standard of construction for party walls which was followed subsequently by rules for external walls. The thickness of three feet was probably dictated by the use of dry walling put together with poor lime mortar. Building owner and adjoining owner had their rights defined, probably for the first time, and these principles have, with variations, persisted through 800 years and the same may be said of the provisions as to obstruction of light, which now forms part of common law.

In Mediaeval London (Ecclesiastical) by Sir Walter Besant the author makes the following remarks on these regulations: "This law, like so many mediaeval laws, was sensible and necessary. It fell through as did all mediaeval laws for want of police to execute it. In London there were thousands of houses at that moment built of wood with roofs of thatch. There does not appear to have been any attempt made to replace wood with stone. That indeed would have been impossible on account of the cost, but at least as houses fell down, and many of them in the narrow courts were only wattle and daub, an attempt might have been made to replace them with more substantial houses having roofs of tile. The mediaeval way was to understand very clearly what ought to be done, then to pass a law commanding that thing to be, and then to sit down with the feeling that duty had been done."

Some further extracts are also given in Besant's Mediaeval History taken from Riley (Introduction Liber Albus). "The upper room of the house was generally known as the 'solar' and is also called in Fitz-Ailwyn's Assize the 'domus' or house. From a deed 1217 or 1218 it appears that the corbels or joists supporting the upper floor were inserted at the height of eight feet from the ground. At the time of the Assize it is evident that the houses in London consisted of but one storey over the ground floor and no more. At what period more storeys were first added does not appear; but in the early part of the 14th century we find houses in London of two or three storeys mentioned. Cellars are not referred to in the Assize but they are noticed as places used for business in the first half of the reign of Henry III. By the Assize a person had full liberty to obstruct a neighbour's ancient lights unless some writing could be produced by that neighbour, showing a right to the contrary. The Assize makes no provisions for the materials to be used for roofing but within a century and a half, however, we find detailed enactments that the houses of the citizens shall be covered with lead, tiles or stone. Windows are mentioned, but glass, however, was used only by the most opulent, and at the time of Richard I they were merely apertures open in the day, crossed perhaps with iron stanchions, and covered by shutters by night. There is no mention of chimneys and they were found only in the abodes of the most wealthy; smoke from fires went by way of doors and windows."

The division of London into Wards occurred in about 1100 and some 200 years later 24 wards and their Aldermen can be traced. Gatherings of the people by summons, termed the 'folkmoots' had been a part of the civic life of the city from very early times, but later, as the population increased, other arrangements became necessary and the inhabitants were called by summons, for separate divisions or Wards. These meetings were known as 'wardmotes' and they were presided over by the head of the ward – the Alderman. They were held for the purpose of correcting defaults – the removal of nuisances – the promotion of the well-being of the Ward.

The following are examples of edicts issued by the Wardmotes – the penthouses and jetties of houses shall be so high that folks on horseback may ride beneath them; and that they shall be of the height of nine feet at the very least – all others shall be forthwith rearranged within 'firty' days under a penalty of forty shillings unto the use of the Sheriffs. And that no stall shall project out from the house beyond the width of two feet and a half: the same shall be movable and flexible for the convenience of neighbours. Lime shall be well measured by quarter and bushellof Assize. The same shall be well burnt according to the ancient ordinance; and every sack shall contain one bushel of Assize. Tiles shall be of the ancient dimensions and they shall be well burnt and well leaded. Furnaces and Reredos[1] were not to be erected near laths, partitions or boards by which a fire might easily arise. Scavagers[2] were to cause the same to be immediately removed and to receive fourpence for the removal of any such nuisance. All masons, carpenters, daubers, tilers[3] and labourers were to be paid the rates ordained by the Common Council of the City. All persons who lived in great houses within the ward to have a ladder or two ready and prepared, to succour their neighbours in case of fire. And also they have in summer time, and especially between the Feast of Pentecost and the Feast of St. Bartholomew (4th August) before their doors a barrel full of water for quenching fires, if it be not a house that has a fountain of its own. No house within the liberties to be covered otherwise than with lead, tile or stone and if any there such be that the same be forthwith rased by the constables and scavagers – their taking for their trouble four pence. No hoards or palings to be made before any tenement, without the sanction of the Mayor and Aldermen. No steps to cellars to project into the streets or lanes. These provisions may be considered to have constituted the first bylaws.

The encroachment of buildings on the highways was also guarded against as the following record indicates:

"Also that all Master Carpenters and Masons of the City shall be sworn. That they make no 'Purprestures'[4] upon the walls or lanes within the City or Suburbs, or prejudice the neighbours, when they make their Buildings against the Statutes of old time ordained." City Records Letter Book F.105-6.

For the more speedy removal also of burning houses each ward was enjoined to provide a strong iron hook with a wooden handle, two chains and two strong cords;

---

1. An open fireplace such as was commonly used in the middle of the ancient halls.
2. At the wardmote officials were elected, e.g. Scavagers, Aleconners, Beadel, etc. The Scavager was an officer to take custom upon the scavage, i.e, inspection and duties on imported goods. The word used by the Normans means show-age, or age added to the old English word schawen, now show. Chaucer was controller of the city customs and he inspected imports of wool, on which there was a duty of twelve pence per cask or load, so Geoffrey Chaucer the poet was by trade a Scavager. At a later date part of the Scavagers' duties were to see that the streets were kept clean, and hence the modern word scavenger, whose present day occupation corresponds with that of the 'Raker' of mediaeval London. The Scavager was required to swear on oath; 'You shall swear that you shall diligently oversee that the pavements within your ward are well and rightly repaired and not made too high in nuisance of the neighbours and that the ways and streets and lanes are cleared of dung and all manner of filth for the decency of the City: and that chimneys, furnaces and reredoses are of stone and sufficiently defended against peril of fire; and if you find anything to the contrary you shall show it unto the Alderman so that the Alderman may ordain for the amendment thereof. And this you shall not fail to do. So God you help and the Saints'.
3. Note that bricks are not referred to – tiles were probably used as bricks, being possibly two inches in thickness.
4. Purprestures – encroachments or illegal enclosures. From the French Pourprist – an enclosure.

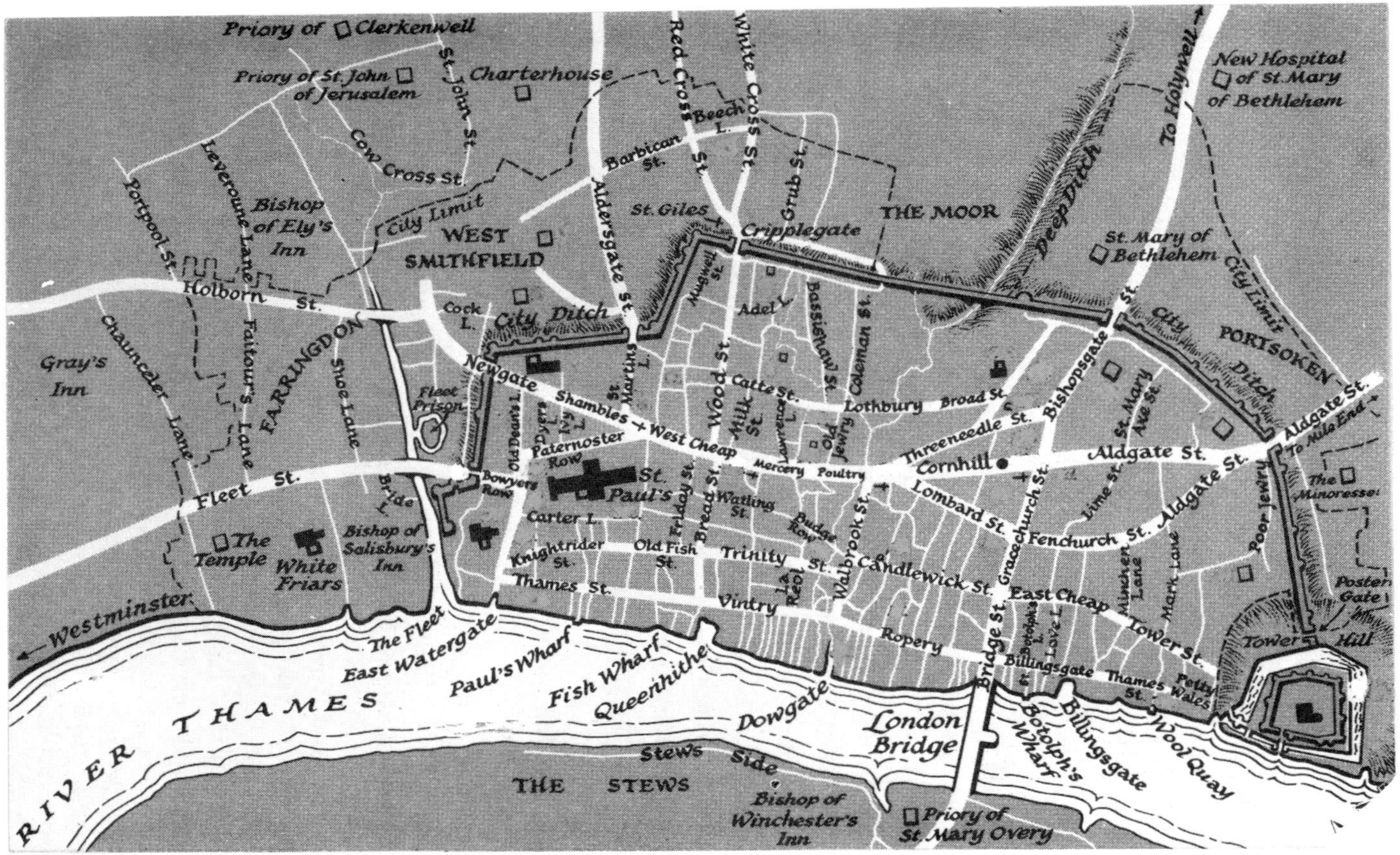

London in the fourteenth century

this to be left in the possession of the Beadel of the Ward, who was also to be provided with a good horn 'loudly sounding'.

Thus restrictions on frontage lines and projections from buildings followed fire walls, and even more provisions of co-operation in escapes from fire were attempted.

The first Building Act case which has come to the writer's notice, is recorded in Besant's Mediaeval London, where it is mentioned – 'In 1302 one Thomas Bat being hailed before the Mayor on a charge of neglecting to put tiles instead of thatch on his houses offered to indemnify the city in case of any fire happening by reason of his thatch. The offer was accepted, on the understanding that the thatch was to be removed by a certain time'. The report continues – 'The naivete of Mr. Bat in offering and the city accepting, an indemnity in case of fire is truly remarkable. What would Mr. Bat have done, how far would his personal estates have gone, if a quarter of the city had been burned down by reason of his thatch.'

In the year 1236 water was brought first into the city by lead pipes from wells at Tyburn in the districts now called St. Marylebone. The Mayor and Aldermen used to inspect the head of the supply once a year, and to hunt a hare before dinner and a fox after dinner in the fields of St. Marylebone. In 1285 the pipes were changed to wood – hollowed out tree trunks being used for the purpose – and various reservoirs were built in the city including one at Cheapside. For many years this conduit was relied upon for the city's supply of water, the only other sources being the foul waters of the Fleet and Walbrook.

Besant records an interesting occurrence in 1331 when King Edward III held a great tournament in Cheapside. – 'In the middle of the City of London in a street called Cheape the stone pavement being covered with sand that the horses might not slide when they strongly set their feet to the ground, the King held a tournament three days together with the nobility, valiant men of the realm, and some other strange knights. And to the end the beholders might with the better ease see the same, there was a wooden scaffold erected, across the street like unto a tower wherein Queen Philippa and many other ladies richly attired and assembled from all parts of the realm did stand to behold the jousts; but the higher frames on which the ladies were placed, brake in sunder, whereby these were with some shame forced to fall down, by reason whereof the knights and such as were underneath were grieviously hurt; wherefore the Queen took great care to save the carpenters from punishment and through her prayers, which she made upon her knees, pacified the King and Council and thereby purchased great love of the people. After which time the King caused a shed to be strongly made of stone for himself, the Queen and other estates to stand on and there to behold the joustings and other shows at their pleasure, by the Church of St. Mary Bow, as is showed in Cordwainer Street Ward.' Through all the centuries the writer has yet to find another royal occasion on which a stand collapsed. There were no District Surveyors in the reign of Edward III, and one shudders to think of the penalty incurred by such a calamity. The responsible officials might easily have been half hanged, drawn and quartered. Some supervision, however, did exist at this early date, one mason and two carpenters being appointed regularly for the purpose by the Mayor and Aldermen. Possibly the carpenters referred to were those two men whose lives were saved by the supplication of the Queen. Further mention is made later on of this office.

London in the thirteenth and fourteenth centuries obtained the highest point ever reached in religion, if churches are any criterion. The Church was everywhere, there being 126 parish churches in London and 25 large or small religious houses. A considerable portion of the population gained their livelihood directly or indirectly from these religious institutions. At the time of the Conquest the churches were constructed mainly of wood in the form of tree trunks split and placed side by side. In the many generations which had passed they had developed, with the loving care bestowed upon them, to buildings in stone of considerable beauty, and now in 1400 their bells were ringing throughout most of the day. In the same way the houses had changed from wattle and daub shacks to timber erections with, at the first, one small room above and later to two and even to three storeys over. The staircase would probably be outside, and the upper floor would in most cases belong to a separate tenant – so flats are not a modern invention. The houses were not built to any definite line, but they fronted in whichever way the builder fancied. Chimneys were fairly common by 1400, but the hard clay earth covered with rushes still formed the ground floor, and this covering was generally in a dirty and verminous condition. Glass was still a luxury and relatively few windows were glazed. Large houses of the Barons with a central hall, in which perhaps two hundred retainers slept, were dotted about the town. Curfew rang at eight o'clock when the city gates where shut. An order made in 1309 required persons to take their refuse to the boats by the river and not to throw it into the streets; but nevertheless the highways became in time saturated with poisonous matter which materially assisted the spread of the plague. Under the Plantagenets men of all trades found their distinct and several places in the city; the mercers, goldsmiths, drapers, skinners, ironmongers, etc. formed separate little communities each with its 'guild'[1] – lawfully created by the grant of a charter by the king. The guilds stood for good craftmanship and fair trading, and before the end of the 14th century they had become distinctly powerful. From 1375 the members of the City Council were no longer elected by the Wards but by the trading guilds; they decided who were to be the 'freemen' of London and they had their own way of dealing with delinquents such as a certain John Penrose who was found guilty in 1364 of selling unsound and unwholesome wine. He was sentenced to imprisonment for one year and a day, to drink a draught of the bad wine – the rest to be poured over his head and to forswear the calling of a vinter in the City of London for ever.

The two hundred and fifty years in which the Plantagenets ruled covered a period of architectural glory; the incomparable gothic builders erected in these years their wondrous cathedrals which are our heritage today. These mighty buildings were erected at a time when the population of the whole country amounted to no more than two millions and in the 14th century the black death accounted for one-third of the people; one authority states that two-thirds of the population of London died. Henry III who by his extravegance caused the city to revolt, left his mark in stone by the building of Westminster Abbey. The magnificent Westminster Hall, now attached to the Houses of Parliament, and originally erected by the Norman King William II was largely reconstructed by the last of the Plantagenet Kings: Richard II (1377–1399). The crypt of St. John's Church, Clerkenwell, which still survives, although the church above was destroyed by fire in the Second World War bombing, is one only of several examples remaining in London today of the master works of these early English builders.

London in the reigns of the Lancastrians and Yorkists 1399–1485

The struggles for supremacy between the Houses of Lancaster and York and known as the Wars of the Roses, occupied thirty years of the fifteenth century (1455–1485). The nobles of the land in fighting among themselves in this long civil war helped materially in bringing about the emancipation of the lowest class. Serfdom or villenage came to an end and during these years the powers of Parliament increased considerably. Printing was introduced in the

---

1. The term Guild is of Saxon derivation signifying 'a payment'. They were formed originally as friendly or benefit societies for succour in age and sickness. They were followed by the Trade Guilds and later they became Companies. Some can be traced to an age before the Norman Conquest, the only one remaining being the Saddlers. For legal recognition the sanction of the Crown was necessary, The Company having the earliest Charter are the Weavers, which they received from Henry I. (The Worshipful Company of Carpenters, Jupp.)

reign of Edward IV by William Caxton, who set up a press at Westminster, and in the brief reign of Richard III the first laws were drawn up and printed in English.

London accepted the changes in the monarchy, following the fortunes of war, as a constitutional issue for the city had ceased to be an independent entity; and was now conscious of the remainder of the country. The merchants, guilds and their Mayor and Aldermen were prepared to agree with the verdict as confirmed by the country as a whole, but they were, at the same time, equally ready to fight against any interference with their rights and privileges. There is evidence of considerable prosperity in London during the fifteenth century and many important buildings were erected. The Guildhall was rebuilt in its present position – originally it stood in Aldermanbury. Leadenhall Market was founded and the old Roman walls were reinstated and strengthened. The walls were about 22 feet in height and the towers 40 feet – after 1477 they were not, apparently, again repaired. In 1415 orders were issued for the streets to be lighted by night. The city's wealth came undoubtedly chiefly from the wool trade for in the thirteenth century wool was produced in greater quantities in England than in any other country and the Port of London became the exchange centre for the commodity. The wars of Henry IV and Henry V with France were financed by the city with a view to keeping open the Port of Calais for the reception of wool. The famous Dick Whittington, Lord Mayor of London, had a share in these ventures.

By a resolution of the Common Council passed in 1475 the election of the new mayors was henceforth to be made by the Mayor, Aldermen, Common Councilmen and Liverymen of the city and so it has remained ever since.

With the defeat and death of Richard III in 1485 we come to the close of the history of Mediaeval London and proceed to the spacious days of the Tudors.

CHAPTER II

London under the Tudors 1485–1603. The first efforts to restrict the erection of new buildings

It is said of the Tudors that they reigned 'by the grace of the people', and certainly under their successful reigns London increased in fame and prestige. The cloth trade became almost a monopoly of the city merchants and capital accumulated in their hands. The new nobility was drawn largely from these wealthy citizens who were able to acquire lands in and around London from which in years to come considerable incomes were obtained through ground rents. In the sixteenth century a wave of immigrants came to London – silk weavers settled in the villages of Shoreditch and Spitalfields – French hatters came to Southwark to make felt hats, while to the same suburb the Flemings introduced the brewing of beer from hops. Printers came from the Netherlands to Westminster, Clerkenwell and elsewhere. London became overcrowded and land values within the walls of the city increased enormously. The cost of living continued to rise and an effort to check and stabilise the position was attempted by an Act passed early in the reign of Elizabeth.

This Act in the fifth year of Elizabeth (1562) restricted the wages of servants, workmen, artificers, apprentices and labourers. Persons were compelled to serve by the year in husbandry between twelve years and sixty years. Punishments for servants not performing duties, and their rights to testimonials, were included, while employers paying higher wages rendered themselves liable to penalties. Sheriffs, Justices of the Peace, etc. settled the rates of pay, which evidently did not provide an adequate standard of living. In spite of these regulations money still decreased in value, one reason apparently being the importation of gold from the New World. The old system by which villeins and serfs paid rents, by the labour of their hands, had ceased, and the worker now received his reward in money. One authority states that at the commencement of the sixteenth century a quarter of wheat cost about six shillings while at the close the price had advanced to thrity-eight shillings and sixpence. The problems of the cost of living today are therefore only a repeat of past history. The rate of pay for one man's work a day under the Tudors is recorded at one shilling for a horse, cart and two men. Low wages and high rents led to overcrowding in the dwellings and the continual influx of people to the capital aggravated the trouble. Roving bands of beggars and vagabonds, friars and others from the dissolved monasteries gathered in and around the town, and in 1580 a curious Proclamation was issued to meet the case.

Queen Elizabeth, on the advice of her 'Counsell' and being 'moved by the considerate opinions of the Lord Mayor, Aldermen and other grave wise men in or about the Citie' charged and commanded all persons:

'To desist and forebeare from any new buildings of any house or tenement, within three miles from any of the gates of the sayd Citie of London, to serve for habitation or lodging for any person, where no former house hath bene knowen to have bene, in the memorie of such as are now living, and also to forebeare from letting or setting, or suffering any more families than one onely to be placed or to inhabit from henceforth in any house that heretofore hath bene inhabited'.

London and its environs in the sixteenth century

The Lord Mayor and all other officials having authority, all Justices of the Peace were charged with the duty of seeing that no person began the foundations of any such house – 'but that they be prohibited and restrained so to do'. The persons attempting to build and workmen (after warning) if they continued to build, were to be committed to 'close prison' – without bail – to remain until they could find sureties with bonds that they would not again attempt to build. The Lord Mayor and other officers concerned with buildings were required to take action and agree among themselves how to proceed against persons responsible during the previous seven years for the increase of 'indwellers, inmates or undersitters' and if there were any 'let or impediment' to consult the 'Privie Counsell' for the remedy.

This Proclamation has been referred to frequently as Elizabeth's attempt at Town Planning, or as one of the first steps toward Town Planning – indirectly it might have been. What the reaction today would be to a proclamation on these lines issued to meet the present shortage of houses is not difficult to imagine – there would be a wholesale riot, but conditions in hygiene are different now. Elizabeth's proclamation was an attempt to drive the people back from whence they came, to avoid the danger of outbreaks of plague. The reasons were explained:

'If any plague of popular sickness shoulde by Gods permission, enter amongst those multitudes, that the same would not onely spread it selfe and invade the whole citie and confines, as great mortalitie shoulde ensue to the same, where her Majesties personall presence is many times required, besides the great confluence of people from all other parts of the Realme, by reason of the ordinary terms of justice there holden, the infection woulde be also dispersed through all other parts of the Realme to the manifest danger of the whole body thereof'.

The proclamation was 'Given at Nonesuch the seventh day of June, 1580, in the two and twentieth yeere of her Majesties Reigne'.

There were, however, other reasons as well. The growth of the town outside the City walls had been restricted in certain directions for a great many years by lands granted as 'fiefs' to the monasteries and other religious houses. When these institutions were repressed by Henry VIII, the opportunity arose for development on these sites. Groups of buildings came into existence and people attracted to the capital arrived to inhabit them. These little communities formed the nuclei for the spreading out which followed in later years and which ultimately led to the scattered township of London we know today. The City Authorities never attempted to move the boundaries of the city and although there were Wards within and Wards without the limits remained unchanged through the centuries. When, however, the early colonies of buildings appeared on the outskirts and throngs of people, struggling to obtain a livelihood, gathered therein, the City Guilds looked with strong disfavour on these newcomers. These intruders were able to compete successfully, in many ways, with the craftsmen within the city, who were called upon to contribute to their guild. The freemen paid their 'scott and lott' and later there were protests against the employment of foreigners – 'who pay noe scott or lott[1] nor beare any office or charge in the city'. The Lord Mayor would certainly be a party to keeping these unwelcome visitors away.

1. The liabilities of the householder, in the city, as laid down by the Common Council, had for many years included the scraping and cleaning of the street in front of his house to the middle of the road or kennel (a shallow channel cut along the centre of the road); there were no distinct footpaths until after the Great Fire in 1666. He was also expected to hang out a light on dark nights and to keep a bucket of water by his street door during summer time. As a citizen – he could further be called upon to act as a beadle or constable. The carrying out of these duties was known as 'bearing lot' and the payment of a rate to avoid bearing lot was termed 'paying scot'.

The Act of 1589

(1) 'For the avoiding of the great inconvenience which are found by experience to grow by the erecting and building of great numbers and multitudes of cottages which are daily more and more increased in many parts of this realm';

(2) 'Be it enacted that – no person shall within this realm of England make, build or erect, or cause to be made, builded or erected, any manner of cottage for habitation or dwelling nor convert – to be used as a cottage for habitation or dwelling unless the same person do assign and lay to the same cottage or building four acres of ground at the least, to be accounted according to the statute or ordinance "de terris mensurandis" being his or her own freehold or inheritance lying near the said cottage to be continually occupied and manured therewith so long as the same cottage shall be inhabited';

(3) 'penalty £10 of lawful money of England for every such offence'.

This Act passed in 1589 restricted building developments over the whole of the country. Incorporated towns were not included and there were certain exemptions on the building of cottages for workmen engaged in mineral works, quarries and also for shepherds and gamekeepers. Subletting or the taking of inmates was also prohibited as follows:–

'That from and after the Feast of All Saints next comyinge there shall not be any inmate of more Famylies in Householde than one dwelling or inhabitinge in any one Cottage made or to be made or erected.'

Cromwell's second Parliament made use of this statute to collect fines on buildings not complying with the requirements and situated within ten miles of the city. The Act was repealed in toto by XV Geo. 3 Ch. 32. (1775).

The Proclamation of 1580 became an Act of Parliament in 1592. This Act was definitely aimed at the lower classes for although it provided that no person should erect a new building for habitation within the Cities of London and Westminster or within three miles of the gates of the City of London it contained exempting clauses for the upper classes. It did not prevent the enlargement of an existing house for certain persons who had been assessed to pay a subsidy to her Majesty at five pounds in goods or three pounds in lands. Ways and means were found to enable a rich person to build a house either outside or inside the two cities. The Act also prevented underletting – 'that no person inhabitinge – a dwelling shall – receive or take into his or their house or houses an inmate or undersitter upon payne'. Thus lodgers were definitely barred in the days of Good Queen Bess. Authorised for seven years only the statute was subsequently renewed periodically by further Proclamations, which sometimes followed the outbreak of plague, such as occurred in 1603. The Act also provided an income useful to the Crown so it remained in force for many years.

The statute did not appear to operate against the rebuilding on old foundations, or on sites occupied in living memory. It certainly contributed to the preservation of some open spaces adjoining the cities, for the recreation, comfort and health of the people and the training of soldiers. Henry VIII was also inadvertently responsible for keeping open large tracts of land adjoining the capital for he fenced in considerable areas to protect game for his personal hunting. The Act did in fact represent the first Town Planning effort, and some restriction of building must have resulted but the officials concerned in administering the Statutes needed a sharp reminder, now and then, to keep them up to their duties. A record of the Privy Council Proceedings, 30th July 1598, contains a letter from the Lord of the Council to certain Knights, Esquires, Justices of the Peace, etc., giving them a severe reprimand for failing to enforce the Act – 'her Majesty fyndinge thereby just occasion to conceave greate offence both against you that have by so many and often warnynges bene chardged to looke to these continewed abuses, and against soch contemptious persons that doe violate those orders taken in that behalfe, wee must let you understand your slack and negligent oversight therein doth deserve some sharp and severe reprehension, and that yf you did performe the care you ought to have used no man durst presume to offend so willfully. Nevertheless once againe wee have thought good to warne you of your duties to have better regarde hereafter to see this dysorder better looked into, and especially at this tyme of the yeere in the vacacion those that doe make new buildinges doe cause the frames to be made in other places, and suddainly sett up the same.' The last few words seemed to suggest that some attempt at prefabrication went on at that time. A similar letter was addressed to the Lord Mayor and his brethren the Aldermen.

Notwithstanding these admonitions the trouble continued for the speculative builder would not stop erecting houses and in June 1602 a further proclamation contained the following: 'that notwithstanding her (Elizabeth's) gracious and Princely commandement signified by her said Proclamation, and the Honourable care of her Privie Councell touching the same, yet it falleth out, partly by the covetous and insatiable dispositions of some persons, that without any respect of the Common good and publicke profite of the Realme, doe onely regard their owne particular lucre and gaine and partly by the negligence and corruption of others, who by reason of their offices and places ought to see the said Proclamation, Orders and Decrees duely perfourmed, and yet doe undutifully neglect the same, that the said mischiefes and inconvenience doe daily encrease and multiplie, to the great contempt of her Majesties Royall commandment and manifest danger to the whole Realme.' From this Proclamation there would appear to be something rotten in the state of Merry England.

By paragraph 6 of this edict – 'all tenements or buildings, not built upon an old foundation of a dwelling house, that are not at this present finished, to be plucked downe, and builders or Leasors that binde or tye the tenants upon their ground, to be bound to appeare in the Starchamber.'

Paragraph 7 – 'those houses and tenements, that are already demised or letten, diligently to enquiry what terme they have, and if they have them from yeere to yeere, then the tenant to be commanded to avoyde and to provide himselfe elsewhere without the precincts aforesaid before the ende of three moneths: and order to be also taken that the house bee not let agine, but in such sort as is before expressed.'

Paragraph 9 – 'and if any shal henceforth offend in new building, or in any dividing of any tenement contrary to the true intent and meaning of this Proclamation and all workemen continuing the same worke, after they shal be forbidden – shal bee committed to prison, untill they shall finde sufficient sureties for their appearance in the Starre chamber, to answere their contempts there, and for their good behaviour in the meane season.'

The Tudors and highways of London

The efforts of the Tudors to deal with local government could not be said to have produced very tangible results. In addition to these unavailing efforts to restrict building the 'Road Acts' which placed the responsibility for the maintenance of bridges and roads on the Justices proved remarkably ineffective. The Act of 1563, called for compulsory service on the roads from every parishioner. Six days per year being the limit, but again, the payment of a fine exempted the person from the duty. In Easterweek, in every parish, the parishioners were summoned by the Churchwardens and Constable and they had to appoint – 'two honest persons to be surveyors for one year of the works for the amendment of the Highways in their parish leading to any market town.' The fine for failing to serve in this capacity was £5, to be paid to the Justices at Quarter Sessions. The Surveyors chosen had to press men into the labour gangs and, naturally, those compelled to join were not over anxious to work. They were termed 'Kings Loiterers', for – 'spending most of their time standing still and prating or asking passengers for a largesse.' Should – 'a common and ancient Kings Highway become ruinous, miry, deep broken and great decay, so as to be a common nuisance – to the King's Loyal subjects' – the whole parish could be indited at Quarter Sessions of Assizes. The badness of the roads made travel difficult and Queen Elizabeth in her coach had sometimes to drive over fields to avoid the impassable highways. Several streets in Finsbury are mentioned in early records. St. John's Street in particular is referred to as leading to Islington Church and being in 1544 – 'very foul, full of pits and sloughs, very perilous and noyous!"

Population of London in the sixteenth century

The population of London in the sixteenth century cannot be estimated with any like certainty. A Dr. Creighton in 1891 published a long account on the subject and from various contemporary figures he estimated the population in the reign of Henry VIII at approximately 50,000; two-thirds being in the walled city and the remainder in the Liberties between the gates and the bars. By 1563 (6th Elizabeth) Dr. Creighton, basing his figures on the Manuscript Bills of Mortality, considered that the number of inhabitants had nearly doubled, being then about 93,000. In spite of plagues and the restrictions on building and sub-letting the population increased steadily and before the end of the century there were probably some 200,000 persons living in the city and suburbs.

For centuries Londoners had been buried in the churchyards within the city and a writer Bullien in his 'Dealogue of the Pestilence' refers to the multitudes of graves in every churchyard and the great heaps of rotten bones. In 1582 certain parishes were ordered by the Lord Mayor to use a new burial ground outside the walls. Dr. Creighton writes that the ground outside the walls, which came in time to be the densely populated Liberties and out-parishes and the seat of later plagues, had for years past received the refuse of the city and a large proportion of the bodies of the dead. By 1605 Dr. Creighton reckoned that the population of the capital had reached nearly 250,000 of which 76,000 lived within the city, some 150,000 in the Liberties, outer suburbs and outer parishes and the remainder about 24,000 in Westminster and certain parishes which did not come within the Bills of Mortality. These figures provide some indication of the progress of the capital in the great days of the Tudors, when, in rather more than one hundred years, the inhabitants increased five-fold, i.e. 50,000 to 250,000.

During the comparatively short period of 118 years during which the Tudors ruled, a radical change occurred in building. The Tudor mansion, built of a warm coloured brick with stone mullioned windows and a characteristic flattened arch and the twisted ornamental chimneys became the home of the wealthy. The old stone structures were discarded and framed buildings four and five storeys high, constructed of heavy framed oak with plaster panels, became the principal houses on the main streets. The wooden members were often carved in various ways and decorative shields and signs coloured in blue, red and gold, gave the Gothic touch to the handsome fronts. Church construction stopped with the Reformation and Grammar Schools were built. The period covers the golden age of literature and in London the plays of Shakespeare were produced in the first open air theatres. The first theatre was a wooden structure erected in Shoreditch.

Finally some mention should be made as to the position of London in connection with the defences of the kingdom. The Crown did not possess a standing army such as we have today. The cities, according to their wealth and position, were expected to provide, in times of emergency, so many trained men. Commissioners were appointed by an Act passed in the reign of Henry VIII to see that the inhabitants of the cities and boroughs were properly provided with arms. London had its trained bands, the militia, whose training, apparently, did not extend to beyond one day per month. Nevertheless the city always came forward readily to offer its services in men, money and ships when so required.

At the coming of the Armada the Queen called on London to equip fifteen ships and to muster five thousand men; actually thirty ships were prepared and manned and ten thousand men of the militia paraded for action.

CHAPTER III

London under the Stuarts and Commonwealth 1603–1659. Restrictions on the erection of new buildings continued and the birth of the London Building Acts.

The Stuarts ascended the throne in the person of James I in 1603 and in this year further restrictions were proclaimed against – 'inmates and multitudes of dwellers in strait rooms and places in and about the City of London; and for the rasing and pulling down of certaine new erected buildings.' The cause of a devastating plague was attributed to – 'the great confluence and accesse of excessive numbers of idle, indigent, dissolute and dangerous persons, and the pestering of many of them in small and strait rooms and habitations.' No house within four miles of the city in which infection had occurred could be occupied by a new tenant. Further, that the Aldermen in the city and the Justices outside should take special care to prevent overcrowding and that houses or places ordered to be pulled down – 'shall forthwith be pulled down' – and after being so demolished no other building should be erected on the site. They, the Aldermen and the Justices of the Peace were to answer any neglect – 'at their utmost perill'.

An Ordinance issued in 1607, again attempted to prevent the erection of new buildings in or near the City of London. If buildings were erected on old foundations they should

'both adorne and beautifie his sayde Citie, and bee lesse subject to danger of fire, and cause lesse waste of timber (fitter to be reserved for the shipping of his Realme) and likewise such as in regard of the charge of building, can not bee inhabited but by persons of some ability.'

A person enlarging his own dwelling house was not regarded as an offender against this Proclamation if the enlargement did not exceed more than one-third of the old building. and that it was used entirely for one habitation. No cellar erected within the last five years was 'to bee used for lodgings, or tipling or victualling houses.'

This Proclamation contained a distinct indication of authority dictating to the Builder or owner as to the quality and style of the front elevation of his premises.

No new buildings were hereafter to be erected (on the foundations of any former dwelling house) unless – 'the front and all the outer walls shall bee built of brick or stone.' The front – 'shall bee made in that uniforme sort and order which shall bee prescribed by the Alderman of the Ward . . . . . or Justices of the Peace.' Offenders were liable to fines, imprisonment and order by Court of Starre Chamber.

In the year following another edict on the same subject came from King James and in 1615, he issued a decree with a long exposition of works executed in his reign of twelve years. The wordy document is a fine example of the grandiloquent style of the man who believed in the 'Divine right of Kings'. The edict starts thus:

'Wee doe well perceive in our princely wisdome and providence now, that our Citie of London is become the greatest, or next the greatest Citie of the Christian World, it is more than time that there bee an utter cessation of further new-buildings, lest the surcharge and overflow of people doe bring upon our said Citie infinite inconveniences, which have bene so often mentioned, both in Our former Proclamations, and in the Degrees of Our high Court of Star Chamber, as it were in vain to repeat them: Our purpose and Princely resolution being now and hereafter, to leave Words, and to act and execute our Princely Ordinances on that behalfe and not to make discourse or recitall of them: Therefore, as wee doe exceedingly approve and commend all Edifices, Structures and Workes which tend to publique use and ornament, in and about Our Citie, as the paving of Smithfield, the planting of Moorefields, the bringing of the New streame unto the West parts of the Cities and Suburbs, the Pesthouse, Suttons Hospital, Britanes Burse, the reedifying of Algate, Hicks Hall, and the like workes, which have bene erected and performed in greater number in these twelve yeares of Our Reigne, then in the whole ages heretofore: So on the other side, for further addition of private buildings, Wee are fully resolved, that this Our Royall Proclamation, and finall and peremptorie commendment, shal be the furthest and utmost period and end of them: Onely, as to private houses, Wee could desire and wish, according to Our former Proclamation and Ordinances touching Brick-buildings, that as it was said by the first Emperor of Rome, that he found the Citie of Rome of Bricks, and left it of Marble, So that Wee whom God hath honoured to be the first King of Great Britaine, might be able to say in some proportion, That Wee had found Our Citie and Suburbs of London of Sticks, and left them of Bricks being a Meteriall farre more durable, safe from fire, beautiful and magnificent.'

The qualification by the words 'some proportion', was evidently necessary having regard to the fire happening in 1666. The edict ratified and confirmed the previous Proclamations.

'His Majesties further pleasure for the matter of buildings' was proclaimed in 1619, when he recalls the previous ordinances and speaks with indignation against the many persons who, for their own gain, were bold enough to violate the commandments. References were made to proceedings taken against certain persons in the High Court of Starre Chamber and of orders given for the demolishing of the houses of the offenders. It also stated:—

'If Wee should have proceeded against all of those in such examplary forms of Justice Wee should have caused great devastation in Our Citie of London and the places adjacent thereunto.'

The Starre Chamber acted as a side line in helping to replenish the Royal purse so King James had some consolation for the perverse ways of his loving subjects. A Commission was created of — 'certaine persons of trust giving them power to call before them such as had offended against Our sayd proclamations and for Us and on Our behalfe to compound with them for their offences, thereby to deter them and others from adventuring the like in time to come.' This Commission at a later date was referred to as "The Commission for Building" to deal with offences against the Proclamations.

1619: The birth of the Building Acts

In this Proclamation of 1619 is detected the birth of the Building Acts, for provisions were contained therein relating to the thickness of walls, windows, shop fronts etc., as follows:—

'Our expresse will and pleasure is, That in erecting of new Buildings hereafter, every whole Story of and in such houses, and Buildings, and all and every the roomes of such whole Story shall be of the height of tenne foot of assize at the least, and every halfe Story of and in such houses, and Buildings shall bee of the height of seven foote, and a halfe at the least:

and that the forefront and outward Walles, and the Jambes Heads and Soyles of the Windowes shall be of Bricke, or of Bricke and Stone, and the Windowes (being of Timber) not to bee put in untill the Jambes and Heads aforesaide bee finished and beare of themselves.'

Walls were to be of the following thicknesses:—

'And if the saide Buildings doe not exceed two Stories in height, then the Walles thereof shall bee of the thickness of one Bricke and halfe a Brickes length from the ground unto the uppermost part of the saide Walles: And where the Building shall be (over) the height of two Stories, the Walles of the first Story shall bee of the thickness of two Brickes length, and from thence to the uppermost part of the Wall, of the thickness of one Bricke and halfe a Brickes length.'

'And that in Building of the saide houses, there shall be no Jutties or Jutting, or Cant-windowes, either upon Timber Joystes or otherwise, but the Walles to goe direct and streight upwards, and at the setting off a water Table to bee made: Also the lights of the Windowes of every whole Story, to be of more height than breadth, to the end the roomes may receive ayre for health, and that there may be a sufficient peere of Bricke betweene the windowes for strength: And likewise the Windowes of every halfe story to be made square every way, or neere thereabouts.'

'And lastly, that all Shops in every Principall Streets of Trade, be made of Pillasters of hard Stone, or Bricke, and the heads of the Shop windowes cut in wedges Archwise, to sustaine the Wall about it, and for ornament of the Streets.'

In the year following, Londoners received some further instructions from the King in the matter of building. The Proclamation for 1620 has an interesting reference to the Assize of Fitz-Ailwyn in the reign of Richard I:—

'. . . . . the diligence and care of our Commissioners authorised for the execution of Our Commandments in that behalfe, And the duetifull obedience and conformitie of Our best disposed Subjects, Hath not onely given Us great content, but confirmed Our Resolution against all opposition of refractory persons, to proceede in a Worke not onely honourable and gracefull, but safe and healthfull for Our sayd Citie: It being not without president of ancient times, even in this Our Citie of London: In the records whereof it is remembered, that in the time of King Richard the first, Henry Fitz-Ailwyn then Mayor, for the prevention of casualties of fire, caused provision to be made, that Buildings in the sayd Citie should be of Stone, which for many yeeres after was observed; But the neglect thereof in succeeding times, especially in the present, the great confluence of Our sayd Citie, pestering of the Streets with Jutties, Stalles, and other annoyances, scarcitie of Timber, and many other occurrents, have turned the policie of those ancient times from conveniencie to necessitie: In which respect, We are now fully determined, not onely to ratifie Our former Commandments, but to use all possible endeavour by Our further care and direction to accomplish Our intention in a matter of such high consequence.'

Old and ruinous buildings were not to be strengthened or continued. The digging of cellars, bringing up of brick walls, new chimneys and staircases, setting on new roofs and thrusting out of dormers were all forbidden in old buildings within two miles of the city unless licensed and allowed by the Commissioners for Buildings.

'And further We do hereby straitly charge and command, That no person or persons, whatsoever within the limits aforesaid, doe at any times hereafter presume or attempt to erect, cover, overlay or inclose any Hovels or other Sheds of Timber, with Reeds, Faggots, Hay, Straw, Boards, or other materials, or doe raise up any wall, pale or banke of earth, to which Sheds may be added: Or doe repairs or new make into the Streets, any manner of Bulkes, Stalles, Windowes, doores, or other offensive issues: Or doe alter or change the use of dwelling house or other building to any more noysome or offensive use, end or purpose, than the same was imployed before the time of the demolishing or altering the same.'

The Building Act was continued –
All new houses and buildings within five miles of the gates of the city must be in brick or stone.
Storey heights of 10'0" and 7'6" confirmed. (The half storey apparently referred to attics and additions).
Outside, division or party walls, to be of brick or stone. Thickness of walls : Not exceeding two storeys – 1½ bricks for full height. Not exceeding three storeys – 2 bricks for first storey and 1½ bricks above. And so proportionally if there should be more storeys. Piers between windows were not to be less than one-half the breadth of the windows.

The final ordinance given by King James is dated 14th July, 1624, in which year he died. This last Proclamation while expressing approval of those who have obeyed the former edicts, especially – 'persons of best ranke and qualitie' – again has cause of complaint and warns others who continue to resist the orders of the paines, penalties and severe punishments which await them. The Lord Mayor, Aldermen, Sheriffs and Justices of Peace were also included in this warning on their being remiss in their duties and not enforcing the commandments.

The first Proclamation of the ill-fated Charles I is dated 2nd May, 1625. It mentions – 'the vigilant care His most Royal Father King James, of blessed memory, took in his lifetime to pursue the good course which the most excellent Princesse Queene Elizabeth had in Her time begun concerning inmates and buildings within the said Citie'.

No building whatsoever was to be erected within two miles of the City except it be on the foundations of a former dwelling house. All buildings built or set up, within the two miles, contrary to any Proclamation since 1615 were to be pulled down. Cellars were to be disused for lodgings or the victualling of houses. All outer walls of buildings within three miles of the gates of the City were to be constructed in brick or stone and erected according to form and proportion, i.e. thickness of walls, size of windows, etc.

1625, standard specification for bricks to be used in London

For the first time the substance of the 'brick' is dealt with. The method and period of digging, weathering, moulding, drying and firing being set out for the various stages of the process of brickmaking, The finished size of the brick was to be: length 9", breadth 4⅜" and the thickness 2¼". The price was fixed at eight shillings per thousand at the kiln and the Commissioners had authority to regulate the charge for cartage to the site. The brick may therefore be considered as being the first important item in building construction to be thoroughly standardised. These provisions constituted in fact, the first 'British Standard Specification', but the regulations were, at that time, restricted to the city and suburbs; they read as follows:

'And, for the better encouragement of His Majesties loving Subjects in their buildings, according to the directions of this Proclamation, His Majestie has thought fit, by the advise aforesaid, to set downe these Orders following, concerning the true making, and rating of the price of Bricke, which is one of the principall Materials, requisite for the said buildings, viz. That the earth, whereof the Bricke shall be made, be good and fit for that purpose: The first digging thereof to bee betweene the Feasts of Saint Michael the Archangel (29th Sept.) and S. Thomas the Apostle (21st Dec.). And the second digging, casting, or turning up of the said earth, to be at, or before the last day of February then following: And that no person whatsoever, doe presume to digge, or make any Bricke, in any place within one mile of the gates of the said Citie of London, or within one mile of his Majesties Palace of Westminster.

That the said Earth bee sufficiently and well wrought and tempered before it bee moulded: And that the Brick makers cause no earth to be moulded for bricke, but onely between the Feast of the Annunciation of the blessed Virgine Mary (25th March) and the last day of August yeerely, and at no other time or season of the yeere.

That in the moulding of the said brickes the moulds bee thoroughly and well filled, and not set in the moulds in the laying downe: And that they bee sufficiently and well dried before they bee put into the Kilne, and then carefully and thoroughly burned; so as for the assize, every bricke being burned, conteine in length nine inches, in breadth foure inches one quarter and a helf a quarter of an inch, and in the thicknesse, two inches and one quarter of an inch.

That the price of Brickes (being thus wrought and made in goodnesse, size and manner, as aforesaid) shall not exceede the rate of eight shillings the thousand at the Kilne: And if any excessive rate bee demanded for the carriage of the said Brickes, from the Kilne, to the place where they shall bee to bee used, the Commissioners for Building to moderate the same, according to equitie, in their good discretions: And that no person or persons shall make, or cause to be made within five miles of any of the gates of the Citie of London, nor bring by water or land, or utter, sell, or put to sale within the said Citie, or any place or places within five miles thereof, as aforesaid, any Brickes made or wrought contrary to the directions aforesaid, nor sell the same at any higher rate, than is before mentioned.'

The extraordinary effrontery with which these Proclamations were disregarded is well illustrated by the case of a certain Arthur Cundall who – 'presumed to erect a new house upon His Majesties owne ground nere the Parliament stairs, to the annoyance of His Majestie's passage that way and the offence of divers gentlemen of qualitye dwelling in those parts.' He was reproved by the Council – 'at several tymes' – but took no notice. At a meeting of the Council in 1627 the King being present, it was decided that – 'this insolent carriage of the said Cundall may not be longer suffered.' Allowed fourteen days in which to prove that the new building had been erected on old foundations, or to pull it down, Cundall still managed to defy the King's Court. Moreover he succeeded in obtaining licences for the buildings to be used as ale-houses. Although threatened many times with destruction the buildings apparently remained, for his name appeared in a list of 450 persons who paid compositions in 1638 for 1,361 houses erected contrary to the royal Proclamation. This case is reported in "The Growth of Stuart London" by Brett-James.

The next Ordinance is dated 16th July 1630, in which all requirements set out in the previous Proclamations, with a few variations, were imposed. There being an interesting proviso – 'Provided always that for so much as concerneth the building with bricke or stone shall not extend to any buildings upon London Bridge which by reason of the situation thereof cannot with convenience be so built.' Possibly these were the first exempted buildings.

A new departure occurred in 1636 when the Starre Chamber issued a Decree which again stressed the unfortunate state of affairs arising from the division of old buildings into tenements and the erection of houses. Parishes became over-burndened with poor and impotent persons and also with – 'idle, loose and dissolute beggars who committed pilfories, cosenges and infinite disorders.' The Court therefore ordered that the owners of these buildings should contribute towards the maintenance of the poor. An action taken by the Attorney General against two persons Rice Griffeth and John Scrips, who had erected tenements and divided them into several rooms, wherein divers poor persons dwelt, with the support of alms given by the Parish was described in the Decree. The offenders were sentenced, but the buildings were not demolished for the charge of rehousing the tenants would have fallen upon the Parish. The occupants were allowed to remain for the term of their natural lives in the buildings living rent free so long as they existed by begging and by assistance from the Parish. The fact that tenants would be allowed to occupy premises, without paying rent, while the landlords could also be called upon to contribute to their keep should have had a material effect in stopping the erection of tenements. Moreover on the departure of these protected dwellers the authorities were – 'to prostrate, pull down and deface the buildings in such sort as the same should be no more fit for habitation.'

The Decree reviewed the various edicts and recorded that 'Exemplarie sentences in this honourable Court have been pronounced against offenders and many houses and buildings have been demolished. Nevertheless such hath been the disobedience and contempt of great multitudes – that the new buildings and dividing of tenements have daily more and more increased – that in many Parishes there are far more householders and families that live by begging and other unlawful ways and by relief and alms of the Parish than are in the same Parish to live by their own means and vocation. So as the burden is growen so heavy that the wealthy are not able to relieve the poor in time of health much less in time of sickness or infection as hath appeared in the late visitation.'

The Decree goes on to indite the landlords of these tenements as being – 'guilte of a Common Nuisance' – and they were to be proceeded against – 'with more rigor and severity.' This extensive Decree contained most stringent orders on the restriction of building and perhaps something should be said on this Court of Starre Chamber.

The Starre Chamber was created by Henry VII in 1487 and abolished in 1641 by Charles I. The Court consisted of the Keeper of the Privy Seal, Lord Chief Justice, Lord Chief Baron and the Judges of His Majesties Courts of Kings Bench, Common Pleas and Court of Exchequer. In theory it was a revival of the judicial power of the King's Privy Council. Offenders could be called before the Court, tried and sentenced without a jury. The Court became known as the hated Starre Chamber, but when originally created it functioned to deal with the high-born rebels for the purpose of maintaining the authority of the Crown. It worked in the interests of the orderly against the disorderly, and in the difficult times of the Reformation it assisted in preserving the peace. Mr. P.J. Black, the late District Surveyor for South Kensington, prepared complete copies of the Proclamations from which extracts have been taken and recorded in the preceding pages. He considered that something could be said for the Starre Chamber's declarations as expressed in their Decree of 1636 and also for the methods they could exploit in calling experts to advise in particular cases. He thought that the Court could be regarded as equivalent of the Tribunal of Appeal, which is the body of arbitrators today under most of the present building law. There is, however, a great and fundamental difference, for the Court of Starre Chamber existed, mainly to pass decrees and prosecute offenders, while the Tribunal of Appeal holds the scales between the rights of the individual to freedom of action and authority seeking by law to control those rights for the benefit of the community, or even perhaps in the interests of the complainant himself.

The Civil War between King Charles and the Parliamentarians commenced in 1642 and dragged on for eight years. London supplied men, money and materials in the fight against the King, and the resources of the city proved a decisive factor in the ultimate result. In 1643 a threatened attack on the capital caused some consternation and defence works were put in hand, but the town was never actually in danger. The struggle developed in many parts of the country: Edgehill 1642, Marsden Moor 1644, and Naseby 1645 settled the fate of Charles, who was executed in Whitehall in 1649. The trouble then started again; to end finally with the battles of Dunbar 1650 and Worcester 1651. Before this date however the population of London had been reduced to dire straits and petitions were sent to Parliament pleading for peace. Trade stopped with the war and deserters, robbers and thieves swarmed in the town; riots and pillages occurred, and the citizens came near to starvation.

One incident in these troublesome times must not be forgotten for the consequences were to have far reaching effects on the destiny of our people. Between 1629 and 1640 some twenty thousand Puritans left these shores to avoid the religious persecution of Bishop Laud and they settled in the New World to become the ancestors of the great English speaking race of America. It is true that they were not the pioneers, but this emigration was by far the most important. Sir Walter Raleigh's attempt to found the colony of Virginia in the reign of Elizabeth failed, and in 1620 the "Mayflower" sailed from Plymouth with a small company of Puritans, who established themselves in the neighbourhood of Cape Cod.

The Commonwealth 1649–1660

The records of the Carpenters' Company contain some interesting details of their efforts to obtain relief from the edicts restricting building and sums of money were paid to – 'Counsell for a tolleracon for buildings.' The Company were also interested in the controversy of the time – timber versus brick buildings. The evidence also shows that a considerable amount of rebuilding went on after the Civil War, there being probably a shortage of housing accommodation. In 1655 the Order Books of the Company contain a resolution by which members were allowed to take an apprentice beyond the usual number – 'because divers persons of this Company have at present great employment in building, work being now very plentiful and still increasing.'

An Act for the preventing of the multiplicity of buildings in and about the suburbs of London, and within ten miles thereof. Year 1656

This Act referred to the excessive number of houses, etc. erected in and about the suburbs being – 'a great annoyance and nuisance to the Commonwealth.' It was enacted that for every dwelling house erected within ten miles of the walls of the city since 25th March 1620, and not having four acres of freehold land, at least, belonging thereto should be the subject of a fine of one year's rent to be paid to the Lord Protector. The Commonwealth Parliament assembled in 1649 so buildings erected twenty-nine years earlier in the reign of James I became liable for the fine. The Stuarts reigning without a Parliament could not think of a tax to equal this outrageous extortion. The order appears to have been based on the Act passed by Elizabeth in 1588 which did not apply to incorporated towns. The suburbs were therefore included in this tax as being outside of the town. It was further enacted that persons who, after September 29th 1657, erected or built – 'any dwelling house, out-house or cottage for habitation in or upon a new foundation, and shall not assign and lay four acres of ground – to every such house – in the suburbs of the city of London, or within ten miles of the said city shall forfeit and lose £100 of lawful English money for every such offence, for the use of the Commonwealth.' There was a continuing penalty of £20 per month if the premises were – 'upheld and continued' – this to be used for the benefit of the poor of the particular Parish. Persons making default in payment were to be apprehended and imprisoned – 'there to lie without bail or mainprize, until they have satisfied and paid the respective sums.' The payment of the fine acquitted the owner of all – 'penalties, forfeitures, suits, informations, indictments, persecutions and molestations whatsoever.' The Commissioners were allowed sixpence in every pound collected to cover their salaries and those of their deputies, clerks and others.

All manner of houses, edifices and cottages erected after the passing of the Act within the Cities of London and Westminster or the Liberties and Suburbs thereof or within the Borough of Southwark were to be built of brick or stone – 'straight up without butting or jetting out into the street'. The penalty for non-compliance being £100 and action had to be taken within one year of the offence. Churches, chapels, hospitals, almshouses, docks and various other buildings including certain houses in course of erection in Lincolne Inn Fields were exempted.

Sir William Petty 1623–1685, a great personality of the age, saw clearly the futility of these restrictions on building. Petty became Professor of Anatomy at Oxford but he is remembered chiefly as the "Father of Statistics". Evelyn considered him to be the second counsellor in the kingdom. Petty in his Treatise of Taxes and Essays in Political Arithmetick discusses the actual and probable size of London. He argued that it was unnecessary to curtail its growth and to discourage building on new foundations as the policy tended to – 'fasten the city to its old seat and ground plot – men being unwilling to build new houses on old sites and so they cobble up old houses until they become fundamentally irreparable, at which time they become either the dwelling of the Rascality or in process of time they return to waste gardens' Petty considered that the population of London would reach five millions by 1802, and over ten millions by 1842, at which figure the growth would stop. Actually the census figures for greater London in 1932 (90 years later) were eight and one-eighth millions.

CHAPTER IV

London under the Restoration, Charles II 1660–1685. The great fire of London and the first comprehensive Building Act.

Thoroughly tired by the exhortations and dour severities of the Puritans, under whose administration sports and pleasures had practically ceased, the city welcomed the restoration of the Stuarts in the person of Charles II in 1660. Bonfires and feastings signified the pleasure of the citizens, but they little knew the danger they were courting in choosing this clever and crafty King, who ultimately deprived them, by orthodox methods, of most of their rights, which his father Charles I failed to secure in his day.

On 16th August 1661, a Proclamation was announced concerning buildings. The former edicts of Queen Elizabeth and of the Royal Father and Grandfather of the king were mentioned – 'also the time of the late confusions', a remarkable reference to the Commonwealth, and it again appears that the people were increasing in great numbers, the price of victuals was going up and so were new unauthorised buildings. There is also a note of frequent fires chiefly occasioned by timber buildings. A point was made that the cost of building in brick or stone is found to be little more, if not less, than the building with timber. The injunctions against the erection of any new building, except on old foundations, were re-enacted – the limit being two miles from any of the gates of the city. All buildings to be of brick or brick and stone – 'Jutties, outwindows, or trussing over, or overchanging (sic) walls or windows, or any post or pillars to support the same towards the street, (other than windows commonly called ballconies) were prohibited. One or more "Ballconies" were allowed to houses of regular construction built with – 'walls upright from the foundations to the top, without jutties, outwindows or trussing over or overhanging as aforesaid.' The new buildings on London Bridge were exempted as before.

In addition to the Lord Mayor and other authorities there was reference to the Surveyor of His Majesties Works being responsible for seeing that the Proclamation – 'be in all things duely pursued and put in effectual execution: And to that end, to revive the former Orders and Proclamations in this behalf – and also touching the proportions and scantling of bricks – shall be observed, as was formerly directed and used, whereby the buildings may be more substantial, and not so slight as of late, and at present they have been in most places within the said cities and Limits aforesaid.'

The London of 1660

What changes had occurred in London, within the eighty years now passed since the first Proclamation of Elizabeth in 1580. By the edicts issued the town should have remained with little alteration. The only new buildings being in brick on sites where others previously existed. Some premises in stone and brick, mainly belonging to the Companies were certainly erected, but in the city the great mass of buildings must have remained as originally constructed in the early days of the Tudors. Probably the edicts had the effect of preventing the rebuilding of the old timber framed constructions, as the owners were not likely to favour the new order of building in brick with consequent loss of their projections over the streets. Although the repairing of old and worn out structures was forbidden under certain ordinances, there can be no doubt that many were in fact partly rebuilt and renovated on the old lines. In 1660 the city remained a perfect example of a mediaeval town; houses with high-pitched roofs and quaint gables with timber framed fronts stepped out in successive stories until the overhanging pent-houses almost met across the narrow lanes formed the bulk of the buildings. The shops were open to the streets as bazaars, in which a goodly store of rich merchandise could be found. Towering above this colourful collection of old structures stood the great grim Gothic Cathedral of St. Paul's[1], while 109 other churches raised their steeples or towers above the clustering pointed roofs of the surrounding dwellings. The one narrow bridge over the Thames carried a strange collection of shops and habitations maintaining their precarious existence by the mutual support given by one to the other. A crescent shaped wall encircled the city extending from the Tower in the east to the Temple in the west, and formed the northern barrier of defence. The Thames, an unpolluted river, in which fish were found in plenty flowed along the southern boundary and watermen plied their busy trade thereon. Practically all transport went by water and even the Lord Mayor proceeding from the city to Westminster went by way of the river in his gilded barge. The main streets, such as Cheapside, were largely blocked by markets, while projecting stalls on other highways formed formidable obstacles to traffic. The elite travelling through the city were carried usually in sedan chairs, which had been a licensed service since 1634. Hackney coaches were also available, but they proved to be of little use in the lanes and congested streets. The springs on these vehicles were practically non-existent, and the discomfort of this means of travel over the uneven roads must have been considerable. All dirt and filth went on to the highways, to be cleared away by the "Rakers" and rain from roofs, by way of spouting gutters poured likewise thereon. Of sewers and foot-pavements there were none, and a centre channel along the roads served to take away the water. Many of the gentry had left the smell, grime and inconvenience of the city to occupy new mansions in Westminster. Possibly King James had these buildings in mind when he referred – 'to finding a city of sticks and leaving one of bricks' – for these remarks were certainly not pertinent to the City of London. Outside the city ample open spaces, such as Moorfields and Hyde Park, had been preserved and the edicts had produced some effect on the newer suburbs, but the waterside communities such as lived in Stepney still inhabited old wooden hovels of an indescribable character. The dwellings growing in numbers between Westminster and the city were mainly of brick construction, on roads of a fair width.

Population of London in the seventeenth century

Astonishing variations in the estimates of contemporary writers on the population of London in the seventeenth century are recorded by Brett James in his book "The Growth of Stuart London". The most reliable information is probably that given by Captain John Graunt in a book published in the early years of the reign of Charles II. He based his figures on the Bills of Mortality and the records of christenings and he points out that in the first forty years of the century burials exceeded births; but the losses were more than equalled by the influx of persons from the country. The Civil War (1642–1651) did not materially affect the rate of increase of the population for although large numbers left the capital, many to fight for the cause they favoured, many more seeking refuge, came in to take their place. Graunt comments on the spread of London westwards where the wider streets could accommodate carriage traffic. He came to the conclusion that the inhabitants in and about

1. Bishop Mauritius commenced the erection of the cathedral after the old church founded by Mellitus had been destroyed by fire in 1087 or 1088. The work was declared complete in 1315 during the reign of Edward II. In 1561 the steeple was struck by lightning and destroyed by fire; it was never re-erected. In the reign of Charles I (1625–1649) the structure was restored and a classic portico added to the west front by Inigo Jones.

London in 1660 numbered approximately 460,000. Sir William Petty (1623–1685) of whom a reference is made on page 25, considered that the population for greater London had risen in the latter part of the century to 670,000. Mr. Walter Bell in his book on the "Great Plague" considers that in 1665 the figures were under half a million for the whole of London, City, Westminster, Liberties and other parishes, so it is certainly safe to say that within and around the city's ancient walls there dwelt some four hundred thousand persons in the year 1664. On this busy hive of folks, mostly crowded into inadequate dwellings, two terrible calamities were about to fall. In the winter of 1665, a plague, brought, apparently, from the Levant, commenced to take toll of the people. Through the hot and sultry summer days the infection spread with increasing intensity. The doors of houses marked with a red cross denoted the presence of the dreaded fever within, and by night carts carried away the dead to be buried in common pits. The winter of 1666 brought relief from the visitation but some 100,000 persons had perished. Towards the close of the summer of 1666 the city was swept away by fire.

The most devastating plagues of London in the 17th century are recorded as follows:–

1603 –	there died of plague	30,500
1625 –	" " " "	35,400
1636 –	" " " "	10,400
1665 –	" " " "	100,000

The Great Fire of London 1666

The fire commenced in the early hours of Sunday morning 2nd September, 1666, in a baker's shop in Pudding Lane, a narrow thoroughfare running north and south of Thames Street. The houses in this quarter were practically all of wood, and the fronts jutted out over the lanes to almost meet in the top storeys. Thames Street adjoining contained warehouses packed with combustible materials from spirits and oil to tar and pitch. Fanned by a strong east wind the fire spread rapidly and raged for four days. On the second day King Charles, realising that the conflagration was out of hand, rode into the city with his brother Duke of York. The King and the Duke gave workers much encouragement by taking part in their labours in passing buckets of water and helping with counter measures. On the third day, seamen brought from the dockyards, commenced to blow up blocks of property to form fire breaks. Towards nightfall the wind abated and on the fourth day the situation was under control, but fires in vaults continued to burn until the end of the year. The narrow lanes were useless to check the flying sparks and leaping flames which swept across them devoured the timber-fronted houses with incredible speed. Nightfall presented the scene as a fearful spectacle, the city being covered with lurid flames crackling and roaring; an old description reads – 'the bellowing wind drove the flames forward and their noise was like to a thousand iron chariots beating together upon the stones.' Pepys describes the flames as a – 'most horrid malicious bloody flame, not like the fine flame of an ordinary fire.' He escaped in his nightgown in a cart with his treasures which he buried in a garden at Bethnal Green.

Nearly four-fifths of the city was destroyed including St. Pauls and eighty-seven Parish Chruches, the Guildhall, the Royal Exchange, The Custom House, forty-four Halls of the City Companies, four Prisons, four Gates, numerous commercial buildings and thirteen thousand two hundred houses. Two hundred thousand people were rendered homeless. The loss was estimated at ten million pounds.

Rumours of plots by foreigners were dispelled by King Charles who addressed the refugees in person and promised to bring them aid. A Frenchman, Robert Hubert, however, insisted that he had fired the city and he was duly tried, convicted and hanged. England was at war with France and the Netherlands and the confession of this Frenchman, although undoubtedly false, did much to save the leasees, as even in those days they could not be

Engraving from a contemporary painting of the Great Fire at Ludgate in the City wall

held liable, by the landlords, for damage caused by the King's enemies. This did not mean that the government would pay for the loss, but the leases held by tenants unable to or unwilling to rebuild, were voided and any question of compensation arranged among the parties.

On 13th September a Proclamation announced the King's decision for dealing with the situation – intended as an interim measure only, it nevertheless contained the essence of the following building act, inasmuch as all new buildings were to be built of brick or stone and the eminent streets were to be widened, so that a fire could not cross from one side to the other. The new city was to have less lanes and alleys with a fair new frontage to the river. The duties known as "Hearth money" were rescinded for seven years and the King gave a promise – 'that though every man must not be suffered to erect what buildings and where he pleases he shall not in any degree be debarred from receiving the reasonable benefit of what ought to accrue to him from such houses or lands, there being nothing less in Our thoughts, than that any particular persons right and interest should be sacrificed to the publick benefit or convenience, without such recompense as in justice he ought to receive for the same: And when all things of this kind shal be prepared and adjusted by such Commissioners, and otherwise, which shal be found expedient, We make no doubt but such an Act of Parliament wil pass, as shal secure all men in what they shal and ought to possess.'

To give effect to this declaration a complete survey was necessary so that the position and extent of each person's holding could be ascertained. Since the whole area was covered with debris this information could not be obtained readily. To deal with this survey the king appointed three representatives: Dr. Wren, Hugh May and Roger Pratt, and the city nominated three also: Robert Hooke, Edward Jerman and Peter Mills. These six men were instructed early in October to press on with the survey and at the same time Beadles' Booths were set up in the various Wards to which the last occupiers of every building were ordered to bring, within fourteen days, a perfect survey of the ground whereon their premises stood with details of their rights thereto. The results were very meagre, and in spite of threats, little resulted. The tenants were in fact unable to clear the debris and unwilling to pay a fee for a survey to be made on their behalf and the scheme finally had to be abandoned.

The failure of the survey had unfortunate results for sites could not be allocated in the new planning to compensate owners for what they would lose, or in other words, the city could not be set out on a different plan with each person having a site or an interest, not necessarily in the original place, equal to that which he had lost, when in fact the holding of each person was unknown.

To get over the deadlock caused by the failure of the survey, the king gave £100 for the clearing of the streets.

The common impression that the opportunity of replanning the city fell through owing to the greed of the shop-keepers and landlords is not upheld by T.F. Reddaway, in his book "The Rebuilding of London after the Great Fire". He gives three reasons why the replanning did not take place:–

Firstly: the failure of the survey.

Secondly: the dire necessity for the rebuilding being commenced without delay otherwise merchants would seek accommodation elsewhere.

Thirdly: Parliament had to find the necessary money to prosecute the war with France and the Netherlands. The considerable expenditure needed for a total replanning could not have been readily repayed, and long term loans were then unknown.

With regard to the second reason it may be noted that in six years most of the houses had been rebuilt, but there were still a number of 'tofts', or empty spaces where a messuage had stood, but what was more important, a large number of the erected houses were vacant and the city had to take measures to induce the tenants to return. Some restriction in the planning did, in fact, take place due to the objections of certain owners and as an example Mr. Reddaway quotes Fetter Lane which the surveyors staked out to a width of twenty feet but which on the petition of one John Saunders became reduced in width to sixteen feet. Others objected to the lanes being increased in width to admit traffic, but very substantial widenings were achieved.

Parliament discussed the rebuilding of the city but they were much occupied by the war and finally the arrangements were left to the city and a Privy Council who sat once a week to receive a report of progress presented by the six Surveyors, or, as the King's three nominees were termed 'Commissioners for Rebuilding'. Of these men it is stated that Dr. Wren, the Professor of Astronomy and member of the Royal Society had the least qualifications in architectural subjects. His greatness was to come. Actually at this time the professional Architect did not exist, and the contractor with the plant and means for executing large works was also non-existent. These six men formed an ideal team and they were, without doubt, responsible for the first comprehensive Building Act for London which set a standard which subsequent Acts did not maintain. On 8th February, 1667, the Royal Assent was given to an Act for the rebuilding of the City of London. It should be noted that King Charles himself seemed to be fully alive to the necessity for the Bill and he certainly exercised his powers in persuading Parliament to expedite the passing of the measure. It is not too much to say that King Charles II was the patron of the original Building Act and that this act resulted from the great interest manifested in Building Regulations by his Stuart ancestors.

An Act for rebuilding the City of London 1667

I. Forasmuch as the City of London, being the imperial seat of his Majesty's kingdoms, and renowned for trade and commerce throughout the world; by reason of a most dreadful fire lately happening therein, was for the most part thereof burnt down and destroyed within the compass of a few days, and now lies buried in its own ruins: for the speedy restauration whereof, and for the better regulation, uniformity and gracefulness of such new Buildings as shall be erected for habitation in orders thereunto; and to the end that great and outrageous fires (through the blessing of Almighty God) so far forth as human providence (with submission to the divine pleasure) can forsee, may be reasonably prevented or obviated for the time to come, both by the matter and form of such building: and further, to the intent that all encouragement and expedition may be given unto, and all impediments and obstructions that may retard or protract the undertaking or carrying on a work so necessary, and of so great honour and importance to his Majesty and his Kingdom, and to the rest of his Majesty's kingdoms and dominions, may be removed;

II. Be it therefore enacted that the King's most excellent Majesty, by and with the advice and consent of the Lords spiritual and temporal, and commons, in this present parliament assembled, and by the authority of the same, That the rules and directions hereafter in this act prescribed, be duly observed by all persons therein concerned.

III. (1) No building or house for habitation whatsoever may hereafter be erected within the limits of the said city and liberties thereof, but such as shall be pursuant to such rules and orders of building and with such materials as are hereinafter particularly appointed and according to such scantlings as are set down and prescribed in the table in this present act hereafter specified.

(2) If any person or persons shall presume to build contrary thereunto, and be convicted of the same by the oaths of two or more credible witnesses, to be taken before the Lord Mayor for the time being or any two or more of the justices of the peace of the said city, who are hereby empowered to administer the same oaths; that then and in such case the said house so irregularly built as aforesaid shall be deemed as a common nuisance.

(3) The builder and levier thereof shall enter into recognizance in such sum as the said

lord mayor and justices respectively in their discretions shall appoint, for abatement and demolishing the same in convenient time, or otherwise to amend the same according to such rules and orders as aforesaid: in default of entering into such recognizance, the offender shall be committed in the common jail of the said city, there to remain without bail or mainprize, till he shall have abated or demolished or otherwise amended the same: or else such irregular house shall or may be demolished or abated by order of the court of aldermen.

IV. (1) And that the said irregular buildings may be the better prevented or more effectively discovered,

(2) be it further enacted by the authority aforesaid that the lord mayor, aldermen and common council of the said city shall and may at their will and pleasure elect, nominate and appoint one or more discreet and intelligent person or persons in the art of building, to be surveyors or supervisors to see the said rules and scantlings well and truly observed;

(3) and that it shall be lawful for the said mayor, aldermen and common council, or for the mayor and aldermen in their court of aldermen, to administer to all the said surveyors or supervisors, an oath upon the holy evangelists, for the true and impartial execution of their office in that behalf and to appoint the several precincts which shall be under their several surveys.

V. (1) And to the end that builders may the better know how to provide and fit their materials for the several buildings,

(2) be it enacted:– that there shall be only four sorts of buildings and no more, and that all manner of houses to be erected shall be of one of these four sorts of buildings and no other, (that is to say)

(a) The first or least sort of house fronting by-lanes
(b) the second sort fronting streets and lanes of note
(c) the third sort fronting high and principal streets
(d) the fourth and largest sort, of mansion houses for citizens or other persons of extraordinary quality not fronting either of the three former ways,

the roofs of each of the said first, second and third sorts of houses respectively shall be uniform.

VI. (1) On fifth April next ensuing the lord mayor, etc., were required to declare which and how many of the streets were to be regarded as coming within the above categories and they were to be marked or staked out by persons appointed under the common seal of the city. The marking out had to include the breadth, length and extent to avoid doubt.

(2) 'And if any person or persons whatsoever shall wittingly or willingly without good authority pluck up or remove any of the said stakes or markstones, thereby to obscure or confound the bounds of such streets or lanes, or any of them and shall be thereof legally convicted of one witness (other than of the informer) to be taken before any one or more justices of the peace... the said justices may send such offender to the common gaol – there to remain by the space of three months without bail or main-prize unless he pay or cause to be paid to the use of the mayor the sum of ten pounds to be employed towards the repairing of the public buildings.'

(3) 'Provided always that where any such offence shall be committed by any person or persons of low and mean condition whom the said justice or justices of the peace shall in his conscience believe to be unable to satisfy the said penalties, that then and in such case the said justice or justices shall and may by order and warrant under his or their hands and seals cause such offender to be openly whipped near unto the place where the offence shall be committed till his body be bloody.'

The Act provided that the outsides of all buildings in and about the city were to be – 'of brick or stone, or bricks and stone' except 'door-cases, window-frames, brest-summers and other parts of the first storey to the front, between the piers, which are to be left to the discretion of the builder to use substantial oaken timber instead of brick or stone for conveniency of shops.' The doors and window-frames also the brest-summers were to be 'discharged of the burden' of carrying the load above by 'arch-work of brick or stone either straight or circular.'

The number of storeys for each of the three sorts of buildings and the thicknesses of the external and party walls were specified in a table to the Act. Those of the fourth sort – being mansion houses were required to have the same scantlings as set out in the table, but the number of storeys and the height thereof was left to the discretion of the builder providing always that not more than four storeys could be erected. A balcony, projecting four feet, and a pent-house were permitted to houses fronting high streets. The pent-house had to be covered with lead, slate or tile and sealed with plaster, and apparently it could extend for the whole width of the building. Down pipes were required to convey rain water from the roofs and from projections to the street channels. Stall-boards to shop fronts could, when let down, extend only eleven inches from the buildings.

The clauses of the Act relating to party walls enacted that they should be built equally on both owners land and a special instruction from the Privy Council issued at Whitehall on 8th May 1667 called for the following procedure:– 'That the Surveyors shall take care for the equal setting out of all party walls and piers, and no persons be permitted to build till that be done; therefore, for the prevention of any exaction in the taking of such surveys, and of all quarrels and contentions that may arise between the builders, that no builder shall lay his foundation untill the Surveyors or one of them, shall view it and see the party walls and piers equally set out and that all persons observe the Surveyors directions concerning the superstructure to be erected over the said foundation.

And that for the defraying that, and all other incident Charges of Measuring, Staking out, Taking the Levell and Surveying the Streets and Ground, each Builder, before he lay his Foundation, or such survey shall be taken, do repair to the Chamber of London (City Treasury) and there enter his Name, with the place where his Building is to be set out, and to pay the Chamberlain the summe of six shillings eight pence for every Foundation to be rebuilt. For which Mr. Chamberlain shall give Acquittances: upon receipt of which Acquittances the Surveyors shall proceed to set out such persons Foundations.' This is the first reference to a builder giving Notice before commencing a work and the procedure is remotely akin to the practice today in respect of surveys for the relicencing of temporary structures – a certificate is not issued until the owner has paid the fee.

In erecting an isolated building the builder was required to complete the party walls, which could not then be used by an adjoining owner until he had paid one half the cost of the walls plus six per cent interest per annum.

Section XV of the Act made provision for the compulsory purchase by the city authorities of sites left vacant for over three years. The value to be assessed by a jury of – 'good and lawful men' – impanelled.

Section XVI dealt with the supply of building materials at reasonable prices and the employment of workmen at moderate wages. Two or more Justices of the King's Bench could summons the makers of bricks, or any other person, accused of unreasonable exactions and they could fix the price to give an honest profit – imprisonment being the penalty for non-compliance. The same procedure could be followed in cases of workmen attempting to extort excessive wages.

The city authorities were definitely required to widen certain streets including the following:– Fleet Street, Ludgate Hill, St. Pauls Churchyard, Cheapside, Poultry, Cornhill, Blowbladder Street, Newgate Market, Ave Maria Lane, Paternoster Row, Gracious Street, and several others – all narrow passages were not to be less than fourteen feet in width. They were also to make, or cause to be made a new street leading from the Guildhall to Cheapside.

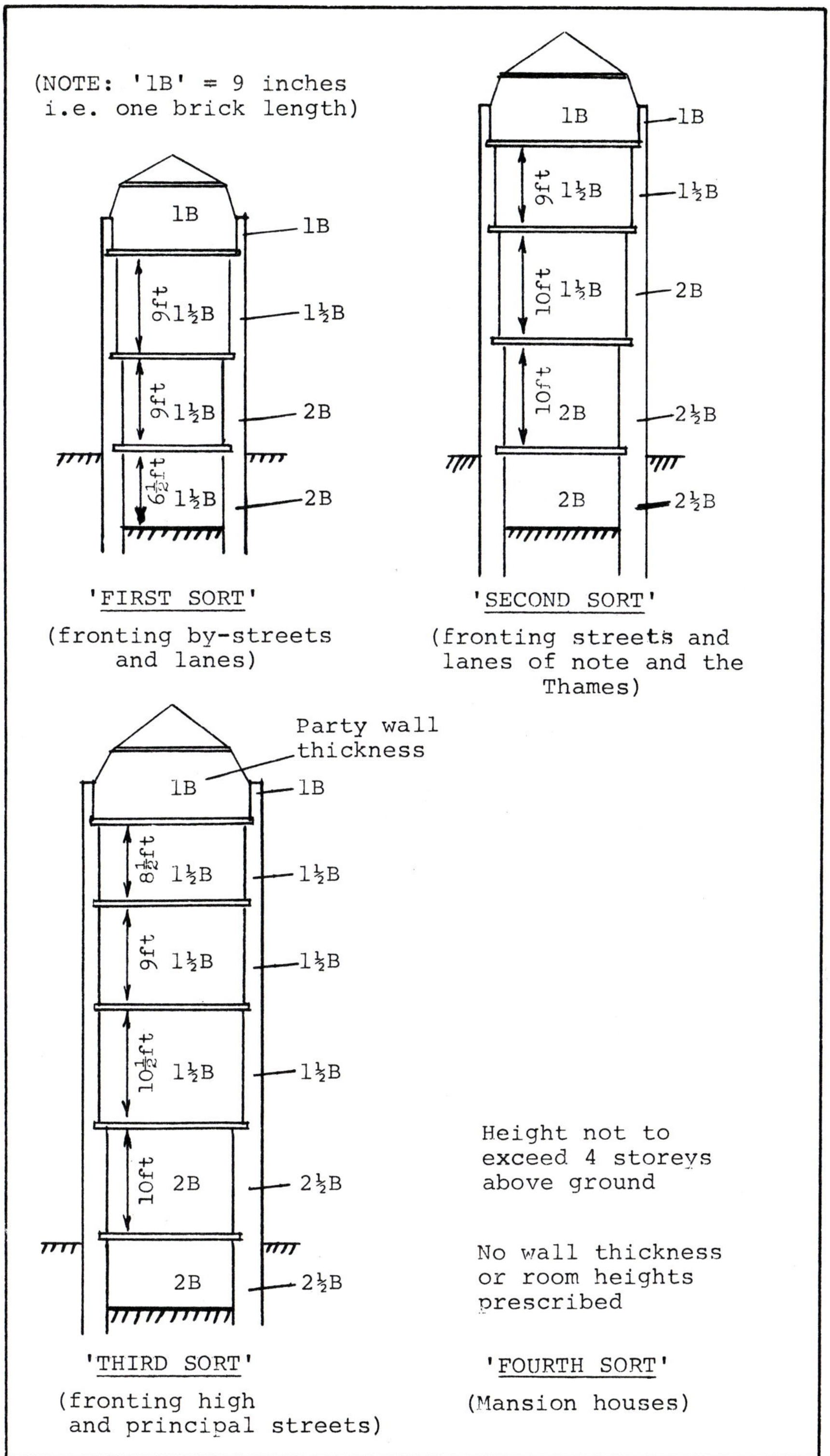

WALL THICKNESSES and ROOM HEIGHTS - 1667 ACT

P

At the Court at WHITEHALL the eighth of *May* 1667.

Present

The KING's most Excellent *Majesty*,

His *Royal Highness* the Duke of YORK,
Lord Arch-Bishop of *Canterbury*,
Lord Chancellor,
Lord Privy-Seal,
Duke of *Albemarle*,
Marquess of *Dorchester*,
Lord Chamberlain,
Earl of *Bridgwater*,
Earl of *Berkshire*,
Earl of *Bathe*,
Earl of *Carlisle*,
Earl of *Craven*,
Earl of *Lauderdaill*,
Earl of *Middleton*,
Lord *Arlington*,
Lord *Ashley*,
Mr. Comptroller,
Mr. Secretary *Morice*,
Mr. Chancellor of the Dutchy,
Sir *William Coventry*.

An ORDER made by the Lord Mayor, Aldermen, and Common Council of the City of *London*, of the 29. of *April* last past, in the ensuing words, (viz.)

IT is Ordered, That the Surveyors take special care, that the Breast-Summ[illegible] houses do range of an equal height house with house, so far as shall be convenient, and there to make [illegible]ions.

And that they do encourage and give Directions to all Builders for orna[illegible] and projections of the Front-Buildings be of rubbed Bricks; and that all the [illegible] of rough Bricks neatly wrought, or all rubbed, at the discretion of the Builder, or th[illegible] inrich their Fronts as they please.

That if any person or persons shall desire in any Street or Lane of Note to Build on each side of the Street or Lane (opposite one to the other) six or more Houses of the Third Rate, or that the upper Rooms or Garrets may be flat Roofs encompassed with Battlements of Bricks covered with Stone, or Gable ends, or Rails, and Bannisters of Iron or Stone, or to vary their Roofs for the greater ornament of Building; the Surveyors, or one of them, shall certifie their opinions therein to the Committee for Re-building, who shall have liberty to give leave for the same, if they see cause.

That in all the Streets no Sign-posts shall hang cross, but the Signs shall be fixed against the [illegible], or some other convenient part of the Side of the house.

It is Ordered that a Postern shall be made on the North-side of Newgate for Conveniency of Foot-passengers, and that Holborn-Bridge shall be enlarged to run straight on a bevil Line from the Timber-House on the North-side thereof, known by the Sign of the Cock, to the Front of the Buildings at the Swan Inne on the said North-side of Holborn-hill.

Forasmuch as it is Provided in the late Act for Re-building, That the Surveyors shall take care for the equal setting out of all party-Walls and Peers, and no person be permitted to build till that be done; therefore, for prevention of any Exaction in the taking of such Surveys, and of all Quarrells and Contentions that may arise between the Builders, it is Ordered, That no Builder shall lay his Foundation, untill the Surveyors, or one of them, (according to the Act) shall view it, and see the party-Walls and Peers equally set out, and that all persons observe the Surveyors Directions concerning the Superstructure to be erected over the said Foundation.

And that for the defraying that, and all other incident Charges of Measuring, Staking out, taking the Levell, and Surveying the Streets and Ground, each Builder, before he lay his Foundation, or such Survey shall be taken, do repair to the Chamber of London, and there enter his Name, with the place where his Building is to be set out, and to pay to the Chamberlain the summe of six shillings eight pence for every Foundation to be re-built. For which Mr. Chamberlain shall give Acquittances: upon Receipt of which Acquittances the Surveyors shall proceed to set out such persons Foundations.

And it is Ordered, That all persons who have already laid any Foundations shall forthwith pay into the Chamber of London six shillings eight pence for every Foundation.

And this Court is consenting and desirous that all streight and narrow Passages, which shall be found convenient for common Benefit and Accommodation, and shall receive his MAJESTIE's Order and Approbation, shall and may be Inlarged and made wider, and otherwise Altered, before the 20. day of May now next ensuing, as shall be fitting for the Beauty, Ornament, and Conveniency thereof, and Staked and set out accordingly.

Several late Inhabitants of Fleetstreet, intending to Re-build their Houses which did formerly stand backward of other Foundations near adjoyning, and desiring liberty to advance their Houses, that the whole Front may run on a straight Line; the Committee did agree to the same, if the Right Honourable the Lord High Chancellor of England and the other Lords shall approve thereof, and procure his MAJESTIE's Approbation to the same: and the Committee do desire liberty may be given for other persons in other places, where it shall be found convenient.

And it is Ordered, That the Committee for Re-building do present the Particulars aforesaid to the Right Honourable the Lord High Chancellor of England and the other Lords, and that the same (if they receive his MAJESTIE's Approbation) shall be forthwith Printed and Published.

Which being this day represented to the Board by the Right Honourable the Lord High Chancellor of *England*, the same was allowed and approved of; and it was Ordered that the same be punctually observed in every part thereof. And all persons concerned are required and commanded to yield due obedience and conform themselves thereunto. And that the said Order be forthwith Printed and Published.

Edw. Walker.

Printed by *James Flesher*, Printer to the Honourable City of LONDON.

Proclamation of 1667

Section XXXVI enabled the Mayor and Commonalty to meet the cost of the street widening and improvements by giving them authority to impose a tax of twelve pence on every chaldron of twenty six bushels, or one ton, of all sorts of coals imported and brought into the City of London. This tax was fixed for ten years from 24th June, 1667.

Trades judged as – 'Noisom or perillous' – in respect of fire could be prohibited on the principal streets. Authority was given for the construction of common sewers, drains or vaults and a reasonable tax could be imposed on property benefiting thereby. The 2nd September was to be observed yearly as – 'a day of publick fasting and humiliation' – in remembrance of the great calamity and a column of brass or stone was to be erected near to the place where the fire began in perpetual remembrance. The column known as "The Monument" was built for this purpose.

Of the many churches destroyed the Act provided that only 39 in number should be rebuilt and the sites of those left vacant were to be sold and the money obtained employed as a contribution towards the cost of those to be re-erected.

Sections XLIII–XLVI dealt with construction matters and included a table of thicknesses for walls and heights of storeys: a schedule of timber scantlings was also set out therein.

Section XLVII contained general rules relating to:–

(1) Foundations.
(2) Timber near chimney jambs.
(3) No timber within the tunnel of any chimney with penalty and weekly continuing penalty against the workmen.
(4) Joists not to exceed 12" apart.
(5) Bearing of joists not longer than 10' or single rafters longer than 9'.
(6) Roofs, window-frames and cellar floors to be made of oak.
(7) Tile-pins of oak.
(8) No summers or girders to lie over the head of doors or windows.
(9) No summer or girder to lie less than 10" in the wall, joists 8" to be laid in loam.

The Privy Council's instructions issued on 8th May, 1667, also contained the following:–

'It is ordered that the Surveyors take special care that the brest summers of all houses do range of an equal height house with house, so far as it shall be convenient and there to make breaks by their directions. And that they do encourage and give directions to all builders for ornament sake, that the ornaments and projections of the front-buildings be of rubbed bricks; and that all the naked parts of the walls may be done of rough bricks neatly wrought, or all rubbed at the discretion of the builder, or that the builders may otherwise inrich their fronts as they please.'

'That in all the streets no sign-posts shall hang across, but the signs shall be fixed against the balconies or some other convenient part of the side of the house.'

Provision is made for other designs subject to the Surveyor "certifying their opinions therein to the Committee for Rebuilding, who shall have liberty to give leave for the same if they see cause". (of the present-day "waiver" system).

The Act of Elizabeth (1562) controlling wages, etc., has been referred to and this Act conferred great advantages on the City Companies interested in building, for the system of apprenticeship for seven years with a master, was confirmed and made law in that statute. The Building Act of 1667 cut across these close trades and admitted foreigners to the crafts. There was some trouble in consequence, and petitions were presented by the Carpenters' Company and others concerned.

The rebuilding of the City

The position was now clear, the old planning would be retained but certain streets widened and other improvements effected. King Charles had approved the plan with many valuable suggestions, including one for the removal of the street markets to market houses, which was duly acted on. But other alterations to the planning proposed by the king were shelved on the grounds that only the widenings authorised by the Act could be carried out. Armed with a comprehensive Building Act the work of setting out the streets and the sites could be proceeded with while disputes could be settled by a special court termed the "Fire Court". The Surveyors chosen for the job were Peter Mills, Robert Hooke, Edward Jerman and John Oliver. The first three were the City's representatives, mentioned previously and Mills, the City Surveyor, and Hooke were sworn in on 14th March 1667, their authority of staking being sealed by the City on 20th March. Jerman and Oliver refused the office but, in Mills' absence due to illness, Oliver acted in his place and in January 1668 he accepted and was duly sworn in. These three men were the first statutory Surveyors for, in addition to their work of staking out streets and sites, they surveyed the buildings and watched to see that the Act was not infringed. Before long the city was calling on these Surveyors for weekly returns of irregular and defective buildings in their respective districts. In 1676 they were ordered to make a full survey to discover irregularities and the Common Sergeant was instructed to advise on the best course for prosecuting those responsible. Five years later the Aldermen were still pursuing irregularities and in 1685 the question of insufficient fall pipes caused some trouble.

The Surveyors had a tough job for they were expected to satisfy and make amicable settlements among the parties interested in the various sites with which they had to deal, but such matters as could not be arranged went to the "Fire Court".

The short description of this truly remarkable Building Act of 1667, given on the preceding pages, indicates, to some extent, the completeness with which the ground was covered and the production of such an Act in about four months with very little in the way of precedent must rank as a distinct achievement. The Act practically covered the construction of buildings and it must have proved an inestimable advantage to many owners who could instruct their builders to erect buildings of the particular grade applicable and then to merely specify the fittings and finishings required.

The rebuilding of the churches and halls extended over many years and the work on St. Pauls, commenced in 1675 continued until 1710, but the houses and commercial buildings were complete by 1676. In ten years London had been reinstated and a very different place it must have seemed to the old inhabitants. The mediaeval city had disappeared. The ramshackle overhanging timber framed structures facing the streets and the indescribable collection of hovels of one sort or another clustering on the lanes, courts and alleys at the rear, had gone for ever. The picturesque city with its quaint signs, many of which extended right across the thoroughfares and its spouting gutters, had vanished as an artist's dream. In place of the colourful motley collection of dwellings, buildings of brick with unbroken elevations, built to definite frontage lines, on widened streets had arisen. Now could the grandson (Charles II) of James I most truly say of the city – 'Wee had found Our Citie of London of sticks and left it of brick being a material farre more durable safe from fire beautiful and magnificent.' The first and perhaps the greatest of all Town Planning Schemes had come into being. It is true that no provisions were made for open spaces at the rear of dwellings, but perhaps that would be asking too much at that time. The Act controlled buildings in the city for over one hundred years until 1774 when its provisions were repealed by an Act which did not possess a vestige of Town Planning and under which buildings were again allowed to be built on any street, wide or narrow, to unlimited heights.

Those who had to deal with the piles of debris and the fire-swept area following the great fire of December 1940 will, at least, have some appreciation of the tremendous difficulties which beset the city in 1666. Every credit is due to those three Surveyors: Robert Hooke, Peter Mills and John Oliver, who brought order and well constructed buildings to that great area of chaos, ruin and desolation; their names should be recorded, with grateful remembrance, in the annals of the city. Theirs was a great work and District Surveyors today can think of them with pride as they were undoubtedly the first Statutory Surveyors. Their salaries are reported to have been £100 per annum increased to £150 after the first six months.

The Act of 1667 applied only to the city and in 1671 King Charles issued a Proclamation against certain mean habitations and cottages being erected in the suburbs. The places named are the Fields called Wind-Mill-Fields, Dog-Fields, and Fields adjoining So-Hoe. He objected to these buildings as they rendered – 'the government of those parts more unmanageable; But especially by choaking up the air of His Majesties Palaces and Parke – whereby His Majesties Palaces may be greatly annoyed, the houses of the nobility and gentry very much offended, the Parishes over charged, the perfecting of the city buildings very much hindered, and the health both of the city and suburbs exceedingly endangered.' The Proclamation required the erection of the buildings to cease and none to be finished without – 'His Majesties licence in that behalf'. The final threat reads – 'His Majesty will cause such buildings to be abased and thrown down and the persons of such offenders to be arrested and seised and further proceeded against according to the utmost rigour and severity of the law.'

The passing of the Stuarts. Developments of the century.

Charles II died somewhat suddenly in 1685 but, before his demise he had reduced the City Authorities and those of other towns to a state of impotence and this he accomplished by playing his own party, the Royalist, against the other parties and obtaining the election to office of the men who would serve him. He also had an army of 10,000 men. He suspended the exchequer, or the payment of interest on money lent to the crown and ruined some of the principal bankers and many who to them had trusted their money. The city had become weak from the several disasters, the Civil War, the Plague, and the Fire and Charles had all the control he would have wished.[1] His death proved opportune or possibly the destiny of the country might have suffered a change. James II, his brother, lacked the ability of Charles and his arbitrary policy cost him the crown. William and Mary were crowned in 1689 – Mary died in 1694 and William in 1702 when Anne the second daughter of James II came to the throne.

The seventeenth century will be remembered for Town Planning other than the rebuilding of the city for some of the most important squares of London were set out in the hundred years. Covent Garden Square, designed by Inigo Jones (1630), Leicester Square laid out fronting Leicester House (1635), Bloomsbury Square (1665), Lincoln Inn Fields and Red Lion Square largely preserved from buildings in about 1684, Soho Square (1681), Grosvenor Square (1695), Berkeley Square (1698), St. James' Square (1684).

The most celebrated speculative builder of the age was undoubtedly Dr. Nicholas Barbon or Barebone – the son of Praisegod Barebone who gave his name to a notorious

1. Sir Laurence Gomme refers, in his book "The Making of London" to the surrender by the City Authorities of their Charter to Charles II as the 'one miserable occasion in the history of the city's fight for liberty and right.' He quotes from John Evelyn's diary (June 18th 1683) – 'I was present and heard the humble submission and petition of the Lord Maior, Sheriffs, and Aldermen on behalf of the Citty of London, on the quo warranto against their charter which they delivered to his Majesty in the Presence Chamber. It was delivered kneeling' . . . They were required – 'that they should neither elect Maior, Sheriff, Aldermen, Recorder, Common Sergeant, Town Clerk, Coroner or Steward of Southwark without His Majesty's approbation.' The occasion called from John Evelyn the bitter remark 'and so they tamely parted with their so ancient privileges after they had dined and been treated by the King.'

Parliament. Nicholas Barbon is referred to by contemporary writers as 'that great builder', so some reference should be made to his works. He demolished two riverside palaces in the Strand, Essex House and York House, and covered the sites with streets and buildings – Essex Street, Villiers Street, etc. He bought Red Lion Fields and fell foul of the lawyers in an attempt to build over the open space. Warrants to stop the building resulted in malicious and vexatious actions by Barbon at law. There appeared to be no easy way to frustrate a speculative builder in those days and the Square was developed but with a considerable saving of open space. Barbon had many other speculations including the Bedford Corporation's estate in Holborn, Devonshire House, Bishopsgate and much of the rebuilding of the city can be traced to him. Some of his work came into the category of jerry-building and he knew how to make the most out of a plot by curtailing the frontages. He published a book, "An Apology for the Builder" in which he pointed out that the natural increase in mankind is the cause of the increase of the city. He further claimed that the building restrictions of Cromwell (The Commonwealth Act of 1656, see pages 24-25) had resulted in immigration and in spite of the restrictions only £20,000 had been collected for infringements of the regulations. He was a pioneer of fire insurance and the Phoenix Office claim him as their founder. Barbon had many other irons in the fire, including the floating of land banks. He lived spendidly, but mostly on credit and he died in 1698 crushed by the failure of his plans. Had he survived to see one only of his many grandiose schemes succeed he would have died a wealthy man. The mentality of this builder of London is indicated clearly by the instructions he left to his executors – 'to pay none of my debts.'

CHAPTER V

Building Enactments 1700–1774.
The Act of 1707.

"An Act for the better preventing mischiefs that may happen by fire." The bogey of fire is still the motive power for the Building Acts and this measure had for its main objective the formation of a fire brigade. The Statute commences with a Statement on the many fires occurring about the Cities of London and Westminster to the utter ruin of many subjects. The churchwardens were made responsible for the fixing of fire cocks and wooden plugs to water mains – 'belonging to any water-works whatsoever' – the plugs – 'to lie even with the pavement – so that such cocks may be opened to let out the water without loss of time in digging down to the pipes, the position of the stop cocks to be marked in the front of the houses. Every Parish to have and keep in good order in a known public place a large engine and a hand engine to throw up water for extinguishing fires.' Defaulting churchwardens were liable to penalties.

Section II. exempted certain watermen retained by Insurance Companies for arresting or extinguishing fires, from being impressed to serve as marines or soldiers.

Section III. provided that servants causing fires by negligence and carelessness should be liable on conviction for a fine of £100 or imprisonment for eighteen months with hard labour.

Section IV. enacted that new houses shall have party walls wholly of brick or stone – two bricks thick in the cellar and ground storeys, thirteen inches thick upwards through all storeys to eighteen inches above the roof. No – 'mundillion or cornish of timber or wood under the eaves', front and rear walls to be built of brick or stone (2′6″ high above the garret floor). The owner or builder of any new house built contrary to the true intent and meaning of this Act was liable to forfeit loss and pay for such default £50, the money to be divided between the informer and the poor of the parish.

Under this Act party wall parapets appear to be required, but further mention is made on this matter later. The administration was evidently left to the common informer.

In the following year a further Act extended the arrangements for fighting fires and confirmed the rules in respect of party walls. A clause added exempted the buildings on London Bridge. Party walls were to be built equally on each owner's land and the adjoining owner had to pay for his part of the wall at the rate of £5 per rod of brickwork. No beams or rafters to be built in the brickwork of gable ends. Chimney jambs and backs were required to be nine inches in thickness with four and a half inch 'withs', all funnels plastered or pargetted inside from bottom to top; hearths, timber near to chimneys and flues, wainscoting, etc. were referred to, gable ends to be rendered on the rough side, all stoves, boilers and coppers were not to be built nearer than nine inches to the adjoining house, timber to be kept at least five inches from any fireplace or flue.

Section XII. referred to the frequent great damage which happens by constant decay occurring by the setting of brickwork upon timber. No brickwork or stonework in the fronts, party or partition walls of any house – shall be supported, depend or otherwise bear upon any sort of timber or woodwork (excepting piles or planks where they are absolutely necessary for foundations in marshy and unsound ground and excepting likewise all houses upon London Bridge and on the river of Thames below bridge). Every person offending liable to three months imprisonment.

Section XIII required the fixing of door frames and window frames of wood to be set into wall four inches.

These two Acts had far reaching effects on the architecture of the day; that well known style termed "Queen Anne", in which the frames of doors and windows were fixed flush with the outsides of the walls, and wooden cornices and hoods over the entrance doorways were distinctive features. This type of house front so much admired in later days and which came undoubtedly from Holland with William, now became illegal in the eighth year of the reign of Queen Anne. Consequently relatively few buildings on these lines could have been erected at that time.

Queen Anne died in 1714 and by decree this date marks the division between old and modern, and all things created after this date cannot be termed ancient, so we now leave the misty past for the definite present.

The Act of 1724

"An Act for the better regulating of buildings and to prevent mischiefs that may happen by fire within the weekly bills of mortality, and other places therein mentioned."

Sections I & II of the Act dealt with procedure in obtaining the rebuilding of old and defective party walls. The decision being left to the verdict of workmen to be appointed by both owners and who were to give their expressed opinions to the Justices who could examine the men on oath and issue a final award. After notice the building owner had the right, if confirmed by the award, to proceed with the rebuilding and to enter the adjoining house to execute all necessary shoring. The adjoining owner on the completion of the wall could be called upon to pay one half of the cost thereof.

Section III enacted that to avoid the spread of fire from one house to another – 'that it was not lawful to make or have in any party wall of a house (after 24th June 1725) any door-case, window, lintol, brest-summer or storey-posts, or plates whatsoever – unless where two or more houses shall be laid together and so used or occupied as one house only.' The penalty £50 could be imposed if the openings were retained and used contrary to this law. This clause did not prevent such openings in the front of the house for the convenience of shops only. This is the first direct permission for the uniting of premises in one occupation.

Other provisions included a requirement that party down pipes should be fixed to take water from roofs, balconies, etc. into the street channels. Penalty for non-compliance £10. All penalties and forfeitures could be sued for, levied and recovered – one half thereof being paid to the informer, and the other half to the poor of the parish.

This Act extended to – 'the Cities of London and Westminster (except houses on London Bridge or on the river Thames below Bridge) St. Marylebone, Paddington, Chelsea and St. Pancras. This is the first time that these Parishes outside the cities are mentioned.

George I died in 1727 and thirty-three years later in 1760 being the last year of the reign of George II an Act was passed for widening certain streets, lanes and passages in the City of London and for opening certain new streets etc. The Act give the Lord Mayor and Aldermen power to acquire lands for the widening of Minories, Bishopsgate Street and several other streets. Compensation for ground taken was to be assessed by a jury impanelled for the purpose. Amendments in the procedure on the rebuilding of party walls were included, the thicknesses being increased to – 'two bricks and one half in the cellar and two bricks upwards'. Further no timbers except as specified were to be laid in party walls and such timbers fixed in either side of the wall were not to meet but to be nine inches distant. Penalty £50, to be divided between the informer and the poor of the parish. Building costs were evidently increasing for a clause inserted raised the price to be paid, by an adjoining owner on the rebuilding of a party wall from £5 per rod to £7 per rod.

Section XXVIII of this Act of 1760 contained the first regulations for dealing with dangerous structures. It refers to certain houses in the City of London being in such a condition – 'that passengers passing thereby are in danger of their lives from the falling thereof, or of bricks or timber therefrom; and often are hurt by the falling of the walls thereof. From 24th June, 1760 if any presentment shall be made by any inquest or grand jury in London that any houses or tenements – are in such ruinous condition it shall be lawful – on notice of any such presentment being made – to cause, with all convenient speed, a proper and sufficient hoard to be put up to guard all such ruinous houses from the public street and to cause notice in writing to be given to the owner, if he can be found, if not, notice to be left at the premises to repair the same or to take down such buildings, as the case shall require, within the space of six days then next ensuing.' If not complied with, the court could authorise the removal of the danger and levy the charges on the owner. The cost could also be recovered by distress and sale of goods or alternatively recovered from the future occupier; the money recovered to go to the credit of the city.

The Euston Road is formed

Before leaving the reign of George II it should be mentioned that several of the main thoroughfares which serve the central portions of the Metropolis were then being developed. These roads were controlled by Turnpike Trusts and one in particular is worthy of special notice.

By an Act of George II a new road was formed in 1757 from the Edgware Road to Islington and that main highway named The Marylebone Road. Euston Road, and Pentonville Road came to be constructed by a Trust having charge of the roads in the vicinity. Under this Act the frontages of all buildings were to be kept to a line of fifty feet from the footways of this new street and any buildings erected on such grounds, contrary to the Act, were to be treated as common nuisances and removed. What a grand highway London would possess today if these regulations had been observed.

George II passed away in 1760 and the next Act came in the year 1764 under George III.

The Act of 1764

Party walls and the rebuilding thereof were again a main item in this Act. Further precautions were included to obtain just decisions from the workmen appointed to pass judgment on defective party walls. The thicknesses required in the preceding Act were confirmed, being two and one half bricks thick in the cellar, two bricks up to the garret floor and from thence one brick and half a brick thick at least eighteen inches above the roofs or gutters which adjoin to such party walls.

A clause excluded all timbers from being laid in party walls except timbers of girders, binding joists, etc. for which rules were prescribed. Further these walls – 'were not to be cut into or wounded for the purpose of making chimneys.' A clause laid down conditions on timber near or under hearths and chimneys and excluded timber buildings from being built adjoining or attached to any house. Also – 'that all houses shall be erected and built of stone or good, sound, hard, well-burnt bricks and none other both in the front and back walls and likewise the party walls and that no brest-summer shall be provided higher than the first floor.'

Section VI enacted that every master builder erecting a building after 1st July 1764, shall within fourteen days after the building is covered in, cause the building to be surveyed by one or more of the Surveyors. The Surveyor to make oath before one of his Majesty's Justices of the Peace that the house has been (to the best of his judgment and belief) built and erected agreeable to the directions of this Act; the affidavit to be filed with the clerk of the peace for the county of Middlesex within ten days, the clerk being entitled to receive the sum of one shilling for his trouble.

An interesting instruction on the payment of fire insurance money is contained in this measure and the procedure suggests that the Insurance Offices may have proposed the method set out – 'for the better preventing mischiefs that may happen by fire and to deter and hinder ill-minded persons from wilfully setting their house or houses or other buildings on fire with a view to gaining to themselves the insurance money whereby the lives and fortunes of many families are lost;' it was enacted that it was lawful for the directors of insurance offices upon application and request from any person – or upon grounds of suspicion that the owners had been guilty of fraud or wilfully setting the houses on fire, to cause the insurance money to be expended so far as it would go towards rebuilding, reinstating etc., such houses – 'so burnt down, demolished and damnified, by fire' – unless the parties claiming the money could give sufficient security that it would be properly expended.

The provisions of this Statute could not be ignored with impunity for the penalties for non-observance extended to a fine of £50 or commital to prison for six months.

The conditions of the highways and lanes of the Metropolis by the middle of the eighteenth century still left much to be desired. Over fifty years had to pass before the efforts of McAdam (1756–1836) with his method of surfacing roads with layers of broken granite came to be adopted. A further menace to the streets had arrived in the operations of the water companies and their depredations are mentioned in an Act of George III which covered the repairing, watching, cleansing and lighting of the streets of the city. Under this Act the Mayor, Commonalty and Citizens were vested with powers to elect Commissioners of Sewers who could appoint surveyors and other officials to supervise works to highways; to collect rates and to deal with nuisances and other matters such as stands for public vehicles. Outside the city the inhabitants had for years taken upon themselves the responsibility for repairing the surfaces of the streets and lanes and the provision of a central authority to take over those works was much overdue. The duties were now about to be delegated to bodies of Commissioners and many Acts were passed subsequently concerning, in this respect, the more congested parishes. In the year 1765 such an Act dealt with the parish of Southwark. Watchmen, beadles and other officers were to be employed, their duties and wages were laid down in the Statute which covered such other matters as the repair of drains and the issue of licences to persons requiring to set up hoardings, etc. Further examples of similar Acts are given later.

The Act of 1765

The Statute applied only to the city and dealt with doubts which had arisen under the Act of 1760. It amended the provisions as to the use of timber in party walls and the thicknesses thereof. Henceforth they were to be two and half bricks in the cellar and two bricks upwards to the top above the tiling and then to rise 9″. Party wall parapets nine inches high are clearly required by this clause to the Act. The reference in the Act of 1764 called for such parapets eighteen inches above the roofs and gutters adjoining thereto. In the preface to "Dicksee's Building Acts" he claims the Act of 1764 as being the first to require party wall parapets, but this seems doubtful having regard to the wording of the Act of 1707 in which the provision reads – 'party walls – and thirteen inches thick upwards from the foundations quite through all the storeys of each house and eighteen inches above the roof.'

This 1765 Act prohibited the use of bond timbers in walls except for short lengths to act as spreaders under the ends of heavier timbers. Precious little notice appears to have been taken of this regulation; few old walls, party or otherwise, are found today without bond timbers. Timber beams under this Statute could bear in and on party walls twelve inches, but they were not allowed to meet or be laid opposite each other. They were to be nine inches distant from each other on the sides.

A variety of buildings at the Bank in the time of George III

Before the Great Fire buildings had exposed timber frames projecting further in each storey. Those rebuilt after the 1667 Act had to 'rise straight up' and have their outsides entirely of brick or stone. The brick buildings on the extreme right and left of this scene are typical of those built soon after the fire and display window frames nearly flush with the outside face of the walls. In the later Building Acts from 1707 the window and door frames had to be set back 4 inches from the face of the walls so that they would be less liable to catch fire – the next two buildings on the left have such windows and therefore date from after 1707.

It will also be noted that none of the buildings has any projecting gables or eaves of timber – these were banned by the Act of 1707 but in later Acts from 1894 they were permitted in detached and semi-detached dwelling houses. An even later building can be seen on the corner on the right – with stuccoed walls and pediments in the style of the Adam brothers which became popular in the 1780's. Stucco became more widely used following improvements in the manufacture of cement, especially by Nash in Regent's Park and Regent Street by which time it was almost universal. The slates shown on the roof of this building came into common use only in the 1770's following the opening of large quarries in Wales then.

Another Act followed, in the year 1765:–

The preamble, after referring to previous Acts continued – 'and notwithstanding the said recited Acts touching the pulling down ruinous, bad, and defective party walls, wilful and litigious persons may endeavour to prevent the same being done, by opposing the entry of the first builder into the house which adjoins to such party wall in order to shore up the same for the purpose of taking down the said party wall.' On such a case arising a complaint could be lodged with a Justice of the Peace who could issue a warrant, and fourteen days after service of this warrant at the premises the builder could – 'between the hours of eight in the morning and four in the afternoon enter into the house adjoining . . . . for the purpose of shoring up etc., and if the outer door should be shut and the owner or occupier or other person refuse to open the same being thereunto demanded, to break open such door and remove any goods, furniture, shelves, or other matter or thing whatsoever which shall obstruct the execution of the said works.' The order by the Justices could be appealed against.

Clauses were added with respect to compensation for the making use of a party wall by an adjoining owner; the amount generally being one half the cost of the part so used.

The regulations on timber in party walls were confirmed and penalties against builders neglecting to build according to the Acts were maintained. Workmen acting contrary to the directions of the Acts were liable to forfiets and in default of payment they could be – 'committed to the house of correction for the space of three months without bail or mainprize unless the said penalty shall be sooner paid.'

A further Act applying only to the city was passed in 1767 by which the sole powers and authority for the pitching, paving, cleaning and enlightening (sic.) the streets, lanes, squares, courts, alleys, passages and places within the city and liberties thereof was conferred upon persons to be appointed by the Mayor, commonalty and citizens; such persons were to be known as Commissioners of Sewers. The Act also had reference to other matters including the prevention of obstructions and annoyances within the city and the Act of 1765 was repealed in this respect. Paragraph 35 contained the following – 'every occupier of every house or tenement within the said City . . . . . and every house owner, shall once in every day, between the hours of eight and ten of the clock in the forenoon of each day, scrape, sweep and cleanse the footway all along the front of their respective houses or tenements or cause the same to be scraped, swept and cleansed and in default thereof shall, for every such offence, forfeit and pay the sum of five shillings.' These requirements constituted an attempt, in part at least, to revive the old duties inflicted upon the householder in earlier years, termed 'bearing lot' (see notes to page 13) although this Act made sure that rates on all properties would also be paid, so the householder was now expected to 'bear lot' (to some extent) and at the same time to 'pay scot'. This Act of 1767 was repealed by a Statute passed in 1770 which consolidated, extended and rendered more effectual the powers granted by several Acts of Parliament for making, enlarging and cleansing the vaults, drains etc. and for paving, cleaning, and lighting the streets etc., and for preventing nuisances etc., in the streets etc. of the City of London. No persons were to slake lime in the streets. The Commissioners could also cause names of streets to be fixed and houses and warehouses etc. to be numbered or marked – 'as they shall judge most proper for distinguishing the same.' The Act also required the Commissioners to provide movable or fixed dust boxes for the collection of dust and ashes for the convenience of the 'Scavengers or Rakers'. So both of these terms were recognised at that time, raker being the old mediaeval word which has now fallen into disuse. The clause referred to above requiring the householder to clean the footway, was reinacted with the stipulation that the work should be done before the hour of ten in the forenoon. Further amending statutes (1793 and 1823) left this requirement on the householder unaltered, and it remained the law, apparently, until repealed in 1848 by XI and XII.

Victoria C.163, a period of eighty-one years. The only obligation of this kind that tenants generally accept today is the clearing away of snow on the footpaths before their premises[1], but a custom which may come from these old requirements was still observed in the East End boroughs before the last war. In houses, the fronts of which abut directly on to the pavement, such as form the frontages of many streets in the vicinity of Hoxton, the housewife, after cleaning and whitening her doorstep, would lean out and wash the pavement in front of the step in a semi-circle, reaching as far out as she could and kneeling on the passage of her house on the inner side of the step.

The Act of 1770. An Act for Continuing and amending several Acts for preventing abuses in making bricks and tiles.

The preamble set out that the laws mentioned had been found to be very useful and beneficial but they were near expiring.

All these Acts related to the abuses in the making of bricks and tiles, the fixing of the dimensions and the prevention of unlawful combinations between brickmakers within a certain distance of London in respect of the price of bricks and tiles.

This Act refers to the treatment of working of the clay for brickmaking, permitting the digging of the clay at any time – subject to its being turned once, before being made into bricks. It further governed the mesh of the seive (one quarter of an inch) for the sifting or screening of sea coal used for burning the bricks, permitting the use of cinders (breeze) for burning bricks in clamps.

The size of the brick was altered to 'not less than eight inches and an half long, nor less than four inches broad, nor less than two inches and an half thick.' It was made clear, however, that this Act should not apply to bricks made more than fifteen miles from London.

The Act further dealt with the imposition and collection of penalties imposed for offences.

The Act of 1771

This Act concerned only the Parish of Saint Botolph, Aldgate, and similar Acts dealing with other parishes outside the city, were passed, from time to time, to deal with like circumstances as the necessity arose, and in this way the various bodies of Commissioners of Paving etc., came to be formed.

The preamble to the Act states that – 'Several lanes in the parish of Saint Botolph, Aldgate, are very ill paved and the passage through the same greatly obstructed by poles, projections and other nuisances and annoyed by sprouts, signs and gutters and present methods presented by law are found ineffectual.'

Powers were given to a body of Commissioners[2], the names of whom were included in the Act; there were eleven esquires, commencing with one John Shakespeare, and fifty-six gentlemen, and this Board was duly authorised to administer the Act. The members were to meet – 'at the house known by the name of The Sign of the White Swan;' at which meetings they were to 'defray their own expenses.' The place of meeting being usually, as in this case, an inn, probably gave rise to a clause which appears to have been general in like Acts that 'No victualler or person who shall sell ale or wine or other spirituous liquors by retail shall be capable of acting as a Commissioner under this Act.'

1. This obligation was placed upon the citizens by Section 63 Michael Angelo Taylor's Act 1817. See page 56.
2. The Commissioners consisted of Knights & Esquires of the County and local officers and men of local importance; the qualification for an ordinary Commissioner being that he should be the owner of lands etc. with a yearly value of £50, or estate valued at £1,000. The Commissioners were required to set themselves up as a business-like organisation and to employ clerks, treasurers, collectors, receivers, surveyors and such other officers as they considered necessary.

In addition to their duties of rating and arranging for the paving and cleaning of the highways, the Commissioners could cause all – 'sign-irons, sign-posts, boards, sprouts, gutters, penthouses, posts, rails and other things occasioning any obstruction or annoyance in the streets etc., to be removed or altered in such manner as they should think proper.' The Act continued – 'When such streets are greatly obstructed and made dangerous to foot passengers by steps being brought out or projecting from the houses and by steps and doors going down into cellars, vaults and other places and by show-cases, show-boards and other matters and things projecting from shops and houses over and beyond the area belonging to such houses, they are to be removed . . . And be it enacted – That all houses and buildings hereafter to be built or new fronted or any part thereof within the district aforesaid shall for the affectual and absolute prevention of all manner of projections, annoyances and inconveniences thereby rise perpendicularly from the foundations.' The Commissioners could cause any premises not built in conformity thereto – 'to be pulled down and removed by any persons they shall think fit, the costs and charges whereof shall be paid and reimbursed to the same Commissioners – by the owners – or other persons ordering or directing the same.' The Act ends – 'This Act shall be taken and allowed in all Courts of Justice as a Public Act and all Judges, Justices and others are hereby required to take notice thereof as such without the same being especially pleaded.'

There were many other sections dealing with the cleaning etc. of the streets and the householders were also required, as mentioned in the Acts for the City, to clean the footpaths – 'of their respective houses between the hours of six and nine in the forenoon (Sunday excepted); a fine of two shillings and sixpence could be imposed in default.'

CHAPTER VI

The administration of the Building Enactments in 1774. The ancient office of City Viewer comes to an end with the appointment of statutory surveyors under the Building Act of 1774

The obligation for enforcing the provisions of the proclamations and edicts on building restrictions and operations outside the city, had been placed, from the reign of the Tudors, on the Justices of the Peace and these important officials had to rely mainly on information laid by the common informer, who, on a conviction, could claim a proportion of the fine inflicted on the offender. This was still the position in the suburbs in 1774, except for the provisions made by Section 6 of the Act of 1764 by which new buildings were to be surveyed and passed by a Surveyor within fourteen days of their being covered in. Some authority had also been delegated, as we have seen, to the various bodies of Commissioners of pavements appointed during the preceding quarter of a century. The Commissioners watched lines of frontage and encroachments on the streets but they had no actual control over the construction of the buildings.

Up to the great fire of 1666 the supervision within the city and the liberties thereof followed on the same lines as that indicated in the suburbs; the authorities being the Lord Mayor and the Aldermen, but there was one important difference, for persons had been appointed from early times to watch building operations and to report irregularities to the Aldermen. In the fifteenth century these persons became known as 'City Viewers'. With the rebuilding Act of 1667 statutory surveyors were sworn in to see that the provisions of that Act were duly complied with, but there appears to be no evidence of anyone else being appointed to take the place of these three men – Robert Hooke, Peter Mills and John Oliver – as they died or resigned, although the Act of 1667 continued in operation until 1774. Commissioners of Sewers were also authorised under that Act to deal with drainage matters within the city and as time passed that body acquired powers similar to those possessed by the Commissioners of pavements in the suburbs. The position in the city by 1774 on the control of building works is somewhat obscure, but all the evidence points to a lack of supervision and neglect in this respect. The City Viewers did not seem to be operating and the age old custom which had been followed for over four hundred years, of filling vacancies in that office as they occurred, appears to have been discontinued; the last appointment dating from 1737. The Viewers certainly did not function after 1774 when a new Building Act covering the cities of London and Westminster, and certain parishes, passed into law. That Act provided for statutory surveyors to be nominated to administer the provisions thereof and the need for the services of the Viewers came to an end. There was an undeniable similarity between the work of the Viewer and that of the District Surveyor, although the Viewers were not statutory officials and therefore what is known of their history should be recorded here. The office appears to have originated before the reign of Edward I (1272–1307) when the persons appointed followed, as a step forward in building control, the even earlier 'Scavagers' who reported nuisances to the Aldermen from 1193. The city records contained many notices relative to these appointments, the first concerning the nomination of one mason and two carpenters in 1300.

1300. 29th Edward 1st

"On the Monday next before the Feast of the Purification of the Blessed Mary in the 29th year of the reign of K. Edward before Elias Russell the Mayor of London, and the Aldermen, Robert Osekyn and John De Wrytele, Carpenters, were sworn to make just consideration concerning the boundaries of Lands, ruined and divisible walls and gutters, and other matters touching their office in the city and suburbs of London, whensoever they shall be required".

A similar statement exists regarding the mason, a certain "Richard de Wycham". These officials were therefore functioning in the reign of Edward III when the stand collapsed as mentioned on page 9.

A further record of 1368 states that two carpenters, John de Tottenham and Richard de Shropshire, also two masons, Richard atte Cherche and Thomas atte Barnet, being sworn – 'on Monday next after the Feast of St. Perpetua and St. Felcitas, in full Husting – to well and faithfully perform their office for dividing the lands, rents and tenements in the city and the suburbs thereof, between whatsoever Persons –. And further to do what appertains to the office of assize of nuisances, and to inform the Mayor and Aldermen of all matters which appertain to the assize of Nuisances, etc.'

The office was of some importance as the holders enjoyed the remarkable privilege of exemption from all taxes, which is recorded by the application of the above-mentioned carpenters and masons in 1371 whereas – 'the Master Masons and Carpenters of the City show that whereas their Ancestors – for 100 years past and upwards have been by authority and colour of the said office discharged of all Taxes.' It was agreed – 'that the aforesaid Master Carpenters and Masons be discharged of such Taxes as their Predecessors have been of old time discharged while they continue in their said office.

In 1454, (33rd Henry VI.) Edward Stone and John Wise, carpenters were admitted by the Court to the office of "Viewers" being sworn in before the Mayor and Aldermen to – 'well and faithfully superintend certain nocuments of the City between neighbours; and thereof truly to report before the Mayor for the time being, and to do and execute well and faithfully all that appertains to the office in this respect.' (City Records. Journals 5.231). This is the first mention of the term "Viewers". Other entries clearly indicate that the office continued through the reigns of the Tudors and in the year 1675 a certain Thomas Seagood, a Tiler and Bricklayer secured the post this being the first departure from the age old custom of appointing a mason and carpenter. Later, in 1679, 1685 and 1695 a Glazier, a Weaver and a Glover were successively chosen as Viewers. In 1697 the office came back again to a Bricklayer and the last person nominated was a Carpenter, one John Norris, who commenced his duties in 1737.

These notes on "The Viewers" have been taken from an Historical Account of the Worshipful Company of Carpenters by Edward Basil Jupp (Clerk to the Company), published 1848. After the above note on John Norris the book continues – 'it does not appear by whom the functions previously discharged by the Viewers were performed during the interval which may have elapsed between the death of the last surviving Viewer and the passing of the Building Act in the year 1774, but it is evident that much that had been previously confided to the Viewers, was by that Act, and continues to be, entrusted to the District Surveyors. We here insert the form of Oath taken by the Viewers on their appointment, which is preserved in the City Records, and was framed, as we are informed, in the reign of Queen Elizabeth:

The Othe of the Viewers Maister Wardens of Masons and Carpenters

Ye shall sweare that ye shall truly present from tyme to tyme to the Maior and Aldermen of this City for the tyme being or to the Chamberleyne All such buildings and Purprestures as ye shall fynd sett or made upon any parts of the comon grounde of the said Citty. And from henceforth ye shall not make nor suffer to your knowledge to be made any newe building in any place within the liberty of this Citty. But ye shall the same shewe vnto the said Maior and Aldermen or Chamberleyne for the tyme being to th'entent that reformation thereof may be had. And also ye shall truly and indifferently search all manner of noysaunces, buildinge and edifyinge betweene party and party, when ye shalbe charged by the Maior of the Cittie of London soe to doe, without any favor shewing to any party. And true reports make to the Maior for the tyme being vpon the premises. And thus ye shall doe as God helpe you." – City Records.

In the year 1664 the Hall of the Carpenters Company was enlarged and an entry in the Company's Account Book reads – '1664 29th Sept. Item paid unto and spent with the Citty viewers upon their coming to view the Brickwall between the Drapers Garden and our Garden before the building was laid to see whome the wall belonged unto. It would be would be interesting to know how they decided the ownership of fence walls separating gardens belonging to different owners.

Referring to the Building Act of 1667, E.B. Jupp makes the following observations:– "This Statute materially affected the interest and diminished the influence of our Company; for besides a renewal of the prohibition of timber buildings, backed by such a convincing argument as the great fire afforded, of its necessity, the City, as we have seen, were to appoint surveyors to inspect the buildings; whereas all buildings, at least as far as concerned the timber used in their construction had previously been under the surveillance of the Carpenters' Company, and of the four City Viewers, two of whom we have shewn were appointed by the Court of Aldermen from and on the presentation of our Company." The powers of search possessed by the Carpenters' Company were still recognised. A case is reported – 1668, 30th July – 'upon the Complainte of Mr. Oliver one of the Citty Survaiers unto this Court, on behalfe of one Mrs. Reeve against Mr. Stantion, Carpenter, touching the insufficiencie of a certain building in Fetter Lane undertaken by him. It is ordered by this Court that the Master and Wardens doe view the same.'

Brett James cites certain cases in his book on the Growth of Stuart London, in which persons were imprisoned and fined for erecting buildings contrary to the proclamations and he includes the following: "A specific case was the alteration of an ancient brewhouse in Southwark, where the Lord Mayor recommended that Nicholas Park should be allowed to divide it into not more than three tenements but this permission should not be taken as a precedent. It is evident from other cases that the Lord Mayor made use of the four sworn viewers, who were able to inspect the buildings and make a report as to whether they were constructed in accordance with the custom of the city and the terms of the various proclamations and Acts of Parliament. Sixty years later the Great Fire added much to the prestige and importance of this very ancient and humble office of viewer; and Ogilby and Morgan, two of the earliest scientific cartographers, were to start merely sworn viewers or surveyors.' This statement comes from a Series of Records known as "The Remembrancia" a book compiled from the Archives of the City of London A.D.1579 to 1664. The note contained in the book reads – 'sworn viewers were appointed by the Court of Aldermen from a very early period. The practice, although in some instances departed from, was to appoint to these offices two Master Carpenters and two Master Masons – the Fire Act of 1666 – 7 Section 2 continued them with greatly increased powers under the title of Surveyors. John Ogilby and William Morgan, two of these Surveyors, or Sworn Viewers, subsequently surveyed the whole City and published a most accurate ground plan 1677, a copy of which is preserved in the Guildhall Library.'

The opinion expressed that the Act of 1667 merely strengthened the powers of the City Viewers is interesting but the fact is that the Viewers continued to exist along with the Surveyors appointed under the Act and none of these officials could apparently take action on irregularities by themselves but they merely reported to higher authorities. In earlier years the Lord Mayor probably passed the information on to the Star Chamber.

It should be remembered that the City Companies had strong powers and they could, in extreme cases, commit members to prison and even order a delinquent to be whipped before the Master and Wardens, so the Lord Mayor had very useful assistance, available in the Companies, for dealing with workmen who failed to respect the ancient customs of the city. The writer, however, cannot agree with Brett James that the Viewers held a humble office, for the appointment was evidently considered to be of some importance by the Worshipful Company of Carpenters, and Masters only to the craft were nominated. It is possible that a nominal salary only went with the office and that a fee was paid to them for each work surveyed, such as the fence wall instanced. In this connection it is worthy of note that the office of King's Carpenter in the sixteenth century carried with it a salary of one shilling only per day and that of the Office of Surveyor of the King's Works two shillings per day. These officers however were remunerated in addition for the works they superintended for the King.

It was the Master Carpenters who designed and built the open timber roofs which remain over many halls and churches to this day, as evidence of their great skill, and from this body of craftsmen the Viewers were chosen and similar remarks can be said of the Masons who, quite frequently, carried out extensive works and acted in the role of contractor.

T.F. Reddaway states – 'the Surveyors did not oust the City Viewers but, in the area of the rebuilding, they did in fact perform some of their functions. In July 1668 Mr. Rawlings, the eldest clerk in the Utter (Mayor's) Court, was ordered to attend them in their views upon disputes and to draw up and enter the same – as hee useth to doe of the views of the common viewers of this Citty.'

There are many reports in the City records signed by Robert Hooke and John Oliver on alleged nuisances, irregular buildings and dangerous structures, and quite often they were accompanied by two City Viewers who also signed the document. It is hardly likely that Robert Hooke, M.D. Curator to the Royal Society, and at times a rival to Wren, would have associated himself with the viewers if their office could have been considered only as a humble one. The records extend to the closing years of the seventeenth century; the following is an example:–

1693 – In pursuance of an order of the Honourable Court bearing date 14th of this present December, we whose names are underwritten have met upon the places and have viewed a certain building near Rope Alley in Bishopsgate Street in the Parish of St. Buttolph without Bishops Gate now erecting by Ralph Hardwicke Esq., or some other, whereof complaint hath been made to the court by the Grand Inquest of the Ward, and we doe find that the said Building is wholly irregular and as we consider very insufficient and it is therefore our opinion that the same ought to be reformed and amended and built according to the Directions and Scantlings prescribed by the act of Parliament for Rebuilding this City. And whereas we find there are Divers other houses building adjoining to the same which we find to be likewise irregularly built we are of opinion that the same ought to be amended also. All which nevertheless we humbly leave to your Lordships and Worships grave wisdome to Determine.

John Freeman. Robert Hooke. Jo. Oliver.

But what happened after the departure of the two Surveyors is not evident; Peter Mills, their associate in the early years of the rebuilding of the city, died in 1670 and so his name does not appear in the records. Robert Hooke died at Gresham College in March 1703; he was buried in St. Helens Church, Bishopsgate Street. There is, apparently, no record of the death of John Oliver, who assisted Wren in the rebuilding of St. Pauls. After 1700 the records cease and they recommence towards the close of the 18th century and continue into the early part of the nineteenth century. These later reports are evidently signed, in some cases, by the Surveyors appointed under the 1774 Act. Reports on the surveying of buildings between 1700 and 1774, however, are conspicuous by their absence, but it is known that the Viewers continued in office and possibly the records have been lost. On the other hand it will be noticed that the Act of 1760 contained a section relative to dangerous buildings within the city and made arrangements for the hoarding in of the same under certain circumstances. The fact that it became necessary to include such provisions in the Act appears to indicate that the City Viewers were either not doing their job, or not being instructed so to do by the Lord Mayor, etc. It does certainly seem obvious that the office must have fallen largely into disuetude, anyway so far as referred to the stability of buildings. Possibly the solution to this intriguing question may yet be found in the records of the City. There are, however, two interesting reports in existence by George Dance (the elder). He was appointed to the office of Clerk of the City Works in December 1735 and possibly the structures referred to therein may have belonged to the city. The reports read as follows:—

To the right honble the Lord Mayor and Court Aldermen.

In obedience to your order of the 15th inst., I have view'd the house late the Rummer Tavern in Queen Street and find that the whole front is very much decay'd, and that one of the Piers is burst out in a very frightful manner, and is in so ruinous condition that it ought to be taken down and secured immediately, it being in the most imminent danger; and if neglected must fall very soon

Which is humbly submitted to this Honble Court by March the 22nd, 1742.

Yr most obedient humble servant
Geo. Dance.

To the rt honble the Lord Mayor and Court of Aldermen.

In pursuance of your order I have view'd a ruinous House near Room Land in Queenhith, lately occupied by John Bonner, Victualler and find that a large Wooden Cornice and a Water Tank and some loose pieces of materials are in a dangerous situation and am of Opinion that if the said Cornice and materials and some part of the Tops of the Chimneys were taken down there would be no occasion to fix a board there all which is humbly submitted to this honble Court.

February 23rd, 1762. Geo. Dance.

It may be noted that Geo. Dance was not quite so evidently humble in 1762 as he had been previously in 1742.

There can be no doubt that the Viewers were in fact the predecessors of District Surveyors and that the words of Mr. E. B. Jupp can be accepted as quite correct – 'it is evident that much that has been previously confided to the Viewer was by that Act (1774) and still continues to be entrusted to the District Surveyor.' The three Surveyors: Peter Mills, Robert Hooke and John Oliver were the first statutory Surveyors for they were appointed by the direct command of an Act of Parliament, whereas the Viewer's office came down the centuries from immemorial custom.

It must be conceded that no other persons were appointed to take the place of the three men who set out the new streets and watched the rebuilding of the City. Their own work was complete when the city had been rebuilt. These men came within the pay-roll of the City Corporation and in the words of the keeper of the City Records: "Had anyone else been appointed to succeed them their names would have appeared on the records we have of all persons to whom the City paid salaries." Something would have been known of the men who filled such positions over the seventy years which elapsed between the death of Robert Hooke in 1703 and the passing of the Act of 1774. A further convincing fact is that the Acts of Queen Anne and George I, make no reference to supervision or supervisers while the Act of 1760, contained the provision for a penalty of £50 to be divided between the informant and the poor of the Parish. It was the Act of George III (1764), which contained the clause requiring every building to be surveyed by one or more Surveyors. Had there been any regular supervision in the city comparable to the Office of District Surveyor surely it would have been made use of or mentioned in these Acts. The Act of 1667 which was an Act for the rebuilding of the City, was allowed to remain in force for there were no reasons why it should have been repealed. It is quite possible that a City Viewer may have used the Act in the course of his duties, but it is curious that reports to substantiate that view do not, apparently, exist, but to say that the Office of District Surveyor continued over these years can be only wishful thinking. It was, undoubtedly, the Act of 1774 with its scale of fees for works surveyed, which brought the Office of District Surveyor into existence both within and without of the city.

The Building Act of 1772

In the twelth year of the reign of George III (c.73) an Act was passed for the better regulation of buildings and party walls within the Cities of London and Westminster, and the liberties thereof, and the other parishes, precincts and places in the weekly bills of mortality, the parishes Saint Marylebone and Paddington, Saint Pancras and Saint Luke at Chelsea, in the County of Middlesex, and for the better prevention of mischiefs by fire within the said cities, liberties, parishes, precincts, and places: and for amending and reducing the laws relating thereto into one Act, and for other purposes.

The Statute dealt in detail with party walls and two surveyors or two able workmen could be appointed by either owner to meet similar representatives of the adjoining owner to settle disputes. The measure repealed all previous enactments in respect of party walls. Rules for the projection of shop fronts and other matters of construction were incorporated, but the administration still remained with the common informer and possibly this is the reason why the statute remained in force only for two years. The Act which followed was of much importance.

The Building Act 1774

The preamble followed that given in the preceding Act, as above and reference was merely made to that Act as – 'being found insufficient to answer the good purposes intended thereby.'

Buildings were divided into seven several rates, or classes, all within rules and directions laid down. The first class included churches, manufacturies, warehouses, large dwellings and other buildings. Dwellings to come within the class had to exceed nine squares in area and all other buildings had either to comprise four storeys at least above the ground or exceed thirty one feet in height measured from the pavement to the top of the front wall. The value of the premises had also to be above £850. The second class dropped a storey, the value being limited to £850 and this procedure continued until the fourth class contained one floor only over the ground storey with a cost not greater than £150.

The thickness of walls, both party and external, were specified for each class. The fifth and sixth classes had reference to isolated buildings those being four feet from any public road and sixteen feet from any other building could be built of any dimensions whatever, while those eight feet from any public road and thirty feet from the nearest building could be built of any dimensions and with any materials whatever.

The seventh class included special structures, such as crane houses; every new enclosure for which had to consist of stone, brick, slate, tile, oak, elm, steel, iron or brass, a truly remarkable selection. Other structures included – 'shamble, windmill or watermill and also every building which shall be situated without the Cities of London and Westminster and the liberties thereof, used for workshops or drying-places for tanners, fell-mongers, gluemakers, size-makers, calico-printers, whitsters, whiting-makers, curriers, leather-dressers, buckram-stiffeners, oil-cloth-painters, wool-staplers, throwsters, parchment-makers and paper-makers so long, and at such times, as they are or shall be used for some or one of those purposes, and no longer; shall be deemed the seventh rate of class of building and may be built of any dimensions whatever.'

The wording of the limits to the first-class of buildings is worthy of consideration, it reads – 'and also every warehouse and other buildings whatsoever (dwellings under nine squares excluded) which does or shall exceed three clear storeys above ground, exclusive of the rooms (if any) in the roof thereof, or which is or shall be of the height of thirty one feet from the surface of the pavement, ground, or way, above the area before either of the fronts thereof, to the top of the blocking-course or the coping on the parapet thereof.' The provisions do not limit the height to thirty one feet and it seems difficult to imagine a four storey building which did not exceed this height. In fact there was no limitation to the height of buildings under this Act. The thicknesses of walls for this class of building reads – and every such wall, from the top of such footing, be of the thickness of two bricks in length, or one foot five inches and an half at the least, up to the under side of the one pair of stairs floor; (two storeys) – and from thence of the thickness of one brick and a half in length, or thirteen inches at the least, up to the under side of the plate under the roof or gutter of every such building.' This clearly provided for two storeys of eighteen inch work and thirteen inch work above for an unlimited number of storeys. Lifts were not in operation in 1774 and possibly the question of high buildings, other than churches, had not received serious consideration. The heights of buildings had never been restricted in the suburbs but the Act of 1667, which applied only to the city, laid down definite rules for such heights in conjunction with the widths of the streets they were to front. Under this Act of 1774 no similar requirements were imposed and a first class building of unlimited height could, so far as the Building Act was concerned, be erected fronting on any width street, lane, alley or court. This Act of 1774 repealed the Act of 1667, under which the city had been rebuilt, and definitely in this respect it constituted a retrograde step from the point of view of Town Planning. The limited height of buildings on narrow streets under the Act of 1667 had gone and the high buildings on narrow thoroughfares, that we know today, began to come into being.

Party walls were dealt with extensively under this Act. Irregular walls and even sound timber partitions erected or begun to be erected before June 1774 could be retained, until extensive alterations to the buildings became necessary. From this it would appear that wooden party structures were still in course of erection in spite of the many past Acts to the contrary. Party wall parapets were to be carried up eighteen inches above the roof or one foot above the gutter of the highest building and when dormers were constructed within four feet of the party wall parapet the same was to be built up two feet wider than the dormer and for the full height thereof. No openings were to be made in party walls – 'except for communication from one stack of warehouses to another, and from one stable building to another; all which communications shall have thereto iron doors in such manner as hereinafter directed'. The stacks of warehouses were limited to thirty-five squares in area on the ground plan and the stable buildings twenty-five squares in area on the ground plan. The openings referred to uniting the stacks of warehouses or stable buildings were to be fitted with a wrought iron door one quarter of an inch in thickness.

Party arches of stated thickness were required under and over public ways, and details of timbers in connection therewith were given. Walls were not to be cut into or maimed and the thicknesses of the backs of chimney openings and many other particulars relating to chimneys, flues, boilers and furnaces which are now incorporated in our modern Bylaws were set out for the first time. Two Surveyors or two able workmen, appointed by each owner of a party wall proposed to be pulled down or repaired, were to meet, and the Justices had power to appoint a further Surveyor or workmen to co-operate with those already appointed. A majority report could be appealed against at the Quarter Sessions when the Justices would hear the evidence on oath and settle the matter.

Section XLVI of the Act called for every external wall or external enclosure of every building of the first to the fifth rate class of building to – 'be of brick, stone, artificial stone, lead, copper, tin, slate, tile or iron, or of brick, stone and such artificial stone, lead, copper, tin, slate, tile and iron together, except the necessary piling, bridging and planking for the foundations of the same, and also except the necessary templates, chains, bond-timbers, and also except the doors, sashes, window-shutters, and door and window frames to such buildings – all which window-frames and door-frames shall be set in reveals, and recessed at least four inches from the front of the building in which they are fixed'. Storey posts under the corners at the meeting of two walls and next the junctions of two streets were to be of oak or stone at least twelve inches square.

Sections XLVII & XLVIII. Roofs dormers, etc. were to be covered with – 'glass, copper, lead, tin, slate, tile, or artificial stone, every coping, cornice, facia, window-dressing, portico, balcony, balustrade, or other external decoration or projection whatsoever, shall externally be of brick, stone, burnt clay, or artificial stone, stucco, lead, or iron; except the cornices and dressings to shop-windows'. All water from roofs was to be taken by pipes to drains or channel stones in or below the surface of the ground. Bow windows were prohibited beyond the general building line, but shop fronts on streets less than thirty feet wide could project five inches and ten inches on streets over thirty feet in width. The shop cornices could project thirteen inches and eighteen inches respectively.

Section LIX provided that no iron, tin, copper or other pipe or funnel for conveying smoke or steam shall – 'be fixed next any public street, etc. on the front of any building.'

Section LXIII brought into existence Surveyors to administer the Act not only in the city but in Westminster and the suburbs mentioned – 'that the Mayor and Aldermen of the said city of London shall and may nominate and appoint such and so many discreet persons skilled in the art of building, as they the said mayor and aldermen think fit, to be, during their will and pleasure, the surveyors or supervisors to see the said rules and regulations well and truly observed in and throughout the said City of London, and the liberties thereof.' The Justices of the Peace for the counties of Middlesex and Surrey and the City of Westminster – 'and the liberty of his Majesty's Tower of London' – were required to nominate and appoint at their general quarter sessions the necessary number of discreet persons to fill the office of surveyors for the respective areas outside the jurisdiction of the city authorities.

The Surveyors were required to take the following oath:–

I A.B. being one of the surveyors or supervisors appointed in pursuance of an act of parliament, passed in the fourteenth year of the reign of King George the Third, for the further and better regulation of buildings and party-walls; and for the more effectually preventing mischiefs by fire within the cities of London and Westminster, and the liberties thereof, and the other parishes, precincts, and places, within the weekly bills of mortality, the parishes of Saint Mary-le-bon, Paddington, Saint Pancras and Saint Luke at Chelsea, in the county of Middlesex; and for indemnifying under certain conditions builders, and other persons, against the penalties to which they are or may be liable for erecting buildings within the limits aforesaid, contrary to law, do swear, that, upon receiving notice of any building or wall to be built, or other builders work to be done, within the district under my inspection, not being by illness or otherwise lawfully prevented, I will diligently and faithfully, survey the same, and to the utmost of my abilities, endeavour to cause the rules and regulations, in the said act prescribed, to be strictly observed; and that without favour or affection, prejudice or malice.

So help me God.

The Surveyors appointed were required to notify the clerks of the peace of their place of abode. Twenty-four hours notice had to be given to the respective surveyor, by the master workman or other person causing the work, before the commencement of the erection of any wall etc. The scale of fees chargeable by the Surveyors was, for the erection of a first-class building £3.10.0, alterations or additions to such a building £1.15.0; Second Class £3.3.0, alterations etc. £1.10.0; Third Class £2.10.0, alterations etc. £1.15.0; Fourth Class £2.2.0, alterations etc. £1.1.0; Fifth Class £1.10.0, alterations etc. 15/-; Sixth Class £1.1.0, alterations etc. 10/6d; Seventh Class 10/6d, alterations etc. 5/-. This scale of fees remained in operation until 1855 or 81 years. The Justices had power to vary these amounts and they could enforce payment to the extent of levying by distress warrant on the master workman, or other person responsible, and by the sale of his goods and chattels. For – 'neglecting to give such notice or for refusing admittance' – the penalty incurred was – 'for every default therein, forfeit and pay to the said surveyor treble the satisfaction which such surveyor would have been entitled to receive for his trouble in viewing such buildings or wall, and seeing the rules and regulations of this Act well and truly observed therein – and also for every such default, forfeit the sum of twenty pounds to be recovered, in any of his Majesty's court'. It is interesting to note that the term "viewing" is used in this clause. Work not executed in accordance with the regulations – 'shall be demolished or amended, by order of the Mayor or two Justices.' Workmen were also liable for a fine of 50s. for executing work contrary to the Act and they could – 'be committed to the house of correction, there to remain without bail or mainprize, for any time not exceeding three months or less than one month unless the penalty be sooner paid'.

Within fourteen days of the completion of the covering in of a building or the completion of a work the person responsible was required to – 'cause the same to be surveyed by the surveyor' – and if such surveyor shall upon such survey find that the same is to the best of his judgment and belief built or made good agreeably to the several directions in this Act contained, then such surveyor shall within fourteen days – 'make oath therefore, by affidavit in writing, before the Mayor of the City, or the Justice, as the case may be.' The affidavit was to be filed by the clerk of the peace – 'within ten days after the making thereof'. The clerk being entitled to one shilling, and no more, for his trouble. For neglecting to require the surveyor to make the survey the person responsible became liable to a fine of £10 and a continuing penalty of this amount for every month until the affidavit had been filed.

Section LXX dealt with dangerous structures – 'and whereas houses and buildings are often in so ruinous a condition that passengers thereby are in danger of their lives or limbs from the falling thereof or of the bricks or timber therefrom'. The procedure called for the erection of hoardings by the churchwardens outside the city and by the Mayor and Aldermen within the city. Service of notices on the owner was to follow and on orders, obtained from the Justices etc., the defective premises could be dealt with further. It is interesting to note that the Surveyors appointed under the Acts were not called upon to deal in any way with the structures and the orders emanated from a grand jury or from other juries mentioned.

Sections LXXIV to LXXXVI laid down rules for the provision of fire engines; penalties which householders were liable to for not keeping their chimneys swept on the occasion of fires occurring in unswept chimbeys and other matters relating to fires and the prevention thereof which were repeats of earlier enactments and which in the main have been referred to previously.

Section CI repealed all the former statutes from the Act of Charles II (1667) so far as related to the regulations of buildings and party walls.

Development in London following the Building Act of 1774

The Act of 1774 remained in force until 1845, or nearly 71 years, and it had important results on the growth of London. The population of these years increased from 800,000 approx. in 1774 to 2,250,000 approx. in 1845, an increase of 2¾ times. It will be noticed that the objects of the Act were firstly and mainly the prevention and control of fire, secondly the restriction of encroachments on streets and thirdly the procedure for dealing with dangerous structures. Although buildings had to be enclosed with incombustible substances, openings for windows etc. could be made therein to an unlimited extent, and with no restrictions on the heights thereof, considerable danger existed from the spread of fire across narrow streets. The fact was that houses were disappearing from the city and tall commercial buildings taking their place. Town planning or the ordinary welfare of the citizens had no part in the Statute. The width of new streets was not controlled and the many narrow courts, cul-de-sacs, bottle-necks etc. must have followed. Buildings could be erected to any height on any such street. Dwellings could be built without open spaces at the rear, with no restrictions on the height of habitable rooms or the lighting or ventilation thereof.

Ill-lighted basement rooms could be constructed for dwellings, although the desirability of preventing the use of such underground rooms for this purpose had been realised as far back as 1625. These underground rooms were to give District Surveyors a deal of trouble in the future. The necessity, however, for an authority to administer the Act had been recognised and the office of District Surveyor developed therefrom

The development of London continued and many areas were covered with small mean dwellings which rapidly deteriorated into slums, or as they came to be called 'rookeries'. The villages of Paddington, St. Pancras and Chelsea, which are mentioned in the Act of 1724 grew steadily in size so that by the middle of the nineteenth century they were to lose their separate identities and become merged in the town.

At least one Town Planning scheme of lasting benefit matured towards the end of the century when the Duke of Bedford proceeded to lay out an estate of a hundred and twelve acres on the northside of Oxford Street. The area of Bloomsbury in the Borough of Holborn was thus developed with the delightful squares of different shapes and sizes. Some twenty acres of ground were allotted to these squares; planted with plane trees bordering on grass plots, they have remained to give pleasure and beauty in what might have been a very congested area. Bedford Square was set out between 1775 and 1780, and the others followed in succeeding years.

The astonishing building speculation of the century concerned the erection of the Adelphi on the south side of the Strand by the Adam brothers. Their financial collapse over this venture would have followed, but Parliament sanctioned a lottery with the houses as prizes and the gamble proved highly popular.

The Georgian architecture reached its climax after the end of the century and during the Regency period, with the use of flat stucco-painted walls; the greatest exponent being John Nash (1752-1835). The Regent's town house occupied a site on which the Duke of York's steps and column now stand facing the Mall and "The First Gentleman of Europe", as he termed himself, conceived the idea for a broad thoroughfare to run from his house to Regent's Park. A country residence, for his occupation, situated in the Park would have completed the scheme. The thoroughfare came into existence but the country house did not. Parliament sanctioned the construction of Regent Street on the grounds that the clearance of an unhealthy area would result. John Nash laid out the street and planned the low classic facades which brought a dignity to the town well in keeping with the period.

Surveyors under the Act of 1774

According to a list of districts and Surveyors included in an edition of the 1774 Act published in 1796 at Cambridge it would appear that the Act covered some eighty-nine parishes and wards of London. These parishes and wards were arranged in the list in alphabetical order and it is not possible to state with certainty the number of districts into which they were grouped, but twenty-seven Surveyors were then acting. The thirty-three wards in the city were combined to form four districts. In contrast to the relatively small and congested districts of the city, the sparsely built over parishes of Paddington and St. Pancras were, in 1774, included to form one district, the Surveyor being Mr. Crunden, who also held the parish of St. Luke, Chelsea. How Mr. Crunden travelled about his district we can only conjecture. He either went on horseback or by coach, but he remained a District Surveyor for fifty years and retired at the age of eighty-four; he must have seen great changes in these parishes in his time.

The Surveyors administering the Act of 1774 did not all expect to make a living from the fees collected under this Act, their principal sources of income were often their private practices as architects or surveyors.

They paid for their own office premises and employed such assistants as they required or could afford. This system (which was to last until 1940) led sometimes to the siting of the Surveyors' offices over shops, up innumerable flights of stairs, where the rents were cheaper and to the employment in many cases of unqualified assistants on low rates of pay. More ambitious assistants, seeking qualifications and eventual office as Surveyor would also be prepared to work for a modest salary. These assistants would often, when the Surveyor was absent on holiday, be permitted to retain the fees earned during this period and perhaps show greater zeal and energy at these times.

In 1832 the Government called for a Report on the work of the Surveyors and their administration of the Act of 1774. This Report required details of the extent of each District with particulars of the training of each Surveyor, whether as Architect, Surveyor or Builder, and the date of his appointment. It also required records of the number of breaches of Statute reported, the number of new buildings erected and of old ones repaired.

The information obtained showed that there were then 32 Surveyors (4 in the City, 5 in Westminster, 18 in Middlesex, 4 in the Surrey Parishes coming within the Weekly Bills of Mortality and 1 in the Tower Royalty).

One of these Surveyors had been appointed in 1774 at the Quarter Sessions at Guildford to the District of St. Mary, Lambeth and St. Mary, Newington so he held office there for at least 58 years. The Surveyors in 2 of the City Districts had received their training in the Office of Works, Guildhall, under George Dance (whose Reports are quoted in Chapter VI). Another later resigned as Surveyor on appointment as 'Clerk to the City Works', a position later renamed 'City Architect'. No less than 4 of the Surveyors had been fellow architectural students with John Nash, perhaps the greatest architect of his time. One, perhaps more versatile, was articled to Pugin, worked for Nash, became Surveyor in Bow and then took to the Stage where he became a celebrated comedian and later opened the Adelphi Theatre.

This Report bore fruit a few years later in the radical re-organisation brought about by the Act of 1844, described in the next Chapter.

Contrasts in the London of 1820

CHAPTER VII

The Nineteenth Century. The Early Years: 1800–1837
The Chimney Sweepers' Acts. Paving Acts.

At the commencement of the nineteenth century London still lacked a comprehensive building Act covering the whole of the Metropolis and forty-four years had yet to pass before such an Act became a reality. The Act of 1774 was still in force and this Act applied only to the cities of London and Westminster, the liberties thereof and other parishes,precincts and places within the weekly bills of mortality, the parishes of St. Marylebone, Paddington, St. Pancras and St. Luke, Chelsea. To the south and west large tracts of land were still unbuilt on and a writer in 1839, Thomas Faulkner, says that – 'the parishes of Hammersmith and Fulham may be denominated the great fruit and kitchen-garden north of the Thames for the supply of the London market'. (History of Hammersmith). The same author mentions that in the strawberry season hundreds of women are employed to carry the fruit to the market, each maid making two journeys per day from Hammersmith carrying on her head a basket containing between forty and fifty pounds of fruit.

The years (1714–1837) over which the Hanoverian Kings reigned cover a period notorious for the exploitation of child labour and in 1788 the first Act was passed for the better regulation of chimney sweeps and their apprentices. The preamble to the Act (28 George III c.48) referred to – 'the complicated miseries to which boys employed in climbing and cleaning chimneys are liable beyond any other employment whatever in which boys of tender years are engaged'. The Act cancelled any apprenticeship of boys under the age of eight years. In 1834 a further Act (4 & 5 William IV c.35) amended the previous Act and limited the age at which boys could be apprenticed to the trade to ten years and all boys under fourteen had to be provided with a leather cap having a brass plate attached thereto giving particulars of the name and address of their employer. Section 18 of this Act referred to the construction of flues and chimneys and required 'all withs and partitions between any chimney or flue built after the passing of the Act to be of brick or stone at least equal to half a brick in thickness – every breast back and with or partition of a chimney to be built of sound materials and the joints well filled in with good mortar or cement and rendered or stuccoed within; and also every chimney or flue – built in any wall of greater length of four feet out of any wall not being a circular chmney of twelve inches diameter shall be in every section fourteen inches by nine inches and no chimney or flue shall be constructed with an angle therein which shall be less obtuse than an angle of one hundred and twenty degrees and every salient or projecting angle in any flue or chimney shall be rounded off four inches at least'. These requirements were evidently intended to be complied with for the penalty for non-observance was £100 to be recovered with full costs of suit from master builder or master workman. The clauses on flues were still contained in a further amending Act of 1840 (3 & 4 Victoria c.85) the penalties being reduced to not more than £50 or less than £10. This Act put an end to the employment of boys for climbing and cleaning flues for by Section 2 anyone compelling or knowingly allowing any young person under the age of twenty-one to enter a flue or chimney for cleaning purposes etc., became liable to a heavy fine. These Acts on the chimney sweepers applied to the whole of Great Britain and the provisions so far as London was concerned remained in force until repealed by the Building Act of 1844 (7 & 8 Victoria c.84).

Questions on roof coverings to comply with the provisions of the Building Acts have arisen constantly and perhaps no other sections of the Acts have produced, so persistently, so much discussion. The subject has centered generally around a material having a bitumastic base and in 1810 an Act to amend the Building Act of 1774 was passed to allow a composition of this nature to be employed. This enactment appears to be one by itself, for the writer knows of no other of its kind; it seems strangely out of place in our legislation on building laws, having a distinct leaning towards favouritism to an individual.

The Act referred to a patent granted under the "Great Seal of Great Britain" in 1806 to "Ambrose Bowden John for his newly invented composition called John's Patent Tessera composed of limestone or any other stone powdered, or road stuff, where stone is made use of for repairing roads, and other articles of a stony, sandy or calcareous nature with a sufficient addition of tar or other bituminous substance mixed together by the application of considerable heat and powerful machinery, and afterwards pressed together and rolled into sheets by means of rollers acting with great pressure, to be used in the covering of buildings. And whereas such composition has been found useful and safe for such purposes and not liable to catch fire so as to communicate the same to any adjoining premises." This Act permitted the material to be used on any flat, roof, gutter etc., and it remained in operation until repealed by the Building Act of 1844. (This material appears to be the fore-runner of the modern multi-layer bituminous felt used increasingly to replace asphalt as a covering for flat roofs following the second World War. This, in turn, in the 1970's is giving way to the new single-layer rubber and plastic types of sheeting welded together by powerful solvents). A note in the minutes for October 1853 refers to a similar Bill having passed the House of Lords to enable a certain Donald Grant to introduce a patent system of ventilation. The Bill had been rejected in the Commons on the representation of the Commissioner of Works on the ground that it merely authorised a private invention.

Michael Angelo Taylor's Act 1817

This was an Act for better paving, improving, and regulating the streets of the Metropolis, and removing and preventing nuisances and obstructions. It was so named after the Member of Parliament who had campaigned for many years to obtain an improvement in London's streets.

This Act applied only to the cities of London and Westminster, the borough of Southwark and certain parishes coming within the weekly bills of mortality, but in 1862 by Section 73 of the Metropolis Management Amendment Act the provisions, except certain sections which had been repealed or superseded, were made applicable to the whole of the Metropolis.

The Statute, parts of which are still in force, was detailed with meticulous care, the object being the preservation of the roads and pavements from all possible damage and encroachments. Powers were inserted by which the Commissioners could arrange widenings with owners of property but the main considerations concerned the surfaces of the pavements and carriageways as the following indicates – Section 64 'If any person shall in any street.....beat or dust any carpet or carpets.....or shall throw, cast or lay....any ashes, dust, dirt, rubbish, offal etc......or shall kill, slaughter, scald, dress or cut up any beast;or shall run, roll, drive, draw, or place or cause, permit or suffer to be run, rolled, driven, drawn, or placed upon any of the said footway pavements.....any waggon, cart, dray sledge or other carriage or any wheel, wheelbarrow, handbarrow or truck or any hogshead, cart or barrel, or shall wilfully ride, lead or drive any horse, ass, mule, or other beast upon any of the footway pavements aforesaid.....shall upon conviction forfeit and pay a sum not less than forty shillings or more than five pounds for each offence.'

Persons were not to cause or permit to be set up any stall, board, chopping block, show board on hinges or otherwise, basket, wares, merchandise, casks or goods of any kind whatsoever; neither were they to hoop, place, wash or cleanse or cause to be hooped, washed or cleansed any pipe, barrel, cask or vessel, in or upon any part of the carriageway or footway.

The cleansing and hooping of barrels does not appear to be customary on the highways today but the writer can vouch for many other practices, not much less reprehensible, for which the streets in the east end were used prior to 1940. The staining and polishing of furniture in the back ways of Hoxton was a usual procedure, while on sultry nights in summertime the inhabitants would bring out their mattresses and sleep on the pavements.

Section 63 of this Act provided – "that every occupier of any house or premises..... during the continuance of frost, or after or during the fall of snow, from time to time, and at all times hereafter shall once in every day before the hour of ten of the clock in the forenoon of each day, except Sunday, sweep and cleanse, or cause to be swept or cleansed, the footway all along the front side or back walls of their respective houses, tenements, chapels, meeting houses etc.' Penalty for non-observance, ten shillings for every offence. This Section remained in force until repealed by Section 142 of the Public Health (London) Act 1891, a period of about seventy-four years.

Section 70 concerned cellars, basements, vaults, kitchens and other parts of premises built under the foot pavements, also the openings in such pavements leading thereto. The Commissioners' Surveyors or Inspectors were authorised to take the necessary action to ensure that these constructions were kept in reasonable repair and that the openings were at all time adequately protected by rails, flaps or trap doors. Fines for failure to observe the Commissioners' requirements in this respect were included. These provisions have at times, led to difficulties arising between District Surveyors and Borough Surveyors, who now operate the clauses; it is one of those cases where unavoidable dual control exists, but it is generally recognised that the Borough Surveyor's liability is that for the maintenance of the surface of the pavements.

Section 72 included the usual clauses giving authority to the Commissioners' Surveyors to – 'regulate or remove in such manner as they shall from time to time judge proper, all signs, sign irons, signposts, and other posts, sheds, penthouses, sprouts, gutters, steps, stairs, cellar doors, bow and other windows, projecting over any part of either the footways or carriageways of any of the said streets or public places, window shutters, stumps, shades, rails, pales, palisades, porches, bulks, show glasses and show boards, pools, cesspools, cisterns and reservoirs for water, and all other or any fixed or moveable projections, on hinges or otherwise, from the fronts or sides of any house or houses or other buildings and now affixed or belonging to or which shall be hereafter affixed or belonging to any house etc. abutting upon or contiguous to any streets, and which in the judgment of the Commissioners.....do or may obstruct the circulation of light and air or are inconvenient or incommodious to any passengers along the carriage or footways.' This Section was repealed and replaced with very similar conditions by Section 119 Metropolis Local Management Act 1855.

The Euston Road

(continued from Chapter V)

Something further should now be written on the above highway for the Act of George II now became obsolete by the passing of an Act of George IV. This Act dated 8th June 1821 is a remarkable example of the legislation then in force for the control of turnpike roads. It was termed an Act for more effectively repairing certain roads and the preamble reads – 'Whereas an Act was passed in the Twenty-ninth year of the reign of His Majesty King George the Second intituled; An Act to enable the respective trustees of the Turnpike

Roads leading to Highgate Gate House and Hampstead and from St. Giles's Pound to Kilbourne Bridge in the County of Middlesex to make a new road from the Great Northern Road at Islington to the Edgware Road near Paddington.' Various provisions were then inserted respecting the control of the new road and of other roads.

At the time of the passing of this Act and for some years afterwards the road appears to have been known only as "The New Road" and maps of Islington of the period show the road extending to Islington High Street at the point now known as 'The Angel'. The term Great Northern Road, mentioned in the Acts does not appear on these maps, but the point is made clear by the Act authorising the extension to the city by the formation of the City Road. Section 23 laid down the rates of tolls which included for each Coach, Berlin, Berlin, Landau, Hearse, Chaise Marine, Chariot, Calash, Curricle, Chair Chaise, or Pleasure Cart drawn by six horses, one and sixpence; if drawn by four horses, one shilling; two horses sixpence, and one horse fourpence. Waggons with carriage having three or four wheels of the breadth of six inches, not laden with hay or straw, sixpence and if so laden twopence. The charge for every ass, pony, mule, horse, mare, was twopence and for droves of oxen or neat cattle sixpence per score; for droves of sheep, hogs, etc., threepence per score. A few droves of neat cattle in the Euston Road today would cause a diversion difficult to imagine. There were numerous exemptions from the toll charges which included any horse or carriage attending the King's most excellent Majesty and for any horses or carriages travelling with vagrants sent by legal passes or prisoners sent to gaol or the House of Correction.

Section 53 provided that any building erected within fifty feet of the new road leading from the Great Northern Road in Islington to Tottenham Court Road shall be deemed a common nuisance. Sixty-five years had now passed since this regulation had been incorporated in the original Act of 1756. Could it be that the land in question had, in fact, been kept clear of buildings; it is indeed doubtful.

The Act of 1821 was repealed by a further Act of George IV passed in 1826 and described as – 'An Act for consolidating the trusts of the several Turnpike Roads in the neighbourhood of the Metropolis north of the River Thames.'

Section 140 of this Act read as follows – 'And be it enacted that no building whatsoever shall be erected on any new foundations by any Person or Persons whomsoever upon any of the Lands adjacent to the Road leading from Edgware Road, Paddington to the Great Northern Road, Islington and from the north end of Great Portland Street to such road within fifty feet from the side of such road other than toll houses or watch houses as shall or may be erected or continued by virtue of this Act.'

Section 141 prohibited the erection of buildings within forty feet of the road known as City Road and described in the ninth part of the schedule of the Act as 'The Road from the North West side of the Goswell Street Road next Islington to the North West corner of Finsbury Square by the Artillery Ground in the County of Middlesex commonly called or known by the name of City Road.

A further period of thirty years had to pass before the Metropolitan Management Act of 1855 came into force and rules were laid down in respect of the frontage lines of buildings generally throughout the Metropolis.

1834. A local Paving Act

Further Acts were being placed on the statute book covering the streets of only small parts of the Metropolis and the Commissioners of Pavements were thereby steadily increasing in number. An Act passed for this purpose in 1834 concerned only the Parish of Saint Mary Magdalen, Bermondsey. Under this Act all Justices of the Peace living in the Parish became Commissioners together with twenty-five other persons.

Section 62 required not only the householder, but Churchwardens, Chapel-wardens, Trustees or Ministers of every Meeting House or place of Public Worship, Directors or

Managers of Hospitals, Theatres etc. to clean or cause the footway in front of their premises to be cleaned every day between the hours of six and ten. Penalty for default ten shillings. The person liable could compound with the Commissioners for the work to be done on his behalf, provided he paid the necessary sum of money in advance.

Section 65 gave the Commissioners power to require down-pipes from buildings to carry off the water – 'down and under the foot pavement through and into the common channel so that the same may not fall from the eaves upon, or commode, any person passing such houses etc.'

By Section 68 the occupiers of houses etc. could be called upon to cause all doors and gates opening over the streets to be reversed to open inwards. (penalty twenty shillings per day).

Section 72 dealt with parts of houses projecting beyond the general line of frontage and the Commissioners could require these projections to be set back when such parts were taken down for rebuilding purposes to the level of the first floor. All new buildings had to conform with the existing frontage lines.

Sections 74 & 75 referred to projections from buildings – 'all steps projecting into the footway, projecting windows, show glasses or show boards, and all trees, blocks and other material matters or things,' also, 'all signs, sign irons, sign posts, barbers poles, dyers poles, stalls, bulks, butchers' hooks, sprouts, water pipes etc.' could be removed or altered by order of the Commissioners or Justices when considered to be a nuisance endangering the public.

Section 76 provided for the impounding of all cattle straying upon the streets. Owners had to pay five shillings for each animal taken in charge.

Section 91 gave the Commissioners authority to deal with dangerous structures and they could pull down and rebuild walls etc. on the owner defaulting after notice.

This Public Act extended in all to 164 sections and it seems remarkable that such an extensive Act was necessary to deal with nuisances in one parish only.

CHAPTER VIII

The opening of Queen Victoria's reign. 1844. The first comprehensive Building Act for London brings difficulties in administration, and the District Surveyors' Association is founded.

Victoria at the age of eighteen came to the throne in 1837. Three years later the Queen married her cousin Albert of Saxe-Coburg Gotha, amid the rejoicings of her people. The period was one of hardship, want and discontent among the masses in the cities, and social disturbances followed. The years 1840–1850 were long remembered as the hungry forties, for many were destitute. The year 1845 however can be claimed to be the turning point in the history of the country. To meet the high cost of living and the low wages, import duties had to be reduced (in an effort to assist trade), but the crisis came in 1845 when both the wheat harvest in England the the potato crop in Ireland failed. Early in 1846, amid scenes of great political excitement, the corn laws were repealed. Free trade became established and the unparalleled era of Victorian prosperity followed. In succeeding years the farming industry declined and people flocked to the towns.

The year 1845 is also associated with great activity in the development of the railways which further assisted the movement of the people to the cities, as the new transport brought the materials and food necessary for the maintenance of concentrated numbers of people. The increase in population in the Metropolis as indicated by the graph in Chapter XIII amounted to 855,000 between 1841 and 1861, or an average of 42,000 persons each year. The development and extension of the capital was clearly forseen in the London Building Act of 1844.

Local Government, Public Health Acts, Public Baths, Compulsory Education and the use of Anaesthetics were all to come in 1845. The sewers of London discharged directly into the Thames; and the Fleet River, little more than a sewer, which flowed down Farrington Road and Bridge Street, was still mainly uncovered. Houses with a water supply were exceptional and plagues or outbreaks of fever were of frequent occurrence. Travel to India, by way of the Cape of Good Hope, usually took about four months, whereas today by air the distance can be covered in a few hours.

An exceptional number of Acts of Parliament were passed between 1841 and 1844 mainly in respect of the new railways, but time had to be found to pass a new Building Act for London, as the old Act had been in operation for over seventy years and revisions and amendments were much overdue. The new measure constituted the first comprehensive Building Act of the Metropolis, for it covered an area rather more extensive than the County of London. (The "County of London" ceased to exist in 1965 when "Greater London" was created by the London Government Act 1963.) Radical alterations in procedure and administration were other features of this new Act of 1844. To meet these changed conditions, to obtain mutual counsel and the interchange of opinions among the Surveyors responsible for operating the Act: for securing uniformity of practice with efficient service to the public, the District Surveyors' Association was founded in January 1845.

The Building Act of 1844

"An Act for regulating the Construction and the Use of Buildings in the Metropolis and its neighbourhood."

The reason for the passing of the measure is given as the extension of buildings and the lines of streets beyond the limits covered by the preceding Act of 1774, all of the clauses of which relating to the construction and regulations of buildings were repealed. The preamble continued – 'And forasmuch as in many parts of the Metropolis and the Neighbourhood thereof the Drainage of the Houses is so imperfect as to endanger the Health of the Inhabitants, it is expedient to make Provision for facilitating and promoting the Improvement of such Drainage: And forasmuch as by reason of the Narrowness of Streets, Lanes and Alleys, and the Want of a Thoroughfare in many Places, the due Ventilation of crowded Neighbourhoods is often impeded, and the Health of the Inhabitants thereby endangered, and from the close Contiguity of the opposite Houses the Risk of Accident by Fire is extended, it is expedient to make provision with regard to the Streets and other Ways of the Metropolis for securing a sufficient Width thereof.' Provisions were included for dealing with noisome or deleterious businesses and other matters. The Act also made provision for regulating the office of District Surveyor and the appointment of officers to superintend the administration thereof.

Section III contained the limits to which the Act should extend: north side of Thames, Parishes of Fulham, Hammersmith, Kensington, Hampstead, Hornsey, Tottenham, Saint Pancras, Islington, Stoke Newington, Hackney, Stratford-le-Bow, Bromley, Poplar and Shadwell, and part of Chelsea. South side of river: Woolwich, Charlton, Greenwich, Deptford, Lee, Lewisham, Camberwell, Lambeth, Streatham, Tooting and Wandsworth. The city and other central parishes are not mentioned but they were covered by the Act as these areas came within the limits to which it extended. Further all places within two hundred yards from the exterior boundaries of the districts defined, except those bounded by the river Lee, came under the jurisdiction of the Act. The area covered was thus rather greater than that known as the County of London.

Section IV mentioned the rapid increase in population, building speculation, and the probability of evils arising in districts not covered by regulations and provided that by Order in Council the Act might be extended to cover any place within twelve miles of Charing Cross; this was never done.

The Act dealt at length with party walls, ruinous buildings, and parts of buildings liable to fall. Also the service of Notices of Irregularity by the Surveyors. The essence of all these provisions is the law today as they were well and truly incorporated in the Act of 1894 and carried forward therefrom by subsequent Statutes.

Section XIII provided that two clear days notice should be given by the builder or owner to the Surveyor, before commencing a work, and the penalty for failing to do so was that the party should forfeit and pay to the Surveyor treble the amount of his fees and in addition a fine of £20, could be imposed.

The Act gave us the official title of District Surveyor which arose as follows:–

Section LXIV – 'And now for the purpose of dividing the District to which this Act is to apply into several smaller Districts for the convenient Execution therein of this Act and for appointing competent Surveyors for superintending the same in each such District, and for regulating the duties of their Office, be it enacted, with regard to such Districts, so far as relates to the Appointment and Alteration thereof. That at any Time after this Act shall come into operation, and from Time to Time it shall be lawful for the Lord Mayor and Aldermen of the City of London, with reference to the City of London and the Liberties thereof, and for the Justices of the Peace for the County of Middlesex, the County of Surrey, the County of Kent, the City and Liberties of Westminster, and the Liberty of Her Majesty's Tower of London in their General Quarter Sessions respectively are hereby empowered, but subject nevertheless to the Consent of One of Her Majesty's Principal Secretaries of State, to appoint the Districts for the purpose of this Act.'

Section LXV – 'And be it enacted with regard to the Surveyors to be assigned to such Districts for the purpose of this Act so far as relates to their Appointment, That at any Time after this Act shall come into operation, and from Time to Time, it shall be lawful for the said Lord Mayor and Aldermen of the City – and for the said Justices to nominate and appoint as Surveyors such and so many discreet persons, of the full Age of Thirty Years and properly educated and skilled in the Art and Practice of Building, as they the said Lord Mayor shall think fit.'

Section LXVI – 'And be it enacted with regard to such Surveyors to be hereafter appointed under this Act, except present District Surveyors appointed to new Districts, so far as relates to the ensuring the Possession of due scientific and practical Qualifications, That it shall be lawful for the Commissioners of Works and Buildings and they are hereby empowered to appoint Three or more Architects, Surveyors, or Builders to examine together with the said Official Referees, any persons who may present themselves to be examined for the Purpose of obtaining a Certificate of Qualification, with a view of becoming Candidates for the Office of Surveyors of Metropolitan Buildings of any District within the Limits of this Act.' It will be noticed that the title 'District Surveyor' is mentioned with reference to the existing Surveyors appointed under the Act of 1774 but the term was not used in the old Act. In Section LXX these existing Surveyors are referred to – 'and they are hereby entitled to continue to be the Surveyors for the Purposes of this Act, and for the Districts assigned to them – and to act in all respects as if they had been appointed under this Act; and that every Provision of this Act applicable to District Surveyors shall apply to them'.

The title 'District Surveyor' however, originated prior to the passing of this Act in 1844. A Report of Commissioners on Municipal Corporations in England and Wales dated 1837 has an entry as follows:– 'City of London four "District Surveyors" superintend the state of buildings in the several districts. The average annual emoluments are from £100 to £150, but they vary in their several districts.' The term District Surveyor' probably dates from soon after the passing of the 1774 Act, but not as an Official title.

A candidate could not be appointed unless he held the qualifying certificate and the tenure of the office was to be – 'during the Pleasure only of the said Lord Mayor and Justices.

Section LXVIII set out the duties of the Surveyors – 'To see that all the Rules and Directions of the Act are well and truly observed. To proceed from Time to Time upon the receipt of any notice – and to cause all the Rules – to be strictly observed. To attend and perform everything required of him by this Act whether with or without Notice. To inspect ruinous buildings and Projections in danger at all Times when needful and to take all necessary Measures thereupon. To survey all buildings built, rebuilt, enlarged or altered under the Superintendence of a District Surveyor within any other District to which he shall be appointed by the Official Referees for that purpose.' This provision referred to work done under the professional private practice of a Surveyor in his own District not being surveyed by himself for the purpose of the Act but by another Surveyor to be appointed by the Referees. The Surveyors were – 'to cause a book for registering all Notices, Information and Complaints to be at all times kept in his Office, and to enter in such Book every Notice, Information or Complaint which shall be delivered or made to him and any Proceeding thereon by him taken.

Every Surveyor on his appointment had to take an oath of Official Fidelity in the following form – 'do solemnly declare That I will diligently, faithfully, and impartially perform the Duties of my Office, and to the utmost of my Power, Skill and Ability endeavour to cause the several Provisions of the said Act to be strictly observed, and that without Favour or Affection, Prejudice or Malice, to any Person whomsoever.'

Section LXXII required every Surveyor to keep an office in his district at his own expense – 'in such public Situation as shall be approved by the Lord Mayor, or justices' –

and he was to attend, or some other person on his behalf – 'every Day (Sundays, Christmas Day, and Good Friday excepted) from Ten of the Clock in the morning till Four of the Clock in the Afternoon.'

Section LXXIII gave the Surveyors the right to appoint a deputy in case of illness or other unavoidable circumstances, subject to the consent and approval of the Official Referees.

Two Official Referees being of the profession of an Architect or Surveyor had to be appointed by a Principal Secretary of State; and a Registrar of Metropolitan Buildings had to be nominated by the Commissioners of Works. These three officials were required to take oaths of Official Fidelity and the salary attached to the office in each case amounted to £1,000 per annum. The income tax in 1845 was about eightpence in the pound and a labourer's wage rarely exceeded two shillings and sixpence per day. The Official Referees had very wide powers as they were responsible for finally passing and issuing certificates on Special Buildings, which included Bridges, Royal Palaces, Prisons and the Bank of England. New public buildings and warehouses also received their final survey. They acted as Arbitrators on questions relating to party walls, and their awards were binding on all parties. They had power to call evidence, to administer the oath to witnesses, and they judged all cases of infringement of the Act which the District Surveyors were required to bring before them. They determined whether the building or work should be amended, or pulled down, and they decided all questions of costs, charges, and expenses arising therefrom.

Monthly returns showing fees collected and notices received had to be submitted by the Surveyors to the Registrar who was provided with a Seal of Office and he registered and retained all the sealed documents.

Buildings were divided by this Act into three classes: Dwellings, Warehouses and Public Buildings and these divisions are retained today. Under the heading – 'Alteration of Class' – any room used for the public or general congregation of persons in a building brought that building into the Public Class, but the Official Referees had power to sanction modifications.

The Schedule for the thicknesses of walls for the first class (Dwellings) catered for four rates: the first rate covered buildings over 70 feet and less than 85 feet in height, and the other three rates concerned buildings of less height. An extra rate, however, provided for walls of unlimited height, and in fact, this Act did not limit the height of buildings on old streets. A similar Schedule gave particulars for the second class (warehouses) while the third class (public buildings) came under special clauses and for the first time the floors of the halls, vestibules, lobbies etc. of such buildings were to be – 'wholly supported, constructed, formed, made and finished Fireproof.' The stone stairs in the dwelling class were also to be supported by fireproof construction, etc.

Rates for isolated buildings which included toll houses were given and many particulars as to footings and the thicknesses of walls for storey heights came in this Act. If a storey height (warehouse class) exceeded 18 feet then the thickness of the enclosing walls was not to be less than 26 inches. All woodwork, including window frames etc. had to be set back four inches from the face of the external walls. Rules for brest-summers, chimneys, projections and roof coverings were set out, and for the most part the regulations of today vary little from those under this Act. The divisions for warehouse buildings were limited to 200,000 cu.ft., and openings in walls separating the divisions (termed party walls) were for the first time, to be protected with double iron doors, one quarter of an inch in thickness. Dwelling houses in the same occupation could be united provided the area, when united, did not exceed fourteen squares.

One Schedule of the Act dealt with drains, cesspools and privies, and another contained important regulations on the width of new streets. Every new street (except Mews) had to be forty feet in width at the least, and most important – 'if the buildings fronting any street (new) be more than forty feet high from the level of the street then such street must be of a width equal at the least to the height of the buildings above such level.' The same provisions applied to Mews and Alleys, the limit in width being twenty feet dependant on the height of the buildings.

Schedule (K) was of considerable importance for it provided for backyards, or open spaces, attached to Dwelling houses and precise rules were given for underground rooms used for dwellings. Rooms used as a separate dwelling had to be seven feet at least in height, and attic rooms of a similar height with certain qualifications.

The Schedule of fees chargeable by the Surveyors was practically a re-enactment of the provisions of the 1774 Act with an extra rate added, so that the maximum fee chargeable amounted to £5.5.0d., whereas under the old Act a fee could not exceed £3.10.0d. A further fee of 10/6d. could be charged on buildings erected for the purposes of collecting tolls.

The principal advances of this Act from the point of view of Town Planning and Public Health may be summarised as follows: – Heights of buildings limited to widths of new streets – every new street not to be less than forty feet in width, every new alley or mews to be at least twenty feet in width – open spaces to dwellings required – rules provided for underground rooms used for habitable purposes, and the eventual prohibition of the use, as dwellings, of any such existing rooms not conforming thereto – limiting heights to habitable rooms let as separate dwellings – rules on drains and cesspools – restrictions on deleterious, noxious and dangerous businesses. But the Act said nothing about ventilation and lighting of habitable rooms other than those underground, and the buildings could be erected to unlimited heights on old streets of any width.

This Act constituted therefore a considerable advance in building legislation over the old Act of 1774, but so far as the District Surveyors were concerned the control by Referees and a Registrar inaugurated a new procedure which must have given the older men many misgivings. No protests or appeals appear to have been lodged by the Surveyors on the passing of the Act but certain other persons, landowners, householders, etc. promoted opposition and the Bill appears to have been modified, possibly in consequence. "The Builder" for April 1843 contained the full text of the proposed Act.

The new Act was dated 9th August, 1844, and its provisions relative to the appointments of the additional Surveyors required to superintend the extended areas came into operation on 1st September of that year. Between that date and the end of the year these Surveyors were assigned to the new districts; the list of Surveyors holding appointments in 1845 given in the Appendix, indicates that eighteen were appointed in the autumn of 1844.

An amending Act passed in 1846 (9 & 10 Vict. c.5) had reference only to the appointment of a third Official Referee. Awards by any two Referees were to be binding; apparently it had been realised that if the two Referees disagreed then a result could not be obtained. It also made provisions for cases where a Referee acted in a professional capacity – the building or structure was then to be surveyed, for the purpose of the Act, by one of the other Referees. As a result of this Act it would appear that one Official Referee only received £1000 per annum and the other two £500 each.

The District Surveyors' Association is founded

On 20th January, 1845 a General Meeting to be held at the London Coffee House, Ludgate Hill, was called by George Pownall, Honorary Secretary. John A. White was elected Chairman and he must have been the oldest Surveyor present for his appointment dated from 1807. These men formed the first recorded meeting of the Association. The new Act had come into operation and the meeting was called to consider some doubtful matters arising therefrom. A list of questions, prepared by the Hon. Sec., G. Pownall and three of the members, had been submitted to the Official Referees for their consideration. The reply received from the Registrar, Arthur Symonds, had merely pointed out that the queries raised by the Surveyors in their letter could not be dealt with until actual cases arose, otherwise the Official Referees might be embarrassed by being charged with having prejudged the case. In other words they were not prepared to give a ruling on anything but a definite case. The reply is interesting as it possibly gave rise to a rule of the association that hypothetical questions are not admissible.

A few questions were asked on Building Act matters including one on water closets projecting from back fronts of buildings and a majority vote decided that such projections were permissible provided that the external covering consisted of incombustible materials. Later, however, the Official Referees held that the enclosures of such projections must consist entirely of bricks, stone, or slates, etc. Many of these projections enclosed with slabs of slate still remain.

In April 1845, the place of meetings was changed to the Grays Inn Coffee House, High Holborn, and a Committee also met there regularly, a day or so before the General Meeting. In 1846 it was decided that the number of members necessary to form a quorum at the meetings should be six.

The year's work revealed many difficulties and troubles of the Surveyors particularly with reference to the procedure to enforce the Act. All proceedings had to be taken, in the first place, before the Official Referees, who after hearing the parties issued their award. The awards, in accordance with the terms of the Act, had then to be sealed by the Registrar, but if he considered that any such document did not comply with the law, he could and he often did, refuse to affix his Seal of Office thereto; the award then came before the Commissioners of Works, who decided whether or not it should be sealed and if not the case automatically dropped. Should the award, however, be duly sealed, the Surveyor had then to obtain a certificate from the Referees and he then had to apply for a summons and appear before a Police Court Magistrate to seek an Order. The Magistrates, although bound by the terms of the awards, sometimes thought that they should hear the case over again. The Surveyors were subject to certain costs and charges in connection with all these proceedings and they were naturally incensed and disheartened by the delays and formalities incidental to such a cumbrous method of administration.

The first appointment of a treasurer followed a meeting in December 1845. Mr. E. M. Foxhall accepted the office. A case reported at this meeting concerned the collapse of two houses in the Wandsworth Road with a loss of life – the cause being attributed to a builder digging basements and carrying on the work after dark to avoid the job being discovered by the Surveyor.

A list of proposed amendments, designed to facilitate the working of the Act, came under consideration towards the end of 1845 and in the following April suggestions were put forward by the Association for a new Metropolitan Building Act. The Minutes record a great deal of work carried out by the Committee, the members of which served practically unchanged until 1854. These men worked continually for the Association and for the simplification of the unwieldy Act with which they had to deal. An appeal was made to Sir James Graham, Commissioner for Works, for consideration of the proposed amendments and a sympathetic reply came from Viscount Canning to whom the Committee's recommendations were duly despatched.

The Minutes of a Committee Meeting on 11th January 1847 include a list of names of forty-four members contributing two guineas each, also the names of four members failing or refusing to contribute and three non-members. The total number of District Surveyors was thus fifty-one. The subscription to the funds of the Association was limited this year to one guinea per member.

The activities of the Association for the years 1847-1851 were chiefly directed to the obtaining of amendments to the Act or the substitution of a new Act and various deputations from the Committee waited upon Lord Morpeth, Lord Carlisle and Lord Seymour, who became successively First Commissioners of Woods, Forests and Land Revenues. It would appear that, in all, five Bills were presented to Parliament, the final one being introduced on 20th February 1851, by Lord Seymour and Sir George Grey. This last attempt to produce a new Act had resulted from a Committee appointed by Lord Carlisle consisting of three builders, three Official Referees and three District Surveyors. None of the measures proved acceptable to Parliament.

CHAPTER IX

A public execution. Proposed new Building Acts. The City and dangerous structures. District Surveyors and underground rooms. Years 1850-1856.

Surveyors today can be thankful for the fact that they are not troubled with circumstances arising from public executions. The following item is taken intact from the Minutes of a meeting held on 9th January, 1850: – 'Mr. Porter then, at the request of the meeting, detailed the course he had adopted with regard to the scaffolding erected opposite the Gaol on the occasion of the Mannings' Execution in which his attention having been called to the dangerous nature of the Erections when loaded with people he served Notices on them in respect of their being irregular, but fearing that they would not be effectual as the Danger would be incurred before the expiration of the Notice he recommended the Magistrates at the Police Court to issue Notices of the penalties of £200 for the public use of such Buildings without a Certificate of the Official Referees as to their secure construction. The Magistrate accordingly issued the Notices which were served on the parties erecting such scaffolding and they proved effectual in most cases in causing them to be abated. The Meeting expressed their thanks to Mr. Porter for the communication.'

A long detailed account of this execution appeared in "The Times" for November 14th 1849, from which the following is an extract – 'A crowd estimated at 30,000 gathered – comprised mostly of the off-scourings of the population of London – Irish labourers smoking their clay pipes and muzzy with beer, while pick-pockets plied their light-fingered art. Windows commanding a view of the scaffold rose to a Californian price – two and three guineas being paid by persons from luxurious homes and clubs – they even watched the proceedings with opera glasses from the roofs of miserable dwellings.' The report continues – 'platforms were run up in every direction with more attention to profit than security, or law, – had matters been suffered to proceed as was then contemplated some very serious loss of life must have happened. But fortunately the authorities intervened; the dangerous platforms were removed and barriers were erected in the most effectual positions to prevent the mob from swaying backwards and forwards and becoming unmanageable – five hundred police were present to keep order.' It will be noticed that the "District Surveyor" receives no credit, merely being hidden under "Authorities".

Charles Dickens witnessed this execution and it is claimed that his report, extracts from which are given below, helped materially to end these unwholesome exhibitions. The last public execution occurred in London in 1868. From a letter to "The Times", 14th November 1849, from Charles Dickens:-

"I believe that a sight so inconceivably awful as the wickedness and levity of the immense crowd collected at the execution this morning could be imagined by no man and could be presented in no heathen land under the sun – when I came upon the scene at midnight the shrillness of the cries and howls that were raised from time to time denoting that they came from a concourse of boys and girls already assembled in the best places, made my blood run cold. As the night went on screeching and laughing and yelling in strong chorus of parodies of Negro melodies with substitution of Mrs. Manning for "Susannah" and the like were added to these. When the day dawned thieves, low prostitutes, ruffians and vagabonds of every kind flocked on to the ground with every variety of offensive and foul behaviour. Fightings, faintings, whistlings, imitations of Punch, brutal jokes, tumultuous demonstrations of indecent delight when swooning women were dragged out of the crowd by the police with their dresses disordered, gave a new zest to the general entertainment. When the sun rose brightly as it did it gilded thousands upon thousands of upturned faces so inexpressibly odious in their brutal mirth and callousness that a man had cause to feel ashamed of the shape he wore and to shrink from himself as fashioned in the image of the devil – I have seen habitually some of the worst sources of general contamination and corruption in this country and I think there are not many phases of London life that could surprise me. I am solemnly convinced that nothing that ingenuity could advise to be done in this city in the same compass of time could work such ruin as one public execution. I do not believe that any community can prosper where such a scene of horror and demoralization as was enacted this morning outside Horsemonger-lane Gaol is presented at the very doors of good citizens and is passed by unknown or forgotten. And when in our prayers and thanksgivings for the season we are humbly expressing before God our desire to remove the moral evils of the land I would ask your readers to consider whether it is not a time to think of this one and root it out." Charles Dickens.

Devonshire Terrace, November 13th.

Horsemonger Lane is now known as Union Street, Southwark, and the gaol has disappeared with others of that period.

Public executions had served always, through many centuries, to excite the morbid passions of certain undesirable elements ever present in the communities of large cities. These black spots on the annals of London were now drawing to a close and the unruly scenes were losing favour with the vast majority of the citizens, who in 1850 were more concerned with the increasing prosperity of the capital and the preparations then in progress for a magnificent International Exhibition to be staged in Hyde Park. The active patronage of the Prince Consort did much to ensure the success of the great fair, which was opened in the summer of 1851. The display of British goods brought thousands of visitors from overseas and the trade of the country benefited materially. The central attraction of the Exhibition consisted of a huge glass structure 2000 feet long and 400 feet wide, designated the 'Crystal Palace'. This remarkable building, designed by Joseph Paxton, was removed subsequently to Sydenham where it became renowned for festivals and pyrotechnic displays. Londoners, as time passed, came to regard 'The Palace' with much affection and there were many expressions of genuine regret when the structure collapsed, destroyed utterly by fire, on 30th November, 1936.

The building of the Crystal Palace and the great Railway termini at Euston and Paddington stimulated improvements in the design and construction of wrought iron and cast iron structures.

In the spring of 1854 the Middlesex Magistrates instituted an inquiry into the duties of District Surveyors and the officers of the Association in welcoming the investigation placed themselves entirely at the disposal of the Committee of Inquiry. A deputation attended at the Sessions House, Clerkenwell, on 24th April, when they respectfully suggested that the Magistrates should lend their influence and weight towards procuring a more satisfactory Building Act. Subsequently the Surrey members petitioned their Magistrates for a similar inquiry with a view to obtaining a more workable Act and on 17th November 1854 a deputation waited upon a Committee of Magistrates at Newington Session House. In a letter dated 9th January 1855 the Secretary of the Association made the following statement – "I may perhaps mention that none have more deprecated the defects of the Act than the District Surveyors' Association. A short time back they were called to account by the Middlesex Magistrates and having appeared by deputation before them and laid the documents before the Magistrates showing the great labour they have undergone in endeavouring to carry out the Act and procure its amendment the Magistrates expressed themselves in a manner most flattering to them as officers."

The following is an extract from a letter dated 28th July 1854 and addressed to the Right Honourable Sir William Molesworth, Bart., First Commissioner of Parks, Palaces and Public Buildings.

"They (District Surveyors) have been quite aware ever since the passing of the present Act of its great defects, the Rules and Regulations relating to Buildings and Works being inadequate to their purpose, ambiguous in their interpretation and vexatious in details as well as complex and dilatory in the legal remedies provided. They have always lent their utmost endeavours, from the very first, for the last nine years, towards obtaining an Act which should together with greater simplicity of operation provide more completely for the various requirements of this great Metropolis."

This letter was written in a protest following an announcement in the 'Observer' for 5th March 1854, that the Government had instructed the General Board of Health to prepare suggestions for a Building Act to cover the whole country as well as the Metropolis.

The City and dangerous structures, 1848–1856

The position in the city over the control of dangerous structures after 1848 is difficult to explain, for the Act of 1844 laid down very precise rules in this respect, both in the city and suburbs. In 1848 the city obtained their City of London Sewers Act and by Section 157 of that Act powers were given to the Commissioners to deal with these structures through their Surveyor, who could hoard in and serve notices. In default of the owner, and on the order of two Justices, the Commissioners could carry out any necessary work and recover the costs. Two methods were thus available for dealing with dangerous structures, one which called for action by the Court of Aldermen on a report, or certificate, from the District Surveyor acting under the Building Act of 1844 and the other the procedure open to the Commissioners of Sewers under their Sewers Act which did not in any way repeal the provisions of the Building Act. The impression one obtains is that the vested interests of the city desired to have these powers in their own hands and at the same time they were not over anxious to use them. The Minutes of the Commissioners of Sewers for March 1854 contains a report from their Medical Officer of Health, concerning certain premises, No.8 Darkhouse Lane and 59 Skinner Street, which he stated – 'Appear to be in a condition of dangerous dilapidation which would bring them within the control of 157 Clause of your Act of 1848, unless you should think it preferable to refer them to the jurisdiction of the District Surveyor.' It was ordered that the necessary notices should be prepared and served and that the Clerk should write to the District Surveyor and call his attention to the houses reported dangerous. The reaction of an owner receiving two sets of notices and possibly being called upon to pay expenses on both, may be imagined. Generally, the Commissioners appear to have been content to leave matters with the District Surveyor although their Act of 1848 provided a much simpler procedure.

The District Surveyors and underground rooms

The year 1855 proved to be of vital importance to the Surveyors. They were charged by the newly appointed President of the General Board of Health with neglecting their duties on noxious trades and underground dwellings; the Official Referees being also included in the accusation. The allegations were published firstly in "The Times" for 8th January 1855 and they were promptly contested by the Association. The leading article of "The Justice of the Peace" for 27th January 1855 contained the following – 'charges so sweeping and condemnatory surely merited the most careful inquiry and consideration before they were committed to paper. We believe them to be not only unwarrantable according to the facts, but they are made under a total misapprehension of the legal powers of the Official Referees and Surveyors. The 68 section, as quoted by the President of the Board of Health, certainly requires the Surveyors to see that all the rules and directions of the act are well and truly observed throughout their respective districts but the rules and directions referred to in this section have no more to do with the habitation of underground cellars in London than they have to do with the undergrounds occupied with the yet "unhutted" British army before Sebastopol.' The issue of "The Builder" dated 13th January also had an article protesting against the accusations.

A deputation from the Association waited upon Sir Benjamin Hall, the President of the General Board of Health, on 24th January 1855, but the interview did not prove very satisfactory. The allegations on noxious trades, however, were restricted to three Surveyors only, all of whom stoutly denied the charges. In the following March Sir B. Hall asked Parliament to sanction the introduction of his Bill for the Better Local Management of the Metropolis. He produced some interesting figures, which are worthy of recording, and he mentioned many curious differences in the methods of the various bodies which controlled local affairs at that time; such as, one authority watering their side of the road in the morning while the other side, coming under another body, did not get watered until the evening. The main part of his speech concerned the Vestrys, the roads and sewers, but he also included an attack on the District Surveyors. The speech is reported fully in "The Times" for 17th March 1855. The following notes are interesting – the Metropolis recognised by the Registrar General extended from Hampstead in the north to Wandsworth in the south, Stepney in the east to Chelsea in the west; greatest dimensions 11 and 15½ miles, area 78,029 acres, inhabited houses 305,933, population in 1801, 958,863 and in 1851, 2,362,236. He continued –

'The officers appointed under the Metropolitan Buildings Act consisted of a registrar – salary of £1,000; official referees, one at £1,000 and others, making a total of £5,510. Besides these there were fifty-two surveyors; income varying from £200 to £1,600 per annum derived from fees and the total amount received by them in 1853 was no less than £24,364, so that the cost of this establishment to the country and to the ratepayers was just £30,000 per annum over which there was no control whatever. – Soon after he was appointed to his present office the cholera was almost at its height and it became his duty to inquire what these officers had done, whether they had prevented dwellings in cellars contrary to the provisions of the Act, and he found that they had greatly neglected their duty.'

The wording of the Act of 1844, Section LIII reads:-

'That from the First Day of July One Thousand Eight Hundred and Forty Six it shall not be lawful to let separately to hire as a Dwelling any such Room or Cellar not constructed according to the Rules specified in Schedule (K) – nor to occupy or suffer to be occupied as such, nor to let, hire, occupy, or suffer to be occupied any such Room (except for a Wareroom or Storeroom).' The procedure to be followed reads – 'and that on or before the First Day of January One Thousand eight hundred and forty five it shall be the Duty of the Overseers of the Poor and they are hereby required to report to the Official Referees the Number and Situation of the Dwellings within their respective Parishes – and thereupon it shall be the Duty of the Official Referees and they are hereby empowered to direct such Notice – to such Owners and Occupiers – of the existence of this Enactment, and that it shall be the Duty of the District Surveyors and they are hereby required to give full effect to the Directions of such Official Referees in this Behalf.'

The District Surveyors certainly never received any instructions on the subject from the Official Referees and the Secretary of the Association was informed at an interview with the senior Referee that – 'the District Surveyors and themselves had no duties to perform with reference to underground cellars since 1846 and that they had no authority to prevent the mere extension of noxious trades established before the Act was in operation.' No doubt someone was at fault in not putting the law into operation but the Surveyors were the last to be mentioned in the section of the Act in connection with the matter and there were no obligations on them to do anything until requested, so to do, by the Official Referees.

The circumstances are clear, there had been an outbreak of cholera and something had to be done about it. The necessity for the Bill introduced by Sir B. Hall could not be denied. This Bill provided for the main drainage of London,[1] the lack of which and the bad water supply, undoubtedly had much to do with these periodical attacks of cholera. (At the height of these attacks 400 deaths were recorded every day.) Parliament had to be impressed with the necessity for the Bill and all means were used to this end. The Surveyors' conduct became amply justified before the end of the year when the new measure on Local Government came before the House of Lords.

The Bill brought in by Sir B. Hall[2] became known as the Metropolis Local Management Act 1855, and the remarkable thing is that although the Statute created District Boards who were required by sections 132-4 to appoint Medical Officers of Health and Inspectors of Nuisances – the former being required to inspect and report on the sanitary conditions of their respective parish, and the latter to report on nuisances etc. – the reporting on underground rooms, used as dwellings contrary to the provisions of the Act, was left with the District Surveyors. Actually nothing appears to have been done to prevent the use of these rooms as habitations after the charges made by Sir B. Hall in March and the month of August had arrived. In fact nothing could be done, as the provisions under that Act (1844) left the administration to the common informer with the inducement that he could claim one half the penalties, on a conviction, while the other half would go to the poor. Parliament evidently realised that unless some provision could be made to alter this state of affairs then these rooms would continue to be so occupied indefinitely. The provisions of section 53 of the Building Act of 1844, referred to previously, were therefore incorporated in two new sections, 103 & 104, of Sir B. Hall's new Act. These sections were added in the final stages of the Bill in the House and the requirements called upon the Surveyors to take legal action to stop the rooms being used for habitable purposes. Nothing could be done in the House of Commons at this late stage but the Committee of the Association appealed, by a petition hurriedly prepared against the provisions, in the House of Lords. They were so desperate at the unfortunate position in which they were being placed that they proceeded to canvas all the noble Lords they could find; some were out of town, and others were about to go out of town, Lord Salisbury was out when they called, but in the Earl of Hardwicke they found a friend who presented their petition and spoke in favour thereof. The legal action clause was struck out but the provisions remaining on reporting were retained and caused considerable trouble until they were finally disposed of by the Public Health (London) Act 1891.

The sections in question, 103 & 104, Metropolis Local Management Act were briefly – 'every District Surveyor – shall without any fee or reward report periodically and otherwise

---

1. On June 11th, in the House of Commons, "Mr. Brady wished to ask whether the noble Lord had taken any measure to mitigate the effluvium from the Thames. Hon. members sitting in the committee rooms and library were scarcely able to bear it." As a temporary measure the windows of the Houses of Parliament were covered with curtains soaked in chloride of lime.
2. Sir Benjamin Hall was a great political figure of his day and the clock over the Houses of Parliament known to all Londoners as 'Big Ben' was named after him.

as the said Metropolitan Board may order – all cases in which rooms or cellars are occupied contrary to this enactment – and it shall be lawful for any District Surveyor to demand admission to inspect the same between nine o'clock in the morning and six o'clock in the evening; and if admission be not granted any Justice may – on oath before him – authorise such District Surveyor or other person to enter.' This Act was accompanied by a new Building Act termed the Metropolitan Building Act 1855 and the two Acts continued to function together; Building Act matters being constantly dealt with by amendments to the Metropolitan Local Management Act until they were largely separated by the Public Health Act 1891 and the Building Act of 1894. The Surveyors' objections to the inspection of underground rooms can be appreciated. They explained, without result, that these "hide-outs" were only opened late at night when the "appy dossers", as the patrons were termed, trooped down into the cellars and turned in for the night. The Surveyors contended rightly that this job should be one for the police.

In commenting on this Metropolis Local Management Act and its provisions to deal with the local sanitary evils, Sherwood Taylor in his book "Century of Science" remarks – 'overcrowding was rather half-heartedly attacked in this Act and it was enacted that no house should be built without drains – constructed to the satisfaction of the Vestry, which as it often consisted mainly of slum landlords, was very easily satisfied. The sanitary inspectors appointed were often unskilled workmen, and they knew that if their actions embarrassed the members of the Vestries they would lose their livelihood. The next thirty years (after the passing of the Act) showed no improvement in overcrowding but rather an exacerbation of it; thus a Marylebone street in 1868 contained ten dilapidated houses having sixty rooms inhabited by 277 persons. There were attempts to relieve the congestion, but the increase of population and the pulling down of slum dwellings, without building new houses, tended to make it worse. It was impossible to close insanitary houses and shut up cellar-dwellings, when those driven out had no prospect of finding a shelter at a rent which they could pay.'

CHAPTER X

1856–1876. The office of Superintending Architect is created and additional authority conferred on District Surveyors. Metropolis Local Management Act, 1855

A few words should be said on this Act is it laid the foundations of the present system of Local Government in London.

The Act headed – 'An Act for the better Local Management of the Metropolis' received the Royal Assent on 14th August 1855. The measure became law following much dissatisfaction in the Parishes with the condition of affairs as controlled by the Metropolitan Commission of Sewers (see page 84), and the many other Commissioners of Pavements etc. who operated by sanction of special Acts passed to prevent nuisances arising on the highways. The Local government of the Metropolis in 1854 is said to have been in the hands of 300 bodies comprising over 10,400 Commissioners who acted, in one way or another, through 250 Acts of Parliament. The new Act, a private member's Bill, was introduced to the House, as mentioned previously, by the President of the Board of Health, Sir Benjamin Hall, M.P., for the Parish of St. Marylebone.

The statute, based entirely upon the principle of local self government, divided the Metropolis into thirty-eight districts. Twenty-three of these districts consisted of separate parishes such as St. Marylebone and St. Pancras; some fifty-nine smaller parishes being grouped to form fifteen districts, thus Hammersmith and Fulham were combined in one district and Hackney and Stoke Newington in another. The twenty-three parishes thus had a district board each, whereas the remaining fifty-nine had fifteen boards among them. The larger parishes were again divided into wards in which elections were held and the persons returned were termed vestrymen. Members of the district boards were elected by the vestries and in turn they elected members to form a central board known as the Metropolitan Board of Works which consisted, originally, of forty-five members. The six principal parishes elected two members each – seventeen parishes, one each while the Common Council of the City Corporation elected three members. The thirteen remaining members came from the fifteen boards comprising the fifty-nine smaller parishes. It will be noticed that the Metropolitan Board of Works was not a body elected directly by the ratepayers, but indirectly through the district boards.

The district boards dealt with local sewers, house drainage, the maintenance, cleansing and lighting of streets, the collecting of refuse, the control of hoardings and scaffolding erected on highways, the abating of nuisances from premises injurious to health and the overcrowding of dwellings. All these services are now performed by the Borough Councils; The Metropolitan Board of Works were definitely charged with the prevention of sewage passing into the Thames near the Metropolis. They had control of main drainage, the improvement of highways, the Building Acts, regulations in theatres and music halls and later flood prevention. All these matters were later dealt with by the London County Council. This very important Act also contained provisions directly affecting District Surveyors, some of which have been referred to. Two other sections concerning Building Act matters should also be mentioned. Section 141 gave authority to the Metropolitan Board of Works to name streets and further provided that – "The owners or occupiers of houses and buildings in the several streets in the Metropolis shall mark such houses or buildings with such numbers or names for the purpose of distinguishing the same, as the said Board may direct."[1] A penalty of 40/- was included for failure to observe the Board's directions. By the following section the Board were required to keep a register of all alterations made by them in the names of streets. This appears to be the first reference in an Act covering the whole of the Metropolis, to the naming of streets and numbering of houses. Subsequent amending Acts repealed and re-enacted the provisions with certain modifications.

Section 143 covered lines of frontages, the main purpose of the requirements being the preservation of adequate widths for those important highways which radiated from the centre of the Metropolis, and which now pass through miles of densely populated suburbs before finally reaching the open country. These thoroughfares, which we now recognise as arterial roads, were by the middle of the 19th century still largely bordered with gardens or terraced houses set well back from the roads, or by the grounds of imposing residences, or well ordered estates. As these estates were developed into business premises and dwellings, efforts were made by those interested to bring forward the building lines and to cover in the open ground between the boundaries of the roads and the frontages of the original buildings. The section provided that "No building, without the consent of the Metropolitan Board of Works, shall be erected beyond the regular line of buildings in the street in which the same is situate, in case the distance of such line of buildings from the highway do not exceed thirty feet, or within thirty feet of the highway where the distance of the line of buildings therefrom amounts to or exceeds thirty feet, notwithstanding there being gardens or vacant spaces between the line of buildings and the highway." The Vestry or District Boards could demolish unauthorised buildings erected contrary to the requirements and recover the costs from the owners. The Metropolitan Board of Works did subsequently grant many licences to build over these open areas and the lines of one-storey projecting shops, which are a feature of these highways, came to be erected.

It is very doubtful whether the above provisions of Section 143 applied to certain inner roads of the Metropolis which had been the subject of special Acts. If so the original requirements of the Acts mentioned in Chapters V and VII, by which all buildings were to be set back fifty feet from the Euston Road, etc., had now been whittled down to thirty feet. There was no specific repeal in this Act of 1855 of any of those special Acts, but a general clause only contained in Section 247 – 'that all Acts of Parliament in force in any parish or place to which this Act extends – shall so far as the same are inconsistent with the provisions of this Act be repealed.' A criticism of this Section states – 'It is to be observed that the loose and vague words of this Section introduced the opportunity of doubt and obstruction. The words are "All Acts of Parliament". It is impossible to conceive anything more fertile in litigation doubt, and therefore difficulty, than such an enactment.' Difficulties no doubt did arise for in the first Amending Act passed in 1862 the old provisions for frontage lines on this street once again became law and the position was made clear.

This Act proved a considerable advance on anything previously attempted and the fact that it ultimately failed was due, not so much to the provisions of the Act, but to the cupidity of human nature. It failed because the administrators and their servants did not in certain circumstances follow the advice of Toulmin Smith, a Barrister-at-law who, in 1855 was a recognised authority on Parish duties. He concluded his remarks on this Act by saying "It need only be added that it is the first duty, and should be the constant effort, of each of these Bodies, to show itself conscious of the responsibilities, and thus worthy of the name of 'The Local Authority'."

---

1. In the days when London's houses were not numbered – the practice of numbering them did not come into use till 1764, first in Burlington Street and secondly in Lincoln's Inn – they were distinguished by signs which everyone could understand – a very necessary precaution in times when but few people could read or write. Then animals of every kind, quadrupeds, birds and fishes, could be seen in most streets. ("London Memories", by C. W. Heckethorn).

The Association and the Building Act of 1855

The efforts of the Committee, appointed by the Association, in contesting certain clauses of the Local Management Act have been mentioned in the last chapter and at the same time the Committee had to contend with the provisions of a new Building Act which proposed to alter, very considerably, the system of administration contained in the old Act. The Association's representatives appeared before the Select Committee dealing with the Bill in the House of Commons on several occasions and on 10th June they formally applied to be heard by Counsel, but the request was peremptorily refused. The Secretary, however, was allowed to speak and state the several objections and on being asked whether he deemed the Surveyors to have their office for life he replied that "he did think so during their good behaviour."

It can be understood that one matter which caused the members much concern was the fact that appointments in the future would be made by an elected authority, The Metropolitan Board of Works, whereas for eighty years the Magistrates or the Lord Mayor and Aldermen had elected the District Surveyor to his office. The members felt some alarm that possibly property owners, builders and others having vested interests in land or buildings might be able to interfere with their rights and appointments. The Committee could do nothing about this change but they secured several important amendments when the Bill came before the whole Committee of the House. The exempting clause on repairs had the words – 'not effecting the construction of any external or party wall' added at their instigation and they obtained important clauses affecting the right of entry, over which there was much opposition.

The Metropolitan Building Act, 1855

Part I – Dealt with the regulations and supervision of buildings including the construction thereof and those exempted therefrom and many of the clauses are incorporated with little change in our present bylaws. The height of habitable rooms followed the lines of the preceding Act; they were not to be less than seven feet in every part from floor to ceiling, but in the roof the restriction applied to one half the area of such rooms. The limitation to cube in warehouse buildings became two hundred and sixteen thousand feet and the time honoured clause – 'no buildings shall be united unless they are wholly in one occupation' came in this Act.

Section 13 allowed recesses and openings in walls subject to the total area thereof not exceeding one half the area of the walls, etc.

Section 14 contained rules relating to woodwork – loophole frames could be fixed within one and a half inches of the face of any external wall, but all other woodwork fixed in such walls, except bressummers and storey-post frames of doors and windows of shops on the ground storey of any building had to be set back four inches at least from the external face of the wall.

Section 30 placed the responsibility for public buildings upon the District Surveyor as follows:- 'Notwithstanding anything herein contained every public building, including the walls, roofs, floors, galleries and staircases, shall be constructed in such manner as may be approved by the District Surveyor, or in the event of disagreement, may be determined by the Metropolitan Board.'

The Metropolitan Board of Works, established as described by the Metropolitan Local Management Act, became the constituted authority for the administration of the Act and under which the Board could exercise powers with regard to District Surveyors. They could alter the limits, subject to compensation of any district and dismiss, or suspend, any existing District Surveyor with the sanction of one of Her Majesty's Principal Secretaries of State. Any future Surveyor might be dismissed or suspended directly by the Board and in such cases they were authorised to appoint temporary substitutes. On a vacancy occurring the Board could nominate any qualified person to fill the same.

Permission was given to the Royal Institute of British Architects to hold examinations, or they were to be conducted in such other manner as the Board might direct. Successful candidates were entitled to a certificate of competency and certificated persons only were eligible for the appointment of District Surveyor. The Board had to approve of every District Surveyors' office including its position in the district. In case of illness, or other cause, the Surveyor could with the sanction of the Board, appoint a deputy. The Board also had the right to direct any District Surveyor to assist any other District Surveyor, or to appoint some other assistant who would then be entitled to receive the fees for the work he surveyed. A Surveyor, acting professionally in his own district, had to notify the Board and the work would then be surveyed for the purpose of the Act, by a Surveyor appointed from an adjoining district.

The provision of the two clear days notice by the builder, before commencing a work, remained in this Act, but the penalty for non-compliance was restricted to £20, for each offence.

The procedure on the service of Notices of Irregularity by Surveyors and penalties for failure to amend work, with fines on workmen committing breaches of the regulations were set out in detail in the statute. The District Surveyor had now to take proceedings directly before a Justice of the Peace and the Official Referees and Registrar, appointed under the Act of 1844, were dispensed with and compensated for their loss of office.

Part II dealt with Dangerous Structures and the controlling bodies were, in the city, the Commissioners of Sewers, and elsewhere the Commissioners of Police of the Metropolis. Whenever a structure was reported as dangerous to one or other of the Commissioners they were required to order a survey to be made by the District Surveyor, or some other competent Surveyor.

Part III contained the procedure to be followed on questions arising on party structures and the clauses thereon are mainly in operation today. The third Surveyor replaced the Official Referee of the Old Act.

Section 62 provided that the Board of Works may appoint some fit person to be called the Superintending Architect of Metropolitan Buildings, and it further stipulated that this Architect should not practise as an Architect or follow any other occupation. Frederick Marrable became the first Superintending Architect.

Section 52 called for monthly returns to be made by the Surveyors to the Board, showing all complaints, notices and fees received in the several districts.

Part IV contained the clauses regulating proceedings in the Courts and conditions relating to appeals from the decisions of the Justices to the Superior Courts. Section 103 provided – 'all penalties under this Act, and all fees, monies, costs or expenses – directed to be recovered in a summary manner, may be recovered in manner directed by an Act passed in 1848.' This Act, the Summary Jurisdiction Act 1848, which has now been superseded by the Magistrates Courts Act 1952, imposed a limit of six months within which time action must be taken before a Metropolitan Police Magistrate.

Part V contained regulations regarding buildings used for the manufacture of explosives, etc., and concerning offensive and noxious businesses. The Act repealed practically all sections of previous statutes relating to the construction of buildings and retained and incorporated so much of the old Acts which dealt with dangerous and noxious businesses, fire engines and precautions to be taken against fire.

The First Schedule to the Act laid down the thicknesses of walls up to 100 feet in height with an unlimited length for domestic and warehouse buildings. The Act contained no specific limitations on the heights of buildings but it provided that – 'buildings to which the preceding rules are inapplicable require the special sanction of the Metropolitan Board of Works' – so presumably buildings with walls above 100 feet in height required a special consent from the Board.

The Second Schedule contained a new scale of fees based on the area and number of storeys of the building surveyed, with a proviso that no fee should exceed ten pounds.

It will be noticed that this amending Act contained radical alterations in the administrative procedure, but otherwise it produced little change in the law relating to buildings other than in the schedules of the thicknesses of walls. The Statute, however, did not cover, in any way, matters relating to the widths of streets, the provisions for which were left to the Metropolis Local Management Act. Section 202 of that Act gave the Metropolitan Board of Works authority to – 'make, alter and repeal bylaws for regulating the plans, level, widths, surface inclination and the material of the pavement and roadways of new streets and roads.'

The bylaws in respect of new streets were made by the Board of Works on the 17th March 1857, at a meeting held at the Guildhall in the City.

Bylaw (1) required four weeks notice to be given to the Board by any person intending to lay out a new street.

Bylaws (2 & 3) limited the least width of new streets, used for carriage traffic, to forty feet and twenty feet where used only for foot traffic – each such street to have at least two entrances of the full width thereof.

Bylaws (5 & 6) dealt with slope of roadway from the crown to channel, height of kerb, etc.

The Board had no power to restrict the height of buildings by bylaws on these new streets and it would appear that no such restrictions existed after the passing of the Metropolitan Building Act 1855 until 1862 when a further enactment amending the Metropolis Local Management Act became law.

Metropolis Management Amendment Act 1862

This important amendment Act covered many matters from rates and loans to Vestries and the Board of Works to the maintenance of sewers, bridges and roads.

Section 62 required District Surveyors to report, without fee or reward, to the Board, Vestries and District Boards in June and December, and at all other times when requested so to do, all underground rooms or cellars, not complying with the law and occupied as dwellings.

Section 74 gave powers to the Board of Works to acquire, subject to compensation, buildings or parts of buildings projecting beyond the general line of buildings, when such projections or properties had been demolished for more than one half of their cubical contents as a result of fire or other causes.

Section 75 provided that Section 143 of the 1757 Act and Section 140 of the 1821 Act – 'are hereby repealed and in lieu thereof be it enacted that no building structure or erection shall without the consent in writing of the Metropolitan Board of Works be erected beyond the general line of buildings in any street, place or row of houses in which the same is situate in case the distance of such line of buildings from the highway does not exceed fifty feet or within fifty feet of the highway when the distance of the line of buildings therefrom amounts to or exceeds fifty feet notwithstanding there being gardens or vacant spaces between the line of buildings and the highway, such general line of buildings to be decided by the Superintending Architect to the Metropolitan Board of Works for the time being.' In cases of contravention, the Vestry or Board of Works could apply for orders from the Justices and on conviction and in default of the owner, they could enter and alter or demolish the building so erected.

Section 85 limited the height of the buildings, except churches or chapels, on new streets less than fifty feet in width, to the width of such streets measured between the buildings.

Section 98 required all new streets used for the purpose of carriage traffic to be not less than forty feet measured between the boundaries next the public way; streets for foot traffic were limited to twenty feet. Any road, passage, or way, formed or laid out, for either of the aforesaid purposes, after the passing of this Act became a new street. The Board had power to afford relief from these clauses.

A further Act to amend the Building Act of 1855 was passed in 1869 for the purpose of transferring the authority for dealing with dangerous structures, outside the city, from the Commissioners of Police to the Board of Works. The Superintending Architect, George Vulliamy, presented a special report to the Board on 15th September 1869 in which he stated – 'that during the last fourteen years about 1,200 buildings or structures have been reported yearly to the Police as dangerous and requiring inspection. He also demanded additional office accommodation, as there were no rooms available for officials administering the duties at Spring Gardens. The District Surveyors were requested subsequently to take over the surveys for the Board of Works.

An Act passed in 1871 exempted a new cattle market on the site of Deptford Dock from the constructional clauses of the 1855 Building Act.

The Acts of 1707 and 1764 referred briefly to in Chapter V, and other enactments, could not be said to have provided an efficient fire service; the parochial fire brigades being anything but adequately equipped. Charles Dickens in "Sketches by Boz" is said to have presented a very fair example of the working of a parish fire brigade. A welcome addition was made to this service in 1833 when the ten leading fire insurance companies formed the London fire engine establishment with a personnel of eighty men under James Braidwood, an officer with much experience in fire fighting. Other voluntary services were also inaugurated including that of the Royal Society for the 'Protection of Life from Fire'. In 1861 a devastating fire occurred in Tooley Street and several persons, including James Braidwood, lost their lives. The disaster cost the Insurance Companies upwards of £2,000,000, and the fire engine establishment came to an end. A select committee of the House of Commons subsequently recommended that a fire brigade for London should be established and on the 1st January 1866 the Metropolitan Fire Act 1865 came into operation under the Metropolitan Board of Works.

Surveyors and new acts (Years 1856–1876) Court cases and other matters

The Building Act of 1855 improved the status of the District Surveyor very considerably. He was now virtually a free agent with complete control over all building operations coming within the Act. Public buildings were now his sole responsibility – the appeal in cases of disagreement being to the Board of Works. In fact the Surveyors were somewhat alarmed at the prospect of having to deal with these buildings with no rules on construction to guide them, and in 1856 the Association appointed six members to form a Public Buildings Committee.

A special general meeting of the association on 21st December 1855 passed certain bylaws for the purpose of establishing the Association on a more efficient basis. A rota of three members was to meet monthly to consider cases and applications for legal assistance – members not attending on the rota were to forfeit a fine of ten shillings, unless they provided a substitute. Two firms of Solicitors were appointed to take, at stated fees, cases in the Police Courts. The subscriptions were altered and based on income, the rate being ten shillings in every fifty pounds, but this scale was reduced subsequently. The Association's funds were also to be available to assist members with costs in special law cases.

Many Police Court cases were taken by the Surveyors and several went to the Queen's Bench Divisional Court. The sum of five guineas from the Association's funds being allowed in most cases to members having to proceed to the Higher Court. Needless to say the expenses incurred in these cases exceeded, very considerably, this amount. The following

The fire brigade in 1820

decisions are interesting: July 1863 – a Magistrate decided that rooms in the roof constituted a storey and that the thicknesses of walls must be determined by measuring the height to the ceiling of such rooms, although the walls may not extend thereto. The decision caused some comment as generally such cases had not been dealt with on these lines. Early in 1864 a ruling was given in the Court of Queens Bench (Carruthers v Legg, District Surveyor) that the Police Court Magistrates had no authority to give decisions on irregularities in public buildings.

In a case heard in the Court of Common Pleas (1864) it was decided that a Police Court Magistrate was not bound to take the opinion of the Superintending Architect as to the frontage line of buildings in a street, but he was at liberty to form his own opinion thereon, notwithstanding the provisions of Section 75 of the Metropolitan Management Amendment Act, 1862.

July 1869 – Association agreed that a Public House with a club room did not constitute a public building. A Magistrate decided that a wooden building on small wheels or rollers did not come within the Act and dismissed the case.

August 1875 – Counsel's opinion given on openings in party wall above roof of lower building was that – 'a wall was only a party wall so far as it actually separated buildings.' This opinion followed the loss of a case in the Police Court.

A case of a different complexion is reported in 'The Builder' for 20th November 1875 when a certain Richard Whaler, a sculptor, was charged in the Police Court with assaulting a District Surveyor's 'managing clerk' by striking him about the head with a wooden mallet. The prisoner had been annoyed at the action taken by the Surveyor and his clerk on some wooden buildings. The Surveyor, Mr. Knightley, had also received an anonymous letter, apparently sent by Mr. Whaler, warning him to be careful, or he would be a corpse and that he ought to be pole-axed and dipped in tar. The case was adjourned, the Magistrate taking a serious view of the matter and the outcome is not recorded.

The years 1850 to 1900 cover a period rich in literary achievements and much that was written concerned the Victorians and their ways of making money. Charles Dickens (1812–1870) wrote on the poor and slums; Thomas Carlyle (1795–1881) preached reforms to all and sundry, and John Ruskin (1819–1900) condemned the methods of building in no uncertain terms. He refers in "Stone of Venice" (Vol. 2) to base principles of building – 'some vaultless floor that drops the staggering crowd through the jagged rents of its rotten timbers; some fungous wall of nascent rottenness that a thunder shower soaks down with its workmen to a heap of slime and death. These we hear of day by day.' He quotes 'The Builder' of 29th January 1853[1] – 'on Thursday the 20th the front walls of two of the new houses now building in Victoria Street, Westminster, fell to the ground.' There is no reference in our records of this accident but in June 1857 Londoners were startled by the collapse of three old houses in Tottenham Court Road with the loss of seven lives. The 'Building News' reported the accident as like an episode from the destruction of Pompeii and claimed that it was due to the unsurpassed stupidity of our system of legislation. It further made some distinctly sarcastic remarks about the District Surveyors and suggested that the Surveyor directly concerned should be court martialled. Alterations were in progress in the buildings at the time of the accident but they had been reported as dangerous structures to the Commissioner of Police. The Association presented a memorial to the

---

1. The report in 'The Builder' refers to the quantity of rain which had fallen but otherwise it did not throw much light on the collapse and from the description it appears difficult to reconcile the buildings with ordinary house construction, for the statement mentioned – 'massive composition cornices and iron roof girders' and further states that the walls had been built over arches springing from the ground floor. Possibly Ruskin had these arches in mind for he was a strong advocate for the Gothic arch. One wonders what he would say to the Council's dwellings of today in which arches are non-existent.

Board of Works deploring with deep concern various erroneous public and official statements in connection with the collapse and suggested that an inquiry should be made into the action taken by the Commissioner, who dealt with dangerous structures through a Surveyor from his own department. The matter eventually faded out without reflection on anyone concerned.

On 15th January 1864 members were present for the last time at Grays Inn Coffee House, Holborn, where they had met together for nearly nineteen years. A note in the Minutes for December 1855 states that the landlord, Mr. Hart, offered a room at seven shillings a day including pens, ink, paper, lights and fires. No mention is made of refreshments but doubtless they could be obtained at the usual charges. The meetings from 1st April 1864 were held in the Architectural Galleries, 9 Conduit Street, the premises then being in use by various professional societies and in 1865 they were, by arrangement with the Royal Institute of British Architects, commenced in their rooms in an upper storey of the building.

A special return of District Surveyors showing the situation and condition of their offices and the times and mode of transacting the business of the respective districts was prepared in 1865 by the Superintending Architect. Each district, with name of Surveyor, is given together with the situation and condition of the office, hours of attendance, use to which offices applied and general remarks. The records under situation were in all cases 'convenient', but those under conditions varied from – 'very respectable, very orderly, very good', one only being designated 'objectionable'. This last office consisted of a letter box in the bar window of a public house and the hours of attendance were none; the letters being forwarded to an office in Westminster. The Surveyor's residence served in many cases for the office, an example being – 'two parlours used as office in private house.' The hours of attendance varied to an extraordinary degree, some being 'all hours, all times', others 'three or four days a week', while some were merely 'occasionally'. The general remarks throw an interesting light on the office conditions of the times. Some items read – 'a clerk and boy assist. District Surveyor attends three or four times a week; District Surveyor has a back parlour, clerk assists out of doors; keeps three clerks to assist out of doors; District Surveyor and his clerk attends three days a week at 11 o'clock; District Surveyor has two rooms, ground floor, attends twice a week and occasionally sleeps there; District Surveyor has a city office, clerk goes to district twice a week.' These arrangements might have met the exigencies of the times, but they would hardly suit this present work-a-day world.

This Return of 1865 gives the amount of fees earned in each District with the expenses incurred – these varied from as little as £47 (£26 net) in Tower Liberty to as much as £1,318 in St. Pancras. The majority of the 56 Districts earned less than £300 gross.

A later Return, in 1889, by which time the London County Council had just come into being, showed that there were 73 Districts, 35 of which produced fees of less than £500 – the lowest being Deptford with £87 net and the highest Fulham with £1,887 net. In few cases were the office expenses more than £150 p.a. so the number of staff employed must have been minimal, probably no more than one or two clerks.

This variation in income was not of serious consequence to those District Surveyors appointed before 1891 as they were still free to continue their private practices and their appointment as District Surveyors doubtless increased the amount of private work they received. It is interesting to note that during this period the majority of building work was taking place on the fringes of London. As the large suburban housing estates grew up here and there so did the fees in the Districts concerned.

As in private practices sons frequently followed their fathers in the post of District Surveyor. There was no official retirement age, most continuing in Office until their death.

The majority of District Surveyors being architects there were strong links with the Royal Institute of British Architects. Professor Donaldson, son of an architect and District Surveyor, himself became District Surveyor in Holborn and played a large part in the foundation of the R.I.B.A., presenting the President's gold badge and chain and his portrait hangs in their Council Chamber. He remained in office until he was 90 and he is remembered today in the annual presentation of the Donaldson medals for architecture. Another founder member of the R.I.B.A. was H.E. Kendall, who retired as District Surveyor at the age of 99 and whose son also became a District Surveyor. One Surveyor, E. I'Anson, became President of the R.I.B.A. for 3 years, was simultaneously President of the Surveyors' Institute and managed also to be the surveyor to the Merchant Taylors Company, in which capacity he designed Charterhouse School.

Apart from the District Surveyors' services to professional bodies and their private practices they had many outside interests, one became Editor of 'The Builder' (now 'Building') and several went on long and difficult journeys to Russia and to the East, returning with full sketch books to write accounts of their experiences.

The District Surveyors' Association meetings were, from 1865, held at the headquarters of the R.I.B.A. in Conduit Street and this tradition continued until 1934 when the new R.I.B.A. building was completed in Portland Place, where they are held today.

CHAPTER XI

Amendment Acts and Bylaws 1878-1886. Dangerous structures, Commissioners of Sewers. The passing of some notable Surveyors. The Metropolis Management and Building Act Amendment Act, 1878.

This amending Act regulated frontage lines of buildings and the terms – 'centre of roadway' and 'prescribed distance' were mentioned and defined therein. It also gave the Board of Works certain powers to insist on alterations in theatres and music halls.

Section 6 required the frontage or the boundaries to forecourts of buildings, erected after the passing of the Act, to be at least twenty feet, i.e. prescribed distance, from the centre of the roadway on streets used for carriage traffic. The limitations on ways used for foot traffic only being ten feet. The Act did not prevent the construction or extension of any building within the limits of any area which may have been lawfully occupied by any building at any time within two years of the passing thereof.

Part II (Section 16) gave the Board authority to make bylaws with respect to the sites, foundations, and the quality of the substances of which walls were authorised to be constructed under the principal Act, also to prescribe the duties of District Surveyors in respect thereof. Penalties were included for non-compliance with such bylaws. Exemptions for the Duchy of Lancaster and the Queen's Hereditaments completed the statute.

The second part of this Act followed on the collapse in 1875 of three houses in course of erection. Following an enquiry the Board of Works called for a report of cases taken by Surveyors on the use of improper materials in the construction of walls, etc. The Act of 1855 contained unfortunate weaknesses in this respect for it merely provided that the foundations, i.e. footings of walls, should rest on the solid ground and there were no requirements regarding the composition of bricks or mortar. Consequently difficulties had arisen in obtaining convictions against speculative builders on these matters and under the circumstances it is strange that a much larger number of collapses is not recorded. There appeared to be some justification for the remarks of John Ruskin as mentioned in Chapter X.

The Association objected to these important items of construction being dealt with in bylaws and suggested that they should be incorporated in a schedule to the Act but the Bill passed without opposition.

The bylaws came into operation, following the sanction given by a Secretary of State, on 6th October 1879. For the first time walls were required to have a concrete foundation nine inches in thickness – the composition of the concrete being specified and the description and quality of the substance of walls being defined. Sites were required to be cleared of any faecal, animal or vegetable matter or slop (road sweepings) or refuse and covered with a six inch bed of concrete. These rules did not apply to walls or sites on gravel, sand or natural virgin soil, or to sheds and stable buildings. Bricks were to be hard, sound and well burnt, and the proportion of sand, lime or cement, with particulars thereof, for use as mortar were specified. Tops of walls were to be protected with bricks set on edge in cement or a coping, and moreover, every wall of a house or building was to have a damp proof course.

That these fundamental rules of building should have been delayed for so long before being incorporated in the law, seems remarkable. Five thousand copies of the bylaws were printed for the Association and distributed to members at cost price.

The Metropolis Management and Building Act Amendment Act, 1882

Part II gave the Board of Works further powers over the naming and forming of certain streets also in respect of buildings, etc. erected beyond the general frontage lines.

Part III dealt with temporary buildings; the Board obtaining authority to licence iron or wooden structures and to require and obtain the removal of iron buildings, or others of a temporary character on the expiration of the licence. Open spaces to dwellings came within this part of the Act. Every new dwelling-house erected on a site not previously occupied in whole or part by a building had to be provided with an open space at the rear above the level of the ceiling of the ground storey. The required space varied from 150 sq.ft. for dwellings with frontages of 15 ft. or less, to 450 sq.ft. for dwellings with frontages of 30 ft. or over.

Section 15 provided that buildings not erected for public purposes could not be converted thereto unless the District Surveyor was satisfied with the whole construction, or in the event of disagreement the Board had authority to settle the issue.

Section 16 provided that the requirements in the 1855 Act in respect to the distance at which pipes for conveying hot water or steam may be placed from any combustible materials shall not apply to pipes conveying hot water or steam at low pressure.

Part IV contained the usual exempting clauses and included the City of London and the liberties thereof as not coming within the provisions relating to streets and temporary wooden structures.

Bylaws for concrete buildings 1886

On 23rd June 1886, bylaws made by the Board under Section 16, Metropolis Management and Building Acts Amendment Act 1878 were passed by a Secretary of State and came into operation. These bylaws covered the erection of walls erected in concrete. Such walls were to be equal at least in thickness to similar walls specified to be constructed of brickwork under the principal Act. Concrete had to be composed of Portland Cement, clean Thames or pit ballast, or gravel or broken brick or stone or furnace clinkers with clean sand in the proportion of one of cement to two of sand and three of coarse material to pass a 2-inch ring. The walls were to be carried up regularly in parallel frames of equal height. Party walls and chimney stacks could also be constructed of concrete; the exposed work above the roofs being rendered. A fifty per cent increase in fees could be charged by the Surveyor for buildings constructed in this manner and this also applied to alterations and additions. It would be interesting to know what demand could have existed to have produced these bylaws. Relatively very few buildings could have been erected to comply with these requirements. The cost would surely have been prohibitive.

Dangerous structures and the Commissioners of Sewers

Constant complaints are recorded between 1879 and 1881 on the vexed question of dangerous structures. The Board of Works acquired control over the procedure on dangerous structures, outside the city, in 1869 after which date the surveyors were called upon to survey and take the necessary action on these cases. Prior to 1869, when the Commissioner of Police had to deal with these structures, a deputation from the Association waited upon that gentleman and expressed the hope that he would call upon the District Surveyors to carry out the surveys, etc. Now they had these duties they certainly did not like them, particularly the Police Court proceedings, for which they received the sum of five shillings for giving evidence and two shillings and sixpence on attending an adjournment. Counsel's opinion, taken to ascertain their liabilities, proved unsatisfactory, so nothing resulted. A Magistrate's opinion on what constituted a dangerous structure, given in 1879, is worthy of recording – 'a dangerous structure is one not sufficiently and permanently secure against ordinary risks or any extraordinary risks which may be fairly anticipated.' A classic case occurred in the autumn of 1879 concerning a party wall between buildings in the Haymarket. The wall had been shored and at the Police Court proceedings the Magistrate decided that the wall could not be considered dangerous in consequence and he dismissed the summons. The Board of Works were then successful in having the case reopened and after a further hearing the Magistrate reversed his decision and made an order for the wall to be pulled down.

Within the city the authority for dealing with dangerous structures remained with the Commissioners of Sewers, as provided by Section 70 of the Metropolitan Building Act, 1855, and something should be said of the ancient office which existed from very early times. The word sewer came, apparently, from the Saxon 'sae-waer', meaning sea-fence and the Commissioners of Sewers were appointed originally to prevent nuisances arising from the failure of river embankments with the consequent flooding of land and for dealing with other annoyances which arose from time to time, on tidal rivers. Various measures were enacted for this purpose through the centuries, one of much importance was passed in the reign of King Henry the Eighth. The meaning attached to the word sewer appears to have changed as the pollution of the streams flowing through the Metropolis together with that of the Thames itself, became of serious importance. The rebuilding Act of 1667 coupled sewers with drains, the subsequent purpose of which was chiefly the disposal of faecal matter. By the Act of 1667 all common sewers, drains and vaults within the city were to be designed and set out by such and so many persons as the Mayor, Aldermen and Commonalty of the City in Common Council assembled should authorise and appoint under their Common Seal. The persons so appointed were known as Commissioners of Sewers and by 1840 there were five such independent bodies acting over the whole of the Metropolis. The Commissioners of the City, numbering about ninety, were elected annually by the Common Council from their own representatives. The Metropolitan Commissioners of Sewers Act 1848 consolidated the powers of the Commissioners, outside the city, into one central Board, the members of which were appointed by the Crown[1]. Wide powers on sanitary matters were given to the Board by this Act, which did not apply to the city, but in this year, 1848, by the City of London Sewers Act much additional authority was acquired by the Commissioners within the city. The Board, known as the Metropolitan Commissioners of Sewers, was not a success and they were abolished by Sir B. Hall's Local Management Act, 1855 – their duties being conferred on District Boards and Vestries, while the Metropolitan Board of Works, created by that Act of 1855, were given sole control over the main sewers of the Metropolis. The powers of the Commissioners of Sewers in the city, the only such body left in London with this title after 1855, were thus analagous to those of the District Boards outside the city; they dealt with local drainage and other health matters. Although, as indicated above, these Commissioners in the city were, in effect, a Committee only of the Corporation of London, they were recognised by subsequent statutes as apart from the Corporation. They were nominated by the Public Health Act of 1891 to carry out the sanitary requirements of that important Act in the city and the L.B. Act 1894, Section 5 (43) defined "city" as meaning all parts now within the jurisdiction of the Commissioners of Sewers. The following sub-section (44) of that Act also defined the City Corporation (which is relatively a new term) as the Mayor, Aldermen

---

1. The Metropolitan Commissioners of Sewers held their meetings in the Court House, No.1 Greek Street, Soho, and in 1850 the Commissioners made a bylaw, under their Act, requiring a weekly return to be delivered to their offices from each District Surveyor outside the city, of all notices of building or rebuilding of houses or buildings received by him during the week. The Association agreed eventually, that the bylaw should be complied with. The Commissioners became defunct following the passing of Sir B. Hall's Local Management Act 1855, when the Metropolitan Board of Works, created by that Act, took over the Commissioners offices at No.1 Greek Street where they remained until 1861 when they removed to Spring Gardens.

and Commons of the City of London. The Commissioners continued to act apart from the Corporation until 1897 when the City of London Sewers Act transferred their duties and liabilities to, and vested their rights in, the City Corporation who then proceeded to form a Public Health Department. In this way the ancient office of Commissioners of Sewers in London came finally to a close. Dangerous structures in the city now come under the Common Council.

Court cases 1876-1889

The records for the years 1876 to 1889 contain many interesting decisions on Court cases and certain works for which we today consider notice necessary, as a matter of course, such as the rebuilding of parts of walls, etc., were doubtful border line cases in those days. An action taken by Bannister Fletcher in 1889 on the rebuilding of the upper part of a wall and two chimney stacks above was lost in the Police Court and again on appeal in the Higher Court. The Lord Chief Justice supported the contention of the learned Magistrate that the replacing of a few old bricks by a few new bricks did not affect the construction of the wall or alter the character of the house. With the event of the 1878 bylaws several intricate questions arose among which may be mentioned the query as to what could be accepted as "virgin soil" and Magistrates were sometimes confronted by exhibits of heaps of muck shown by the District Surveyor and the counter evidence of pails of sand and gravel produced by the builder – both samples taken according to witnesses from the same site. At times a claim would be put forward that the term 'virgin soil' consisted of ground never broken by the plough; probably this definition came from rural areas. The Surveyors were mostly successful in these cases but an attempt in 1884 to extend the bylaws to cover a cemetery did not prove successful. In this case a builder proceeded to erect a dwelling over a disused burial ground in which some eighteen to twenty thousand persons had been interred following a cholera plague in 1840. In the resulting action at the Police Court the Magistrate came to the conclusion that dead cats, cabbage stalks and other fetid materials might be considered as coming within the definition of obnoxious substances required to be cleared by the bylaw, but he did not think that bodies in coffins came within that category, or that they could be described as materials mixed or impregnated with animal matter. Moreover the builder would be committing an offence if he attempted to remove the bodies. The District Surveyor concerned, Mr. T. Blashill, appealed when the case again went against him. It could not be said that these Surveyors in any way attempted to avoid the issue.

CHAPTER XII

The London County Council replaces the Metropolitan Board of Works. The Tribunal of Appeal is constituted. The Association and the Building Act of 1894.

The Metropolitan Board of Works came to an unseemly end in 1888 following questions raised on their action in letting privately, without competition, certain building sites resulting from the formation of Shaftesbury Avenue. The outcome of an inquiry held by the Board and the censuring of one of their officers did not stop the allegations then prevalent. A Royal Commission of inquiry, consisting of three members, was appointed with the consensus of the Board, from which it received every assistance. The Commission found that two members of the Board and some of its officers had been guilty of malpractices resulting in personal profit to themselves. The Commission generally praised the work of the Board and stated of its members – 'that against the vast majority of them not even suspicion of corruption or misconduct has been breathed.' The concluding passage of the last report of the Board contained a pathetic appeal – 'It has been a source of pain and sorrow to the Board that at the close of thirty years administration of the local affairs of London, which has been attended with at least some measure of success, and in the course of which the Board has carried out some of the greatest works of public utility of which any city can boast, its good name has during the last year of its existence been sullied by iniquitous proceedings of which, though carried on in its midst, its members as a body were entirely without knowledge.' The works referred to included the construction of the outfall sewers, which carried the sewage away from the Metropolis – the embankments of the Thames[1] – the acquisition and maintenance of some thirty parks and the formation of many important highways including Northumberland Avenue, Victoria Street and Charing Cross Road. The Board also initiated the first slum clearance and in sixteen schemes they dealt with forty-two acres of unhealthy properties. They sold the sites for development by Artisan Dwellings Companies. The Board also established the London Fire Brigade and in Building Act matters they procured the passing of several amending Acts and bylaws thereunder.

Public opinion, forever fickle, demanded a change and this came about through the Local Government Act 1888, the main purpose for the passing of which was to provide for elected Councils in counties where the local matters were still in the hands of the Justices of Peace. The Act (Section 40) provided that the area covered by the old Board should constitute a new administrative county and that the portions thereof previously included

---

1. The great works were carried out under the supervision of Sir Joseph William Bazalgette, who was born at Enfield, Greater London, of French descent in March 1819. He commenced his duties as Chief Engineer to the Metropolitan Board of Works in 1856 and his scheme for the main drainage of the Metropolis was sanctioned in 1858. The major works were completed by 1875 at a cost of over £4,000,000. In 1863 the Board obtained powers to construct the Albert Embankment on the Surrey side of the Thames; the work was completed by 1869 – St. Thomas's Hospital being erected subsequently on a part of the surplus land resulting from the great undertaking. The Victoria Embankment, on the Middlesex side, was constructed between 1862 and 1870, and the Chelsea Embankment from Chelsea Hospital to Battersea Bridge, was commenced in 1871 and finished by 1874. Sir Joseph Bazalgette had also much to do with the maintenance and improvements of the bridges over the river. He received a knighthood in 1874 and he remained with the Board until its close in 1889. He died at Wimbledon in March 1891. A record of his services for London is contained on a memorial attached to the Embankment wall near Charing Cross.

in Surrey, Kent and Middlesex should be detached to form 'The County of London.' The city came within the new county, but its many privileges were not affected.

The replacement of the Board of Works by a directly elected authority was hailed with wide approval. In January 1889 the elections were held and The London County Council commenced its duties on 21st March 1889, the first Chairman being Lord Rosebery.

In October 1889 a letter from the Clerk of the Council, H. de la Hooke, came before the meeting for consideration. This is the first reference to the Clerk of the Council. The letter addressed to the Honorary Secretary put forward tentative proposals for the payment of District Surveyors by salaries and contained other suggestions as to the terms of their appointment. In a printed reply the Association gave eight reasons why the system of payment by fees should not be altered. Reason five might be mentioned as it called attention to the old difficulty in the suburbs of the fluctuation of work – 'That the payment of District Surveyors by fees is preferable to payment by fixed salary because it ensures a proper relation between the duties performed and the emolument received. If a fixed salary were paid a disproportion in this respect would in many cases shortly arise and this would more especially be the case in suburban districts, where at one time great numbers of houses are in progress of erection, and at another comparatively little work is being done. Further, payment by fees is an incentive to the District Surveyor to take care that all works to which the regulations of the Building Acts apply are 'brought under his notice and supervision'. It is interesting to note that the Council raised the question of salaries, in lieu of fees, in the first year of their existence and also that half a century was to elapse before the idea became a reality.

The Council pursued their proposal to pay salaries with the Surveyors' Institute and this is the first instance of the mention of that Institute in the Minutes. The following is an extract from the reply the Council received – 'Their (The Institute's) general experience in dealing with officials paid by salary and not in independent practice is that their habits of thought and business frequently led to great delay and to the interposition of frivolous and vexatious objections.'

The Council proceeded, however, to make serious alterations in the conditions under which new applicants to the office of District Surveyor were appointed. The Association raised questions as to the legality of these new conditions in a printed letter of protest, but no attempt was made to test the matter in a court of law. In 1890 the Council made their first appointments, and these men were required to give an undertaking that they would devote the whole of their time to the work of a District Surveyor and that they would not carry on business as an architect, surveyor, or builder, either directly or indirectly; also that they would retire on reaching the age of sixty-five. All appointments thereafter were subject to these conditions, which also had to be accepted by any existing Surveyor wishing to change to another district. It should be mentioned that an alteration in this direction had been contemplated by the Board of Works and in 1886 they passed a resolution by which all future applicants for the office had to give an undertaking that they would not practice in their own districts.

A full account of the Council's meeting at which the alterations in the status of future District Surveyors was passed, appeared in 'The Land Agents' Record' for July 5th of 1890. The further particulars are of interest – the Chairman of the Building Acts Committee, Mr. J. Hutton mentioned – 'there was no sweeping change involved – the Committee sought rather the gradual introduction of a good system, leaving time to do the rest for the Council (Hear, hear).'By way of giving a happy illustration of what time would do he 'might mention that during the time the Committee had been deliberating the question, death had removed two District Surveyors from the ranks.' The recommendations accepted included a stated time for the personal attendance of the Surveyor at his office, that no candidate should be appointed unless he had attained the age of 28 and was under 50; the declaration binding him to the conditions to be entered on the Council's Minutes. The age limit of 65, on reaching which a Surveyor could be called upon to retire, was to stop the very general practice of having the work "devilled" (done by an assistant). The statement continued that 'at the present time there were 74 District Surveyors in London.' This number must have been the maximum ever acting at one time. In 1846 there were 51 Surveyors in office. and by 1882 they had increased to 64. Between 1882 and 1890 there were 14 deaths, 4 retirements and 26 new appointments, so in January 1890 there were 73 Surveyors acting and during the year there was one death and two appointments. As the volume of work increased and districts became vacant they were reduced in area and additional appointments made; the number being increased by eight between 1882 and 1890. In these years there was a very considerable boom in building in London.

In the discussion which ensued on the motion by the Building Acts Committee it was disclosed that 36 districts produced less than £500 each per annum and the declared policy of the Committee was, that they would be rearranged so that an income of not less than that amount would be assured from each district, and the trend of the arguments indicated that the alterations in the status of the District Surveyor, as proposed by the Committee, would not have been agreed to without this assurance. The policy did not materialise for a number of years, and in 1906 there were still 13 districts producing less than £500 each per annum.

With the demise of the Board of Works the Local District Boards evidently thought that an excellent opportunity then existed for the elimination of District Surveyors and the transference of their duties and incomes to themselves. They therefore put forward a proposal to Parliament to this effect. Nothing came of their efforts, for public opinion did not appear to be too favourably impressed by these local bodies and in fact they were the next on the list to be liquidated. The Association, however, addressed a 'Memorial' on the subject to the Prime Minister, the Most Honourable the Marquis of Salisbury from which the following is an extract – 'That the present system whereby the regulations of buildings in the Metropolis is entrusted to a thoroughly independent body of professional men, holding the Certificate of Competency from the Royal Institute of British Architects is in every way preferable to one which would create a class of local inspectors dependent for their salaries upon the caprices and interests of local wirepullers.'

The Tribunal of Appeal is constituted

The first London County Council (General Powers) Act passed through Parliament in 1890. The Act conferred powers on the Council for the acquisition and maintenance of certain parks and open spaces and contained some highly important regulations on Building Act matters.

Section 28 set out the procedure to be followed on the certification by the Superintending Architect of a general line of buildings. A copy of the certificate had to be served on the Vestry or District Board of the Parish in which the buildings were situated, in addition to other persons interested. The Vestry or Board or any other person could, within fourteen days after notice of the certificate, appeal to a tribunal to be constituted as follows – One member to be appointed by the Council, who could not be a member of the Council, one member to be nominated by the Council of the R.I.B.A. and the other by the Council of the Surveyors' Institute. The tribunal could call upon the Superintending Architect for evidence and on any other person and they could confirm, reverse, or vary any such certificate.

In this way the 'Tribunal of Appeal' was constituted and it will be noted that its functions were at that time limited to deciding questions on lines of frontages and they could deal also with disputes on heights of buildings. No specific reasons can be stated for the formation of 'The Tribunal' but possibly the authority given to 'The Architect' by the amending Act of 1862, to decide the general lines of buildings in any street, had resulted in criticism being directed against such an important matter being left to the sole discretion of one person with no appeal therefrom. Decisions, however, on this subject had rested with 'The Architect' for twenty-eight years before the necessity of providing an appeal from his decisions had been discovered.[1]

Section 29 gave the Council power to consent to the erection of a building, coming within the cube limitation contained in the Act, to an extent not exceeding 450,000 cubic feet,subject to a report from the chief officer of the Fire Brigade, but a consent could not be given to a building over 60 feet in height.

Section 31 conferred powers on the Council to make bylaws with respect to (1) materials for plastering; (2) the filling in of excavations made within three feet of buildings; (3) duties of District Surveyors in relation thereto.

Section 34 provided that buildings could not be extended on sites not previously occupied so that any part came within a less distance than 20 feet from the centre of the roadway.

Section 36 limited the height of buildings, except churches and chapels, to 90 feet exclusive of two storeys in the roof and ornamental towers, etc. This regulated height applied on old and new streets – subject to appeal to the Tribunal – penalty for non-compliance £100.

These sections of this Act were incorporated afterwards in the 1894 Act, the height of buildings therein being reduced to 80 feet, but this 1890 General Powers Act was important as it created the first independent body of men with power to vary or reverse official decisions and although the Tribunal of Appeal may function only very occasionally, it is there, and the fact that it does exist may and doubtless does exert a restraining influence on what might otherwise easily develop into inelastic and oppressive decisions on building Act matters. For the first time since passing of the Rebuilding (after the great fire) Act of 1667 buildings on old streets were limited in height. From 1667 to 1774 the height of buildings in the city had been restricted by the 1667 Act, but in the suburbs no limitation had existed previously on streets laid out prior to the passing of the 1844 Act.

The first Act regulating sky signs.

On 3rd July 1891 the Royal Assent was given to the London Sky Sign Act the measure being described as – 'an Act for the Prohibition of Future and Regulation of Existing Sky Signs in the Administrative County of London'. The Act, as stated in the preamble, had for its object the safety of the public and the prevention of unsightly erections in the County and to provide for the prohibition of certain erections above buildings or public streets for purposes of advertisement or announcements etc., and for the regulation of such erections now existing. The provisions covered any sign in the nature of an advertisement visible against the sky from any point in any street including balloons and flags so used, and any open work sign device not used in connection with a Railway Company. Signs resting on the top of a wall and being in one continuous face were exempt. All future sky signs were prohibited and any such existing sign could be retained only on the owner obtaining a certificate of stability from the District Surveyor and upon payment of a fee of two guineas therefor. The Council, or in the case of the city the Commission of Sewers, were authorised to issue licences for two years on existing sky signs on the receipt of a satisfactory certificate from the Surveyor. These licences could be renewed for two further periods of two years making six years in all, the same procedure being followed; after the expiration of the six years such signs were to be removed. The Surveyor's fee had to be paid for the grant or refusal of

1. A conflict of opinion had occurred between the Courts of Queen's Bench and Common Pleas as to whether a Magistrate could question the line defined by the Superintending Architect and possibly this was the reason for the constitution of the Tribunal.

the certificate. In the case of a refusal the applicant could appeal to the Committee of Appeal appointed by the Council under Section 212 of The Metropolitan Management Act 1855.

The Public Health (London) Act 1891 must have come as a considerable relief to District Surveyors for Sections 96 and97 repealed the clauses of Section 62 of the Amending Act of 1862 and delegated the duties on inspecting and reporting on underground rooms to any officer of a sanitary authority. Action had to be taken by that authority before a Petty Sessional Court. District Surveyors were now relieved of all duties in this respect.

On 19th October 1891 new bylaws were passed under Section 16 Metropolis Management and Buildings Act Amendment Act 1878. These bylaws replaced those passed in 1879 and 1886. They dealt with the foundations and sites of buildings, the description and quality of the substances of walls, the duties of District Surveyors and the payment therefor. Relatively few alterations were included in the new bylaws which maintained the original requirements including those on concrete buildings, but to most of the clauses the words – 'to be approved by the District Surveyor' were added.

A curious omission in these bylaws in relation to the construction of party and cross walls is worth mentioning; the regulations with reference to bricks were as follows – 'The external walls of every house, building or other erection shall, except in the case of concrete buildings, be constructed of good, hard, sound, well-burnt bricks or of stone. Similar bricks shall be used in the portions of party and cross walls below the surface or level of the ground and above the roof, including the chimney stacks.' Party and cross walls could therefore be constructed of any poor type of brick between ground and roof levels and in fact they were often built with old soft red bricks, bats and other similar materials obtained from the ancient structures which had to be demolished in the clearing of the site.

The new bylaws under Section 31 London County Council (General Powers) Act 1890 were also passed on the 19th October 1891. For the first time the materials for plastering and the supports therefor were specified, a wide range being included and much being left to the satisfaction of the District Surveyor. The filling in of excavations within three feet of walls of buildings with natural soil, dry rubbish or other suitable materials to be approved by the District Surveyor and the exclusion of slop, refuse, animal or vegetable matter for such purpose became the law under these bylaws.
The supervision was left to the District Surveyor, and a nominal fee could be charged.

The L.C.C. (General Powers) Act 1893 (Section 17) contained amendments to the Sky Sign Act of 1891. The definition of such signs being slightly altered to cover those erected over any structure and the exemption for signs in one continuous face being changed to – 'Any sign on any board, frame or other contrivance securely fixed on to the top of a wall or parapet of any building or the cornice or blocking course of any wall or to the ridge of a roof. Provided that such board or frame or contrivance be of a continuous face and not open work and do not extend in height more that three feet above the part of the wall or parapet or ridge, etc.

The Association and the Building Act of 1894

The year 1894 produced the most comprehensive Act on streets and buildings since the passing of the rebuilding Act of 1667, and at the July meeting a special report on the proposed Bill came before the Association. A Sub-Committee had worked on the suggested new legislation since early in the year and they had achieved considerable success in obtaining the necessary amendments to secure the efficient working of the Act and to safeguard the interests of District Surveyors. The Sub-Committee's list of amendments had been discussed at several conferences with a Sub-Committee of the Building Acts Committee of the Council and in the main they had been accepted by that Sub-Committee. But the Bill, as introduced into Parliament, did not embrace some of these amendments and instructions were given to Parliamentary Agents to lodge a petition; a Mr. Castle being engaged as Counsel and briefed to oppose the Bill.

The following advantages were obtained – the limit of £10 for a fee withdrawn and an extra half fee added for public buildings, concrete buildings, and buildings divided into separate tenements by party structures. An objectionable clause – 'that unless all the provisions of the Act had been observed in carrying out any work the District Surveyor could not claim his fee' – was withdrawn. Another clause under which the Council could appoint officers to carry out any of the provisions of the Act was also struck out.

Amendments were obtained to Part V which controlled open spaces about buildings and the heights thereof. With regard to certifying plans of old buildings the requirements in the Bill, that the District Surveyor should make the plans when called upon so to do, was altered so that he had only to certify to correctness of plans submitted. Other amendments secured were – application of Act to additions and alterations, or other work, as well as to new buildings inserted – rules for scantlings of timber expunged – insertion of words giving power to District Surveyor to enter a building to see that a notice, or order, has been complied with – services of notice, orders, etc. by registered post legalised, and many other matters. When the Bill reached the House of Lords unsuccessful attempts were made to obtain the insertion of a clause to the effect that District Surveyors should not be debarred from private practice. Although this Sub-Committee opposed and obtained many modifications on this Bill they were able, nevertheless, to keep the Association on good terms with the Council.

Article in "Punch"

Modern writers cannot be accused of being squeamish in their use of the English language and since the advent of Shaw's "Pygmalion" books have contained a choice selection of profanity; while indelicate situations have been freely discussed in a way that would have shocked the doyens of the Victorian novels. They made up for this lack of candour in their day by developing a type of broad humour, based partly on moral precepts but often mainly on fanciful and exaggerated circumstances, by which persons of influence in professions and trades came under the lash of a libellous satire. Charles Dickens and W. Makepeace Thackeray were masters of this craft but in the hands of lesser scribes the attacks degenerated into pointless accusations devoid of wit, and covering thegerm of truth with a bushel of lies. Such an article provoked the protest of a Committee of the Association in 1890 to make a request that the President should interview the editor of "Punch" and endeavour to obtain some correction to statements made which were described as – 'exceeding the bounds of facetious criticism'. The President probably obtained little satisfaction from his interview, for he was up against a feature of the times and the claims of freedom for the press. A new series of sketches entitled 'How it's done' – 'A Handbook to Honesty' commenced in the issue of "Punch" for 11th October 1890 – number one being headed "I'm Monarch of all I Survey".The scene depicts a builder meeting a Surveyor in a newly erected building. The builder timidly foxy and clinking in his breeches pocket some metallic substances which might have been keys or coins. The Surveyor, knowingly pompous and self-important, a burly mass of broadcloth and carrying an intimidating notebook and a menacing stub then makes memos in a staccato and stabbing fashion, which is singularly nerve shaking. After some exchanges the following dialogue takes place –

Surveyor: By the way, I suppose this wall is properly underpinned?

Builder: (nervously) Well – er – not exackly – but er er – well the fact is I thought ––

Surveyor: (sternly) What you thought Sir doesn't affect the matter. The question is what the Building Act says. The whole thing must come down.

Builder: But I say, that'll run me into ten pounds at least, and really the thing's as safe as ––

Surveyor: Maybe, maybe. In fact I don't say it isn't. But the Act says it's got to be done.

Builder: Well well, if there is no help for it I must do it of course.

Surveyor: (looking somewhat disappointed) Very sorry of course, but you see what must be, must.

Builder: Yes, yes, no doubt. Well (brightening) anyhow we may as well slip over to the 'Crown and Thistle' and crack a bottle of champagne.

Surveyor: (also brightening) Well ours is a dusty job and I don't care if I do.

They proceed to discuss diverse devices for "dodging the Act" over their champagne and cigars. Finally –

Surveyor: Now look here my boy, suppose you and me just divide that tenner between us, five to you and five to me, and as to the "underpinning" – well nobody'll be a bit the wiser and the building won't be a halfpenny the worse I'll bet my boots. Come, is it a bargain?

The scene ends on the builder paying the Surveyor a fiver, thus evading the law, saving the builder a few pounds and supplementing the salary of the Surveyor. "Punch" would not print articles in this strain today.

CHAPTER XIII

The last of the Victorians and the end of the nineteenth century
The London Building Act 1894. The Borough Councils are formed

Overcrowding and insanitary conditions still prevailed in the housing of the poorer classes, for property and the rights of the individual were still held to be of paramount importance. Conditions were improving gradually and the necessity for the clearing away of slums and the provision of light and air to dwellings had become recognised. Several Acts for this purpose were passed in 1866, 1868, 1875 and 1891. The Building Act of 1894 contained the first detailed regulations for dealing with the complicated problem of providing open spaces to domestic buildings.

The London Building Act, 1894.

The Statute incorporated all the Acts previously mentioned from 1844 to 1893 and it came into operation on 1st January, 1895.

The legislation in this Act made distinct efforts to regulate – 'widths of streets, lines of frontages, open spaces to dwellings, heights of buildings and projections therefrom, ventilation and height of habitable rooms and the control and prevention of the spread of fire.'

Part IV of the Act incorporated the earlier regulations of the Metropolis Local Management Acts in respect of the naming of streets and numbering of houses. For the first time these provisions appear in a Building Act. The Council were given full authority over the provisions and they were required to continue to keep registers of the alterations in the names of streets which they authorised. (Part IV did not apply to the city.)

Part V contained the regulations for open spaces about domestic buildings and the height thereof and its provisions were unique, for nothing approaching them had been attempted previously. The rules were remarkable for the comprehensive, or perhaps incomprehensive way in which they attempted to cover the multitude of cases which could arise. Buildings with and without basements on old and new streets – irregular sites, inclined sites – courts within buildings were all dealt with and the inclusion of a diagonal line drawn from a rear boundary of the required open space had the effect of bringing the heights of dwellings into relation with the open area provided.

The Act reduced the maximum height of buildings from 90 feet to 80 feet exclusive of two storeys in the roof, but many of the old rules on the construction of buildings remained very much as before, including the procedure on party walls and dangerous structures. The certification of frontage lines of old buildings within the prescribed distance by the District Surveyor and also of the irregular open space at the rear of domestic premises constituted a new departure. For the first time two sections were added, 61 (2) and 63 covering requirements for means of escape in case of fire from certain buildings, while a new schedule of materials deemed to be fire-resisting came with the Act.

Section 78 to 80 contained the rules relative to public buildings, the District Surveyor's control being maintained as hitherto, but the last mentioned section included definite regulations on the width of staircases etc., to churches, chapels and other public places of assembly. Of these requirements Mr. Dicksee states "The enactments of this section are not to be found in any previous Act but they are an incorporation of some of the Regulations for the Construction of Theatres made by the Council under the Metropolitan Management and Building Amendment Act 1878." The provisions continued in force until 1940.

The authority of the Tribunal of Appeal created by the L.C.C. (General Powers) Act 1890 became much extended. All decisions under the Act, where left to the discretion of the Council, the Superintending Architect or the District Surveyor could be the subject of appeal to the Tribunal. The Council lost the privilege of nominating one member to the Tribunal – the appointment being transferred to a Secretary of State. This alteration followed on the setting aside of a decision of the Tribunal by the High Court on the grounds that the person appointed by the Council had been found to be a member of the Building Acts Committee. The Tribunal had authority to administer oaths, to hear and receive evidence and to require the production of books or documents and their decisions may be enforced by the High Court as if it had been an order of that Court. In fact their powers were somewhat similar to those possessed by the Official Referees under the Act of 1844 but they were certainly more final.

Doubtless the legislators of the time considered that they had done much to solve the question of building in London and they must be given due credit for a great effort. It is doubtful however whether they realised the outcome of allowing a loophole for the rebuilding of old buildings on narrow streets on a certificate, as to the frontage lines, from the District Surveyor; for in this rebuilding new structures were not limited to the heights of the old buildings and they could be erected to the full height of 80 feet. High commercial buildings arose on narrow ways previously fronted by two storey cottages. At a Town Planning conference held in 1910 at the R.I.B.A. Mr. Arthur Crow, District Surveyor for Whitechapel, read an interesting paper in which many examples of the legal erection of high buildings on narrow streets, some less than 20 feet in width, were illustrated. He stated 'It is sometimes said that the law governing the question of ancient lights is sufficient to prevent any serious increase in the height of buildings on the opposite side of the street, but this is not always to be relied upon; in one case within the writer's experience the owner of a row of two-roomed cottages, let at 4s. a week, threatened a building owner opposite with an action for damages for loss of light. The building owner bought the cottages and raised the rent to 5s. Of course the tenants were at liberty to move away, but the mischief was done.' He further stated 'The result of the present law is, therefore, to foster the retention of narrow streets, and to render them still more unhealthy by allowing buildings to be erected to a much greater height, and providing an increased population on an area already overcrowded.' In the case of dwellings intended for working-class occupation the Act did require that the front walls should be set back 20 feet from the centre of the road. Nevertheless no amending Act has ever been enacted to alter the law in this respect and probably Town Planning is now the only answer.

In this Act the height of habitable rooms became 8'6" at least (8 feet for storeys in the roof) in place of the old limit of 7 feet, and for the first time rules were included for the lighting and ventilating of all such rooms.

It should be noted that, although the Building Act of 1894 recognised the right of District Surveyors to act as independent Architects and although the Association made strong protests against the Council's action in requiring new entrants and those seeking reappointments to contract out of those rights, there was no apparent lack of candidates ready to accept the Council's conditions. Similarly in 1934 when the Council attached onerous conditions to new appointments by which candidates were required to declare that they would not claim compensation in the event of the terms of appointment being altered by Statute, there was still no difficulty in the supply of candidates although some Surveyors holding office did refuse to accept this unreasonable agreement and they were, in consequence, stalemated in the districts they held.

The Borough Councils are formed

The legislation following in 1899 abolished the District Boards and Vestries. These authorities had remained unaffected by the establishment of the London County Council in place of the Metropolitan Board of Works, but it appears evident that several of the Boards represented a policy of stagnation and in fact they were, in some cases, elected for that purpose. Their sanitary inspectors were badly paid, £2 a week being considered a good wage, while some received much less. These officials were subject to pressure from members of the Boards many of whom had interests in slum property, but records indicate that the Medical Officers carried out conscientious and valuable work – often against opposition and threats.[1] The general public evinced little interest in the activities of the Vestries and a Parliamentary return for 1885 recorded that four per cent only of the electors had registered their votes at the election. Nevertheless under their regime cesspools practically disappeared and drains were installed to the vast majority of buildings. A well known authority stated in 1876 – 'With all their faults and defects, the Vestries have done much for London, whilst there is now one-tenth of the London houses which are not drained into the main sewer, there probably was not in 1856 one-tenth that had the advantage of sewer drainage.'

Mr. Balfour introduced the Local Government Bill in February 1899 which substituted the Metropolitan Borough Councils for the District Boards and Vestries. The London County Council fought the Bill to avert what in their words amounted to 'The principle of disintegration'. Lord Salisbury's view prevailed – 'that small municipalities were necessary to counterweight the authority of the London County Council.' The Act divided the County of London, outside the City, into twenty-eight districts closely following the boundaries of the District Boards. Each district became a Metropolitan Borough with full civic regalia – a mayor, aldermen and councillors, complete with mace, robes and gilt chains of office; each borough having its own town hall and town clerk. London became divided into twenty-nine townships (with the city) all having rights independent of the London County Council, which possessed little or none of their civic splendours. The boroughs have the right to promote Bills in Parliament and to appeal for loans to the appriate department of the Government against a refusal of the Council.

The London Government Act 1899 referred to above, transferred from the Council to the newly formed Borough Councils – inter alia – rights in respect of the licensing of wooden structures coming within the provisions of Section 84 L.B. Act, 1894.

Developments of the century

The nineteenth century drawing towards its close had produced much in the way of domestic building in and around the central areas of London that could only be described as undesirable and frightful. A Dr. Southwood Smith in giving evidence before a Select Committee of the House of Commons in 1840 stated – 'At present no more regard is paid in the construction of houses to the health of the inhabitants than is paid to the health of pigs in making sties for them. In point of fact there is not so much attention paid to it.' The window tax Act (1798) remained in force until 1851 and the circumstances arising from this imposition can be well imagined. This tax on light and air simply added a barrier to the health of the people, the wellbeing of whom had been merely ignored by the Building Act of 1774. Early efforts in the construction of blocks of flats for the working classes, built on expensive restricted sites, with no regard to the lighting of habitable rooms resulted in tenement structures in which human beings were buried alive. In the eighteen

1. The Vestry of St. James, Westminster (1866) checked the zeal of their Medical Officer, Dr. Lankester, whose salary was £200 a year by reducing it to £150 after a year or two when they found he was in earnest in his work. (Jephson "Sanitary Evolution of London" p.189.)

hundred and forties New Oxford Street was formed – cut through the densely populated parish of St. Giles – the home of the Irish labouring community. Five thousand persons were displaced to crowd into adjoining boroughs.

In the suburbs, during the latter half of the century, streets upon streets of monotonous dwellings, all similarly arranged in rows, had arisen to provide shelter for the increasing multitudes. Each dwelling sent up its quota of smoke and soot which, on windless days, formed a curtain of gloom over the Metropolis. The peak of this building came in 1881.

The population in 1801, the first census year, amounted to 960,000 and by the middle of the century (1851) the number had risen to 2,360,000 an increase of nearly two and a half times. By 1881 there were 3,816,000 persons in London or nearly four times the number at the commencement of the century, and by 1901 the total amounted to 4,536,000 or in 100 years the population had multiplied itself by four and a half. The figures after 1901 declined as persons moved out of the County.

The population by the 1871 census amounted to 3,254,000 and the inhabited houses numbered at that time 418,802 as recorded by Henry Jephson in his book 'The Sanitary Evolution of London'. By the same authority the number of houses increased to 488,116 by 1881. Jephson lays much stress on overcrowding and gives many examples from the returns of Medical Officers and there can be no question but that this evil, with its serious consequences, was rife. The average of some eight persons to each additional building, on the above figures, does not perhaps appear to be excessive. The figure of 69,314 quoted by Jephson as additional dwellings (inhabited) could not have comprised anything like the total number of houses erected, for all those demolished had to be replaced by new dwellings before any additional houses could be counted. The total of new buildings returned by the District Surveyors as completed for the ten years amounted to 114,341. The difference in the figures, 114,341 and 69,314 amounts to 45,027, and this figure would, on this basis, represent commercial buildings, out-buildings, workshops and houses to make up for those demolished under clearance schemes.

One thing that can be stated with certainty is that the maximum number of building works in 1881, 29,275, including new buildings (15,404) followed the maximum increase in population and that this figure of works was not reached again for over twenty-one years (1904).

The total of new buildings from the District Surveyors' returns which includes, of course, various out-buildings and premises rebuilt indicates that an average of over ten thousand buildings were erected each year or two hundred per week.

Many new thoroughfares were formed in the hundred years and some have been referred to in connection with a review of the work of the Metropolitan Board of Works. Architects drew their inspirations mainly from the past, evidence for which can be seen in two of London's masterpieces in stone – the vast gothic structures of the Houses of Parliament at Westminster and the Law Courts in the Strand. The distinct architecture of the century came with the increase in knowledge of mechanical science and engineers were encroaching on the province of the Architect using big span roofs to cover the new railway termini. Great engineering projects were accomplished including the construction of the first tunnel under the Thames at Rotherhithe (1825–1843) and the erection of the Tower Bridge, commenced 1886, opened 1894. Of all these works, by far the most important was the development of the docks, especially in the first twenty-five years of the century. In these years six docks were completed commencing with the West India Docks established in 1800, and ending with St. Katherine's Docks completed in 1823. Four further great docks were constructed between 1850 and 1888. Without the facilities thus afforded for the accommodation of the shipping of the port, the capital could not possibly have developed in the amazing way it did between 1850 and 1900. The age of iron was ousting that of stone; suspension bridges, iron-arched bridges and flat girder types came into practical use through the genius of those masters of civil engineering, Telford and Brunel.

Nineteenth century houses, showing parapets at party walls, as required by Building Acts since 1707. Modern bylaws do not require these if the party walls are widened to 18″ width just beneath the roof covering, so they are rarely seen now. This picture illustrates two points: firstly, that compliance with bylaws does not necessarily create good housing conditions, and secondly that standards of housing and environment have risen rapidly.

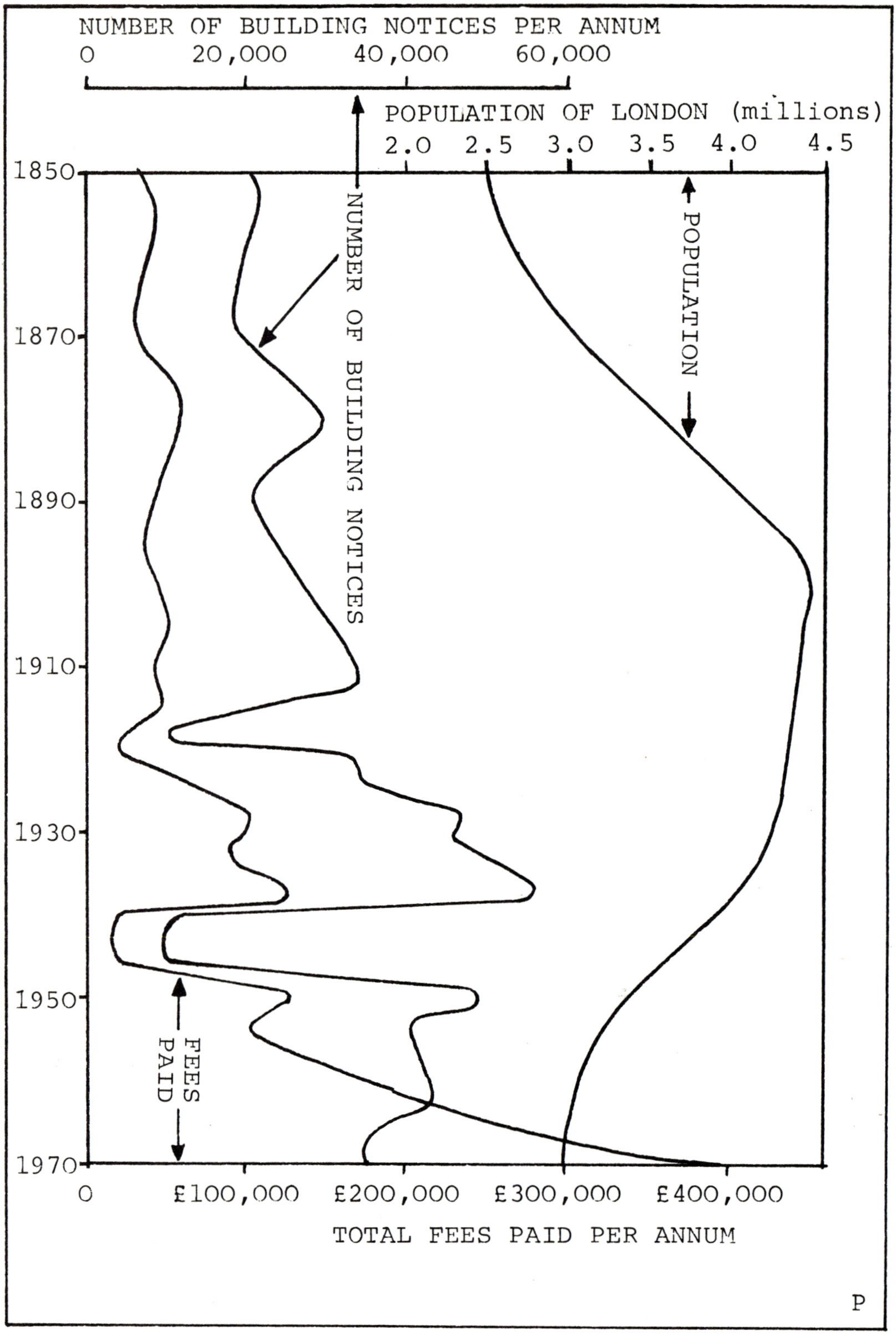

Graph of London's population, building operations, and fees

CHAPTER XIV

The twentieth century. New Building Enactments. The London County Council and District Surveyors. Years 1900–1915

During 1905 the Council deposited a further Bill in Parliament proposing many alterations in the 1894 Act, some of which would have affected vitally the status of the District Surveyor. Provisions were inserted with the object of facilitating the introduction of payment by salaries. The Bill aroused much opposition and a petition presented by the R.I.B.A. described the proposed Act as – 'an ill-considered measure badly framed and one which ought to be withdrawn.' The Association also entered a petition and engaged counsel – Mr. E.J. Castle, K.C. – to conduct the appeal. The only clauses which passed into law those dealing with means of escape in case of fire from certain buildings. This Act constituted the first comprehensive attempt to deal with the difficult problem of escape in case of fire from old and new buildings. A futile effort had been made in Sections 61(2) and 63 of the 1894 Act to cover the ground, but nothing of consequence resulted until this new Act came into operation on 1st January 1906.

The London Building Acts (Amendment) Act, 1905

Under its provisions new buildings, subject to certain limitations, were required to be provided with reasonable means of escape in case of fire and plans and particulars were required to be deposited with the Council before erection was commenced. The Council also obtained the necessary powers enabling them to require protection against fire in certain existing buildings. Section 12 resulted in much trouble to all concerned, particularly the District Surveyors, as it called for escape to the roof by way of counter-weighted trap doors, dormer windows or other means of access thereto and it's application extended to most buildings over thirty feet in height, except dwelling houses occupied by not more than two families. All requirements made under these provisions were subject to appeal to the Tribunal of Appeal. Sections 61(2) and 63 L.B. Act 1894, previously referred to, were repealed together with the Schedule of fire-resisting materials under that statute which became replaced by an extended list contained in the first schedule to the new Act. As a result of this new legislation many additional duties devolved on the District Surveyors the payment for which came in the Second Schedule.

Reference in the records is made in 1905 to a Committee of the R.I.B.A. on Reinforced Concrete – this Committee continued to function until 1932.

Towards the end of the year the Council once again returned to the question of changing the mode of payment from fees to salaries and once again the Association appealed against the proposal. It was now proposed that salaries should be paid to all existing Surveyors, commencing on 1st April 1906; the amounts being equal, in each case, to the average of the fees received in the respective districts over the preceding seven years. New entrants were to come within a 'model' scheme which would have entailed, ultimately, a rearrangement of the districts. The Council would, in all probability, have sanctioned and pressed forward with this recommendation of the Building Acts Committee but for the vigorous opposition of the Finance Committee. A point made by this Committee being –

'that the County would soon be built over entirely and that the Surveyors' income from fees would fall with a consequent loss to the Council.'

The Return of fees earned by each of the 29 District Surveyors in 1906 showed a wide variation from £152 gross (£30 net) in Battersea South to £2,327 (£1,807 net) in St. James, Westminster. Those of the District Surveyors who had been appointed after 1891 were without private practices and the inadequacy of the incomes to enable these men to maintain their position is evident. The Association in 1907 protested and pressed for the removal of the restrictions against private work. In a printed application it was pointed out to the Council that the alteration had not stood the test of time and that in the past men eminent in the profession, including no fewer than five who became Presidents of the R.I.B.A. had presented themselves as candidates but such men would not apply unless they could be assured of an adequate income. The R.I.B.A. and the Surveyors' Institute supported the application which did not prove successful and although in 1908 certain moves were made by extending the boundaries of some districts the position still remained unsatisfactory.

Three appeals against the Council's requirements, made under the 1905 Act, for ventilated lobbies, in lieu of a secondary means of escape, went to the Tribunal of Appeal in 1907 and the Tribunal allowed the appeal in each case. None of the buildings exceeded 1,000 sq.ft. in area and the Building Acts Committee decided that in future smoke lobbies would not be required where a building came within this figure in superficial area, provided an upward escape was available.

Public notice being given in November 1908 by the Council of their intention to include amendments of the Building Act in their (General Powers) Bill, 1909, the Association reacted without delay and secured the loan of a copy of the Bill. The amendments were to provide for buildings of skeleton-framed construction and of reinforced concrete. By the middle of December the Committee of the Association had prepared a complete review of the Bill with many suggestions which are generally contained in the clauses, relating to this type of construction, in operation today.

The London County Council (General Powers) Act, 1909

This Act made it lawful to erect – "buildings wherein the loads and stresses are transmitted through each storey to the foundations by a skeleton framework of metal, or partly by a skeleton framework of metal and partly by a party wall or party walls."

Party walls could not be framed and their construction remained unaltered by this Act. Thicknesses of panel walls, between framing, and the permissible loading on floors and roofs together with the limiting stresses on structural members and the casing thereof as a protection from fire were specified and set out in the statute. Plans, particulars and calculations were to be deposited with the District Surveyor, who could call for reasonable proof as to the quality of metal to be used. He could also require any tests to be carried out that he might consider necessary.

Section 23 gave the Council power to make Regulations with respect to the construction of buildings wholly or partly of reinforced concrete.

Appeals against decisions of the District Surveyor could be made to a Petty Sessional Court provided they were taken within fourteen days of service of notice of such decisions. The Council could modify or waive most of the requirements and in connection therewith they could make such conditions as they thought fit. Appeals against the Council's refusal to modify or waive the provisions under their direction, or objection to such conditions imposed by the Council, could be made to the Tribunal of Appeal.

The contents of this Act were the most technical by far of all the Acts previously passed in connection with buildings within the Metropolis. The Statute made the District Surveyor responsible for steel framed buildings from the foundations and bearing on the ground to such details as the pitch of rivets. The end of the century saw the passing of the old wooden floor and cast iron construction in practically all important buildings. The age of steel and concrete had arrived. Mention is made in the records for 1909 of a member inviting his colleagues to visit his district for the purpose of inspecting two buildings then in course of erection in reinforced concrete, one of which, an electric generating station, probably received a constructional consent from the Council, but the other, being a public building, came without question directly under the control of the District Surveyor.

The water supply of London came under the Metropolitan Water Board following the passing of 'The Metropolis Water Act' in 1902. The Board, first constituted in 1903, is not directly elected by the ratepayers, but the members are delegated from representatives of the London County Council, the Common Council of the City of London, the Metropolitan Borough Councils and by other Boroughs and Urban districts outside London previously supplied by the Companies. A Bill presented by the Board in 1913 would have exempted their buildings from the provisions of the Building Acts. The Association prepared a petition against the measure and negotiations followed; the exemptions were limited finally to pumping stations and to apparatus, such as hydrants, placed under the public way.

Other measures passed included Factory and Workshop Acts 1901 and 1907, Housing and Town Planning Acts 1909, Cinematograph Act 1909, City of London (Various Powers) Act, 1911, Education (Administrative Provisions) Act 1911, Bylaws on Lamps and signs overhanging Public Ways, 1914. These measures had little effect on the District Surveyor, but by the terms of the Education Act they lost their authority over new school buildings.

The Minutes for 1913 and 1914 contain numerous notes on complaints from the Borough Councils who were then raising questions and objections to the authority of the District Surveyor. Some Councils considered that notices for works of underpinning in connection with redrainage should not be given. Following a fire at Barkers' premises, Kensington, in 1913, at which a number of lives were lost, the Kensington Borough Council requested the London County Council to consider whether any of the duties imposed by the Building Acts could not better be discharged by the Metropolitan Borough Councils, especially the provisions on means of escape in case of fire from old buildings. The Building Acts Committee invited representations from the Borough's Standing Joint Committee on the subject and later that body presented a report proposing that District Surveyors should be abolished and their powers transferred to the Borough Councils. The County Council took no action and later in 1914 there is a note in the records of a reply from the Building Acts Committee to the Fulham Borough Council pointing out that the proposed change in authority would result in lack of uniformity of practice and considerable expenditure would be necessary to compensate District Surveyors for their loss of office.

Case law 1900–1915

Numerous important cases were decided in the Police Courts during these years and several actions against the Superintending Architect's decision on lines of frontage went to the Tribunal of Appeal. The following decisions affected District Surveyors: The Council claimed exemption for their schools, mainly on the grounds that they came under clauses of the 1894 Act exempting them from Part VI i.e. construction of buildings. A friendly case in the Police Court went in favour of the Surveyors and in 1909 the Higher Court confirmed the decision.

The Local Government Act of 1899 transferred from the County Council to the Borough Councils the authority to licence wooden structures coming within the provisions of Section 84 of the 1894 Act, and an action followed in 1902 between the District Surveyors and the Westminster City Council. The Lord Chief Justice decided that the powers and duties of the District Surveyors had not been transferred to the City Council and its officers. Although the judgment was not completely favourable to the Surveyors it gave them sufficient authority to claim notice and fees on such structures which included wooden stands erected to enable persons to view processions.

For many years after District Surveyors benefited by these legal decisions in having the necessary authority to survey these works. A number of actions however did not prove successful. A case taken by Mr. Dicksee in 1915, against a builder for renewing cellar-flap doors in soft wood under the public way, did not succeed. The Magistrate found that the doors did not constitute a construction under the public way as they were on a level with the surface and the work constituted a necessary repair – five guineas costs being allowed against Mr. Dicksee. Another case decided against the Surveyors in the Police Court and again in the Higher Court referred to a demand for a fire-resisting floor between the ground storey of a public house exceeding ten squares in area, and the living rooms over. It was held that a licensee could use the whole of the premises for his trade so the question of separation did not arise.

CHAPTER XV

The First World War. The bombing of London 1915–1919.
The reinforced concrete regulations. Years 1915–1920

The bombing of London in the years 1915 to 1919, although a minor affair compared with the terrible events of 1940 to 1945, was nevertheless a matter of serious consequence to the inhabitants. No provisions had been made in the way of public shelters and at times the morale of the citizens had much to endure. Warnings of the approach of hostile aircraft were given by exploding shells – 'maroons' – fired by the Fire Brigade, and during the few daylight raids policemen rode around on bicycles carrying notice boards reading "Police Notice, take cover". The underground stations were available for shelters and at times they were grossly overcrowded by numbers of people seeking cover for whom no adequate sanitary arrangements were available, so conditions became intolerable.

A booklet entitled 'The Council and the War', by the Clerk of the Council, Sir James Bird, and published in 1920 contains an interesting summary of the ways and means adopted to deal with raids and the questions arising therefrom. The elementary nature of the precautions taken is illustrated by the following extract from the book – 'During daylight raids children in the Council's schools were retained in the buildings until the danger had passed. At first no objection was made to their remaining on the top floor of a school, but experience showed this to be undesirable. The provision of dug-outs or sandbags was found to be impracticable. Some 330 of the Council's schools were opened after school hours as shelters.' Many schools, were, in fact, damaged by enemy action and on the 13th June 1917 a bomb fell on Upper North Street School, Poplar, killing nine boys and seven girls and seriously wounding thirty-one, of whom two afterwards died.

The book records that 'Five vans loaded with materials for hoardings were kept ready at depots in East London in charge of the Council's contractors for work on dangerous structures. Eight other contractors agreed to assist in the work if abnormal conditions arose. Arrangements were made with the Metropolitan Borough Councils whereby poles and trestles could be obtained for the blocking of streets, the diversion of traffic, etc. Twenty-two anti-aircraft stations were established at different parks and open spaces. A complete station usually comprised two separate areas, one for the gun and another for the searchlight, whilst at many a range-finder was added.' Airships (Zeppelins) were responsible for a number of raids and it seems incredible today that these vulnerable ships of the air should have been able to penetrate the defences, float over London, drop their bombs thereon and sail away as the following account by Sir J. Bird suggests. – 'It was occasionally possible, however, to anticipate to a certain extent the district the enemy might be intending to attack. For instance, on 13th–14th October 1915, when a Zeppelin approached London from the south, it appeared probable, from its reported movements near Croydon and Beckenham, that Woolwich would be attacked. A number of motor fire engines were therefore concentrated and arrived in Woolwich before the enemy airship commenced bombing the district, with the result that although twenty-four incendiary bombs were dropped, the fires were speedily subdued and no serious outbreak occurred.'

Sir James Bird records the following particulars:
First air raid on London occurred on 31st May 1915, two more followed in September

and one in October, In 1916 there were three raids, in 1917, thirteen, and in 1918 five, making a total of twenty-five. There were also several raids in the neighbourhood of London. Seven raids were carried out by airships and eighteen by aeroplanes – twenty-two by night and three by day. The last raid took place on the night of 19th–20th May 1918. Bombs dropped: 567 explosive, 355 incendiary; total 922.
Persons killed 524, injured 1264.
Persons rescued by fire brigade 138.
Number of fires attended by fire brigade 224
Calls for Council's Ambulance Service 373, cases dealt with 622
Buildings destroyed 174; seriously damaged 619
Buildings dealt with by Council as dangerous structures 2072
Cost of damage roughly £2,042,000.

The buildings included Gray's Inn, Lincoln's Inn, Law Courts, Middle Temple, Inner Temple, Royal Mint (4 killed and 30 injured), Central Telegraph Office, Burlington House, a large number of schools, twelve theatres, ten fire stations, the Midland Hotel (20 killed), several hospitals and a number of railway stations including Liverpool Street (16 killed and 13 injured). A bomb fell on Victoria Embankment and scarred the base of Cleopatra's Needle.

New Building Law, 1915–1920

The L.C.C. (General Powers) Act, 1915, gave the Council further powers for dealing with buildings erected in proximity to dangerous businesses. Exemptions relative to certain of these concerns were also included. The Bylaws for the Regulation of lamps and signs or other Structures Overhanging the Public Way, not in the City of London, came into operation on 1st May 1915. These two enactments had little effect on the Surveyors but a third measure – The Reinforced Concrete Regulations, also passed this year, proved a very different proposition, for the provisions therein demanded much technical knowledge and attention to details on the part of the District Surveyor, not only in the consideration of plans and particulars submitted under the regulations but also in the supervision of the actual work.

The regulations applied only to buildings of reinforced concrete in which the loads and stresses were transmitted through each storey to the foundations by a skeleton framework of reinforced concrete. Loads could, however, be taken on party walls of the thicknesses prescribed by the principal Act, but provisions were also included by which such walls could be constructed of reinforced concrete not less than 8 inches in thickness. The thickness of external panel walls could not be less than 8½ inches and 4 inches if constructed of reinforced concrete. The regulations actually covered only slab and beam construction resting on reinforced pillars – comprehensive formulae for calculating stresses being included – based entirely on theories providing that all tensile stresses must be taken by the steel reinforcement. Rules for lateral binding, relative to permissible stresses, were included for pillars and struts – the cover and spacing of rods being specified. The permissible stresses on steel and concrete according to grading, pressure on brickwork and foundations and the loading on floors for different types of buildings were all provided for in the regulations.

Notice was to be given and plans and calculations were to be deposited with the District Surveyor and he had to be furnished with reasonable proof as to the quality of materials used – he could also require any reasonable test that might be necessary.

These regulations marked a further step forward in the application of structural engineering to every day building and the work of the District Surveyor was changing accordingly, being taken out of the realm of the Architect and brought into the province of the structural Engineer.

CHAPTER XVI

London after the first World War. Great building activity. Districts re-arranged and made coterminous with Borough boundaries. Town planning develops. Years 1920–1930

January 1920 marks the seventy-fifth anniversary of the Association and a considerable change has come over the scene in London since the fiftieth anniversary in 1895. The commencement of the century saw the rise of Labour as a political force. In the election of 1906 twenty-nine Labour members of Parliament were elected and in 1924 the Labour Party took office as a minority Government. The authority of the House of Lords had largely vanished and high taxation, not only on incomes, but in death duties also, was producing its effect on landed estates.

The housing of the working classes had become mainly the affair of the Local Authorities and their control, in many directions, was increasing steadily. Rules and regulations were surrounding the employment of labour and the army of inspectors had received considerable reinforcements. They watched not only the goods the shopman sold but also the time he opened and closed his shop.

The growth in the activities of Local Government as represented by the Metropolitan Board of Works and the London County Council over the years 1855 to 1925 can be appreciated, to some extent, by the increase in the number of officials forming the staff and the extension of the accommodation necessary to house them. The Metropolitan Board of Works in 1856 had their headquarters at No.1 Greek Street, Soho, which soon became inadequate for its purpose. During 1860 the Board built new offices at Spring Gardens, Trafalgar Square, to accommodate a staff of about two hundred, and it was not long before additions to these premises became necessary. The London County Council occupied Old County Hall, Spring Gardens, until 1922, when New County Hall, on the east side of Westminster Bridge, was opened by King George V and Queen Mary. The new building, designed by Ralph Knott in a free-treatment of the English Renaissance style, was expected to house a staff, in about 900 rooms, of approximately 3,700, but the number working in the building soon reached 5,000, and in 1936 the building of further offices was commenced next to York Road.

The development of the internal combustion engine had produced an amazing change in travel. The railways were losing their grip on transport and great quantities of goods now travelled over the original routes, the highways. The Red Flag Law had been repealed in 1896, but the few motor cars on the roads at that time were run generally on solid tyres at about twelve miles per hour. By 1910 there existed one car to about every thousand persons and by 1940 the number had increased to one to every twenty-six persons. A great influx occurred between 1919 and 1921 when the number of motor cars in England increased from about 50,000 to 250,000. By night heavy lorries thundered into London and by day an unsolvable problem of congestion, caused by the new transport, had arisen on the main thoroughfares. The age of machinery and speed had arrived, but in some respects they were doubtful blessings. Heavy casualties, specially among children and old persons on the roads, caused much comment, but they still continue; while unemployment due in some measure at least to the reign of machinery, presented a difficult question. The friendly horse was now rather the exception than the rule and the last horse-bus of the

General Omnibus Company was withdrawn in 1911, but other horse buses continued to run until 1916.

Between 1920 and 1930 many old familiar landmarks in London disappeared. The Regency facades of Nash in Regent Street were demolished to make way for massive steel-framed buildings; other renowned old mansions of the great went the same way to provide sites for large hotels, multiple stores, blocks of offices or terraces of expensive flats. Offices resounded with the click of adding machines and typewriters and even the old copying-ink press of the District Surveyors' office fell into disuse, while the Minutes of the Association which in 1845 were commenced in perfect copperplate style and which later, at times, deteriorated to an almost indecipherable scrawl, were by the end of 1922 being neatly and concisely produced by a lady assistant using a typewriter.

In 1920 a revival in building commenced and the Council issued an invitation to each District Surveyor to attend a meeting on the 17th May at County Hall, Spring Gardens, to consider proposals of the Building Acts Committee for the redistribution of districts. The Council's suggestions that the districts in future should be coterminous with Borough boundaries met with general approval. This conference between the whole body of Surveyors and the Building Acts Committee was, apparently, the first of its kind in the history of the Association. Thirty-nine districts in all were formed, the larger boroughs being sub-divided and no new appointments were made. The following boroughs became distinct districts: Battersea, Bethnal Green, Camberwell, Hackney, Islington, Southwark, Poplar, St. Pancras and Shoreditch – each with its respective Surveyor. To supervise these districts there were thirty-six District Surveyors acting in October when the change-over operated.

During the year negotiations were concluded with Colonel Norton, Chief Administrative Officer of the London Housing Board, and with the Council and the Ministry of Health respecting reduced fees to be charged on Municipal Housing Schemes. The provisions of Section 24 of the Housing and Town Planning Act, 1919, were designed to enable the Ministry of Health to override Bylaws and the Building Acts, but the Ministry desired to make use of the District Surveyors and a satisfactory compromise was arranged. A further Housing Act came into operation in 1923, and under these Acts some 13,600 houses were erected and surveyed during the years 1921 to 1923 and 1925 to 1928. The total abatements in fees during the seven years amounted to approximately £6,400. The scheme did not apply to blocks of flats.

There were still restrictions on building, other than for housing, and works costing over £1,000 had to be reported to the Council. The housing drive was the main consideration of the Government and anything reasonable in the way of a house, or anything that had behind it the prospect of securing the erection of a house, received the blessing of the Ministry.

During 1920 the R.I.B.A. invited the Association to nominate members to the Statutory Board of Examiners and in due course Mr. Perkins and Mr. Fillary were appointed.

In 1921 all districts had been filled satisfactorily with thirty-five regular Surveyors of which thirty-three were members of the Association. Conditions had returned to normal and the upward tendency of building works, shown by the returns, pointed clearly to a coming boom in building and it seemed that the schemes delayed over the four years of war would be made up. Everything seemed set for a quiet, progressive and prosperous period.

A deputation attended at County Hall in February 1922, at the request of the Building Acts Committee, to consider their proposals – 'That the Surveyors should take over the supervision of the work done by the Council's contractors on dangerous structures when owners defaulted on Magistrates' Orders.' Figures given indicated that in eleven years – 1910 to 1921 – the average number of these cases amounted to 150 per year. In 1920 to 1921 there were 214 cases of which 117 came within the Borough of Stepney, and the cost in this Borough amounted to £2,401. Of the remainder, 30 cases occurred in

Shoreditch, cost £428, and 12 in Islington, cost £241. The balance of 55 being spread over all the other districts. Considerable correspondence followed but finally the matter dropped.

During 1922–1923 a Royal Commission sat to consider Local Government over Greater London. The evidence given by the Borough Councils included proposals on District Surveyors which called forth much criticism from the Association. The members considered that this evidence was, to say the least of it, a gross distortion of facts. The Boroughs, apparently, suggested that District Surveyors should be transferred and become salaried officials under their control. The Association placed a written statement before the Commission and it is recorded in a summary of the Minutes for 1923 that the proposals of this Commission might have destroyed the position of the District Surveyor had they materialised. Actually this expensive investigation resulted in no alterations of moment in either the Local Government of the county or of Greater London.

In 1925 the Council communicated with the Association on the subject of control of Town Planning. At that time the duties arising were purely nominal and the Surveyors in the districts then under consideration agreed to accept them without remuneration, on the understanding that the position would be reviewed by the end of 1926. Following a conference held at County Hall for this purpose in 1927 the Association agreed to co-operate with the Council and with their proposals in pursuance of a policy of Town Planning. The Council were to supply the members with plot plans and they were to see that buildings were sited in accordance with these plans and to report deviations therefrom. Alterations to other premises were also to be reported upon if it appeared that the regulations might be applicable. The Council agreed to pay for these services at the rate of fifty guineas per year, when whole districts were covered by the regulations, and pro rata for districts partly covered.

A note in the Minutes for February 1928 recalls the disastrous floods which occurred in January of that year, when the Thames overflowed and a break occurred in the embankment by which the basements of many houses were inundated. The entry called attention to the Metropolis Management (Thames River Prevention of Floods) Amendment Act, 1879 by which certain duties could be imposed on District Surveyors. Those duties are referred to in Section 24 of the Act under the provisions of which the Metropolitan Board of Works could call for a survey from the District Surveyor, or some other competent surveyor on any bank of the river reported as being out of repair, dangerous or insufficient for the effectual protection of any premises within the limits of the Act. Upon the completion of the survey the District or other Surveyor was required to certify to the Board his opinion on such bank. If the bank was found to be out of repair, etc., the Board had then to cause notice to be served on the Commissioner of Sewers of the City of London, the Vestry or Parish, or owner of premises liable to execute flood works, specifying the works considered necessary for repairing such bank. There are no records of any District Surveyor ever having been called upon to perform duties under this Act which is still, apparently, in force. Further the Act appears to have passed into law with no comments on the part of District Surveyors.

The Building Acts Committee in 1927 announced the intention of the Council to hold qualifying examinations, under Section 140 of the 1894 Act, for the office of District Surveyor. Examinations followed in January 1928 and April 1929 and in 1930 an invitation was extended to the Association to nominate two members to serve on the examination board if so required. The Association finally agreed to the suggestion and Mr. W.G. Perkins and Mr. A.C. Meston were appointed and they acted in this capacity for some years.

New Building Law and Amendments to Acts 1920–1930

The London County Council (General Powers) Act 1920 contained restrictions on the erection of dwellinghouses on low-lying lands. Section 7 provided that such buildings should not be erected upon land the surface of which is below the level of Trinity high water mark and which is so situated as not to admit of being efficiently drained by gravitation, at all times, into an existing sewer of the Council. The restrictions extended to the rebuilding of houses which had been pulled down to ground floor level, and certain powers were also conferred on the Council enabling them to make regulations in respect of the adaptation of buildings for dwellinghouses, etc. on such land. Appeals from the Council's decisions could be taken to the Tribunal of Appeal.

The London County Council (General Powers) Act 1923, included under Part II amendments of the L.B. Acts enabling the Council to modify or waive, upon and subject to such conditions as they thought fit, any of the requirements of most of the sub-sections of Section 22, 1909 Act, respecting the construction of skeleton metal framed buildings.

The London County Council (General Powers) Act 1926, Part II, Section 5, conferred upon the Council the right to make and enforce regulations with respect to the conversion of any building, or part of a building, constructed wholly or partly in reinforced concrete. Sub-Section (3) provided that in the erection of any particular building, or part of a building, intended to be constructed wholly or partly of reinforced concrete or the conversion of any particular building, or part of a building, so constructed, the Council may waive or modify on such conditions as they may consider necessary any of the requirements of the reinforced concrete regulations. Sub-Section (6) defined the term "conversion" as applying not only to buildings structurally altered, but also if and whenever any change is made which in the opinion of the District Surveyor affects, or is likely to affect the stability thereof or imperil the safety of persons occupying or resorting thereto. The Council's decisions could be the subject of appeal to the Tribunal of Appeal.

The London County Council (General Powers) Act 1928, Part II contained the amendments to the 1894 Act relating to the remuneration of District Surveyors. Section 4 defined "cubical extent" and "cost" also other items incidental to the computation of fees chargeable on this basis. Section 5 set out the procedure to be followed by builders, or other persons, in connection with the returns of costs of works etc.

The Local Government Act 1929 transferred the Institutional Buildings, previously under the control of Boards of Guardians and the Metropolitan Asylums Boards, to the London County Council who could then claim that such public buildings, all came within the exemptions from the constructural clauses of the Act of 1894. Counsel's opinion, which the Association obtained, supported the Council's contention and so the surveying and control of works to these important buildings passed out of the hands of District Surveyors.

CHAPTER XVII

New methods in building. District Surveyors become officials of the London County Council. Scientific basis for new Building By-laws. The Acts of 1930, 1935 and the London Building Act (Amendment) Act, 1939. Years 1930–1940

The records contained in these notes, after the world war, give little indication of the actual amount of useful work carried out by the Association. By the end of the nineteenth century a gradual change in building procedure became apparent. The old method by which the Architect and his staff produced detailed plans and particulars covering the whole work, and the builder, or contractor, had sole control in the execution of the work and produced in his own workshops the joinery and numerous other items which together constitute a building, ceased to be the usual practice. The Architect now prepared general plans and elevations while steel constructional members, floors, window frames, possibly a sprinkler installation, fire-escape staircases, lifts and other items were dealt with by sub-contractors who specialised in their particular line. The age of the specialist had arrived and many new forms of construction, from different types of piling to new methods of floor and roof construction were on the market. Questions by members occupied much time at the meetings of the Association when the merits and demerits were discussed of such varying matters as the effects of the use of special liquids used to produce smooth surfaces on concrete, to new makes of bricks, materials for damp-proof courses, coverings for roofs, special floor constructions and Nissen type roofs. The Association functioned to encourage sound construction with the use of proper materials and to discourage doubtful propositions and dubious materials.

The new methods of building resulted in additional work being passed on to the District Surveyor. A practice grew up by which Architects would invite tenders from different firms of structural Engineers for the supply and erection of steel work in their buildings and to merely specify that the work must meet with all requirements of the authorities. By so doing they dispensed with the services of a consulting engineer and additional responsibility fell upon the District Surveyor. At times several enquiries would be made by separate firms tendering for the same job, for information on such items as bearing value of the ground, floor loads, etc. The trade depression from 1930-1933 did not affect London to anything like the extent experienced in the provinces, and firms from outside seeking work in the Metropolis, would sometimes fail to realise that they would have to comply with the more stringent rules of construction peculiar to London. The District Surveyor, in this respect, often acts as an arbitrator, for he must endeavour to see that the standard of work does not fall below that laid down by the Acts and bylaws so that speculators cannot obtain an advantage over bona fide builders.

The Code of Practice for the use of structural steel and other materials came into operation in 1932. The Code followed a request from the steelwork firms for some relaxation in law which would reduce cost in steel-framed buildings: there being at that time a trade depression and a financial crisis. The clauses giving the Council authority to waive most of the provisions covering the construction of skeleton framed buildings were contained in Section 58 of the L.B. Act 1930, and the Code set out the basis by which applications for relief under that section would be considered by the Council. A flexural stress of 8T/sq.in. replaced the limit of seven and a half in the Act – higher stresses were allowed on pillars and the floor loads specified were reduced. A definite consent from the Council was necessary in each case. The British Steelwork Association asked for the co-operation of the Association in the interpretation of the Code.

The trade depression during the years 1932–1934 caused much unemployment among the professional classes and the Association contributed fifty guineas in 1932 and forty guineas in 1933 to the unemployment fund of the R.I.B.A.

Town Planning had moved a stage further with the passing of the Town and Country Planning Act 1932, which came into operation in April 1933, and meetings between the Association's representatives and the Council's officers followed. In June 1934, the Council announced their intention of Town Planning the whole of London. A year later the Clerk of the Council notified the Association that the Minister of Health had approved the resolution of the Council to prepare the County of London Town Planning Scheme No.19, which would cover the whole of the County. A Sub-Committee consisting of the Past-Presidents subsequently had an interview with Mr. Berry, Chairman of the Building Acts Committee and their report to the Association indicated that the greatest co-operation would be necessary between the Surveyors and the Council to ensure the success of the new regime. Also that the building public would look to this co-operation to produce smooth running administration.

A scheme for remuneration, prepared by the Council, to meet the conditions arising under the new Town Planning Act was accepted in due course by the Association.

In September 1932, Mr. Woodward reported that welding was in progress to certain balconies of a Hospital in his district of Hammersmith and he invited members to inspect the work and to be present when tests would be applied. Subsequently a number of members attended together with a representative of the Architects' Department, and general satisfaction was expressed with the results achieved. Mr. Bylander, an old friend in the structural world, had control of this work and all who knew him will recollect that he was always in the forefront with new methods of construction.

The British Standards Institute invited the Association in February 1934, to nominate representatives to serve on a Committee formed to consider standardisation of steel sections for welding construction. The members were of the opinion that no useful purpose would be served thereby as the use of welding in connection with the steel work of buildings had yet to be recognised. In this year, however, the subject had to receive serious consideration, and in April twenty members attended a demonstration by films at the Regent Street Polytechnic. In May the British Standards Association asked for the co-operation of members in connection with a proposal to use welding in steel-framed buildings. The Association felt that shop-welding should be allowed, in certain cases, but not site welding. At the end of October the Council announced their decision that welding would be permitted in steel-framed buildings subject to their approval; the procedure being that an application must be made in each case accompanied by drawings and calculations with a description of the proposed method of welding. The applicant would be required to satisfy the District Surveyor that competent welders only would be employed. The consents would also specify that the welding must comply with the appropriate British Standard Specifications.

In March 1935, twenty-seven members visited Bexhill to inspect a welded steel-framed entertainment hall then in course of erection. They were received by the Town Clerk and the engineers responsible, who afforded them every facility for inspecting the work.

Subsequently most of the members attended a course on welding arranged by Messrs. Murex Welding Processes Ltd. when demonstrations were given and facilities afforded for some practical work.

The Association held its last general meeting at No.9 Conduit Street on 4th October 1934. This building had been the members' rendezvous, except for a short time in 1880, since April 1864, or for about seventy years. The Royal Institute of British Architects were about to move to their fine modern building in Portland Place.

The members made a contribution of sixty guineas towards the building fund of the R.I.B.A. and the first meeting at the new headquarters, No.66 Portland Place, occurred on Thursday 6th December 1934.

The Building Acts Revision Sub-Committee reported in April 1935 that the new draft bylaws prepared by the Council provided that walls of public buildings should be subject to the Council's approval. This proposal constituted a direct challenge to the authority of the District Surveyor, for the construction of public buildings had been under his sole control since 1855. The members decided at a special Committee meeting that the enabling Bill should be opposed to safeguard the status of the District Surveyors under the proposed bylaws. The District Surveyors' petition, duly sealed, came before the House of Lords' Committee in May 1935, when Mr. Wrotteslay, K.C. appeared on behalf of the Association. The result afforded some protection, for by the addition of a clause to the Bill the amendments to the principal Act were limited and the sections relating to public buildings were omitted in the Schedule.

Mr. Watkinson, the Association's representative on the British Standards Institute Committee in respect of the Unit Weights of Materials, reported in 1935 that the Committee had completed its work and that he had served therewith for three years during which time thirty-five meetings had been held. Mr. Hall, the Association's representative on the British Standards Institution Committee on the Standard Specification of Structural Steel reported that in nearly all cases the amendments proposed by the Association had been adopted by the Committee and that the work was now complete.

The bylaws authorised by the 1935 Act provided a continuous problem between 1935 and 1938. Proposed bylaws were published by the Council in 1936 to which the Association objected. The impasse resulted mainly from the contention of the Council that appeals from the District Surveyors' decisions should be settled by application to the Council. Mr. Wrotteslay K.C. gave the Association his considered opinion that appeals to the Council would be contrary to the Building Acts and ultra vires and the Minister of Health was informed accordingly. In May 1937 objections were lodged with the Minister on the proposed bylaws on timber.

During 1937 the suggested building bylaws underwent revision, further clauses being added. They were published in May 1937 and came into operation together with the timber bylaws on 1st January 1938; the hearing of appeals from the District Surveyors' decisions being to the Courts of Summary Jurisdiction.

The technical nature of the constructional items of the new bylaws demanded little to the vocation of the engineer.
to the location of the engineer. The District Surveyors' work could now be said to have moved definitely into the sphere of the structural engineer. Appointments were now being filled by men with a science degree.

A number of cinemas were in course of erection during 1936 and 1937 and with a view to uniformity of practice the question of the protection against fire of the steelwork, particularly that supporting the balconies, came under discussion between certain members and the Council's officers. The principles agreed to were 'that where the ventilation to the building came by way of gratings in the risers of the balcony seats, then the individual steelwork members should be encased with two inches of concrete, but where it came through openings arranged in the ceiling under the balconies then the case would be met by the ceiling being constructed of incombustible materials two inches in thickness. Ordinary roof trusses over the auditorium need not be encased.'

King George and Queen Elizabeth were crowned on 12th May 1937, the town being decked in lavish profusion with streamers, standards, banners, flags and masses of symbolical decorations representing Britain and her Empire. District Surveyors in the central districts had much responsibility in connection with these demonstrations of loyalty. They also had to examine and pass numerous stands and balconies on the route of the coronation procession. Excited cheering crowds lined the streets and filled to overflowing all possible sight-seeing places on the adjoining buildings from the shop windows to the roofs. The national day of rejoicing passed without a collapse or failure of any structure used by the public which reflected considerable credit on the Surveyors and workmen concerned. The Council agreed to pay for the inspections on a mileage basis and they extended this arrangement to cover the coronation drives through the suburbs which were also accomplished without accidents due to failure of stands or balconies, etc.

The Council's scheme by which District Surveyors were to lose the freedom they had enjoyed for so many years became known in April 1936. The Association's deputation attending at County Hall, in response to a request from the Clerk, were informed by Mr. Herbert Morrison, the leader of the Council, that both political parties had agreed that District Surveyors should become salaried officials. The reasons given being that Town Planning would be developed further and that the static functions of the Building Acts would fluctuate in consequence. The deputation received an assurance that, in the words of the report, 'a change will only be made in the interests of good administration and not to lower the status of the District Surveyor.' Districts were to be graded and each grade would carry its appropriate salary.

Over the protracted negotiations it is unnecessary to dwell, but the Association stuck to its rights under the Act by which each Surveyor was entitled to a salary based on the last seven years average income from his district and finally the Council agreed to recognise this right which had been incorporated for the first time, in the Act of 1855, the limit then being a three years' average. The Council also gave an assurance that a Surveyor would not be required to move from his district if he did not wish to do so. They also agreed to take over the district offices and the staffs. Each Surveyor received a sealed agreement and one and all became salaried officials of the Council on 1st January 1940. Those having ten or more years to run, before reaching the retiring age of sixty-five, came under the Council's superannuation scheme.

At the end of June 1939 District Surveyors were answering queries on possible sites on buildings for anti-aircraft guns and war seemed inevitable. In view of this situation there is every possibility that the Association might have been successful in opposing the Bill and avoiding temporarily the change over. Opposition from outside sources would not have been difficult to obtain, as many London Architects were not in favour of District Surveyors becoming officials of the Council. There was certainly a chance of the Bill, or the clauses thereof affecting District Surveyors, being delayed until after the war, but there can be no doubt that ultimately the Council would have obtained the control they desired and probably on conditions less advantageous to the existing District Surveyors. The fact is that for a number of years the terms of the office had been recognised as an anachronism, or a survival of times past, as nothing comparative existed in any other part of the country. The attitude of the Parliamentary Committee who heard the Association's appeal against the 1928 Act gave a clear indication of what would be the final result. Further, the Association had been reminded that Coroners and Income Tax Collectors had become, in recent years, salaried officials, but members were not amused by the comparison. The freedom of at least two great professional bodies, the doctors and dentists, had been slowly but surely encroached upon for some years by the Government under the Health Acts, and today we stand on the threshold of nationalisation on a gigantic scale which means, of course, the transfer of many thousands of persons to the realm of officialdom. The march of events could not be stopped by forty odd District Surveyors with a few supporters from outside. The time had arrived when their limited powers were hopeless against the might of that great controlling authority the London County Council, whose yearly financial budgets exceed most of those of the smaller European Countries.

The substitution of a salary for income from fees was of little consequence compared with the loss of independence of action. In the old days a member, or the Association, did not hesitate to challenge the ruling of the Council on questions under the Acts, but this is hardly possible today. All Court actions are now referred to the Solicitor to the Council to whom details must be given and who decides whether or not proceedings should be taken. The Association will, in future, have a very limited scope. Gone are the days when petitions were prepared, sealed and presented to the House of Commons. The Association's functions must now be mainly limited to petitions to the Council and the discussion of questions brought by members. It will, however, still perform much useful work, particularly in settling questions arising under the Acts and so obtaining uniformity of practice. Moreover, a united front of members will always achieve more than individual efforts.

The right to give decisions, where left in the Acts to the discretion of the District Surveyor (and this, of course, applies to new entrants to the office) remains as hitherto and appeals therefrom where so expressly stated must still be taken to the Tribunal of Appeal. We therefore have the interesting position that persons wishing to appeal against certain decisions given by officials of the Council must proceed, not to the Council, but to an independent body.

To meet the position created by the Council the members elected Mr. P.J. Black as President in 1937, and this is the first time in the history of the Association that a member has again occupied the chair after an interval of some years. Mr. Black retained his leadership for four years, until February 1941, and on more than one occasion Mr. Herbert Morrison, who eventually became Home Secretary and Leader of the House of Commons, testified to the ability shown by Mr. Black in the difficult negotiations which followed.

Acts and Bylaws passed 1930 to 1940. The London Building Act. 1930

This was an Act to consolidate the enactments relating to streets and buildings in London. Mr. Dicksee remarks in his book on the statute that 'a consolidating Act should contain no alteration on the previous law; but the Act must, of course, be interpreted as it stands.' A Sub-Committee appointed in January 1929 examined the clauses of the proposed Bill and discovered many variations of words, the effects of which were duly discussed with the Council's Parliamentary Agents. A few minor alterations actually passed into law.

The Town and Country Planning Act 1932 came into operation in April 1933. The Association had watched the passing of the Bill and they secured an amendment safeguarding the provisions of the L.B. Act, 1930. An account amounting to £24 of Messrs. Sherwood & Co. Parliamentary Agents, was subsequently paid for their services in this respect. This Act moved matters a step further from the very definite control outlined by the previous Town Planning Act of 1925. The new Act, however, could still be said to leave the position in a fluid state, but Architects and the public came to understand the necessity for the submission of plans and particulars to the Council under this Act, not only with regard to new buildings but also in connection with alterations involving additions or change of user. Applications on Building Act matters to County Hall came automatically under Town Planning and subsequently they were dealt with together under a combined consent. The Council could not even now, apparently, take immediate action against anyone refusing to make an application in respect of Town Planning or for failing to abide with any conditions imposed in any consent given, but any such persons would run the risk of having to amend the work to the satisfaction of the Council at some time in the future when definite rules and zoning had become law.

The London Building Act (Amendment) Act, 1935

The passing of this enabling Act gave the Council powers to make bylaws covering practically all constructional matters from the laying out of streets, foundations and sites of buildings, the construction and conversion of buildings and structures and any part thereof. Such matters as the taking of samples of building materials by the District Surveyor; the means of escape from buildings over sixty feet in height; lamps, signs, and other structures overhanging the public way and not within the City of London and matters connected with or ancilliary to any of the fore-going could be the subject of bylaws.

Section (7) provided that any person entitled under any bylaw made in pursuance of the Act to appeal to a Court of Summary Jurisdiction, may do so within a period of not more than fourteen days after the service of the notice from the District Surveyor of the requirement which is the subject of the appeal.

Section (9) gave the Council power to modify or waive, upon such terms and conditions as they might think fit, any of the requirements of any bylaws made under the Act, Appeals against the Council's refusal to so modify or waive any of the requirements in respect of metal skeleton or reinforced concrete construction could be taken to the Tribunal of Appeal.

Under the Restriction of Ribbon Development Act 1935, the Provision of Means of Entrance and Egress to Buildings, London, Order 1936, came into operation and the Council issued requirements on new commercial buildings for the loading and unloading of vehicles within the curtilages thereof.

Building Bylaws

A volume of bylaws came into operation on 1st January 1938, replacing most of the Sections in Part VI of the London Building Act, 1930, also the bylaws made under the Metropolis Management Act 1878 and the London County Council (General Powers) Act, 1890.

These new bylaws dealt with loading and wind pressure and they were more detailed as regards grades of concrete and stresses in brickwork, steelwork and reinforced concrete.

At the same time a separate set of bylaws came into operation dealing with timber, giving maximum stresses and containing tables of safe loads. These were the first detailed regulations for timber since those of the 1667 Act.

All the above bylaws were later superseded.

London Building Acts (Amendment) Act, 1939

An Act to amend the enactments relating to streets, buildings and structures in London.

Part II – contains extended clauses on the naming and numbering of streets and buildings.

Part III (Sections 16 to 28 inclusive) – Construction of Buildings. Many alterations are incorporated therein. Section 20 clearly contemplates buildings of greater height than allowed by the 1930 Act, the provisions read 'Unless the Council otherwise consent, no building shall be erected with a storey or part of a storey at a greater height than one hundred feet; or eighty feet if the area of the building exceeds ten thousand square feet.' Authority is given to the Council to allow a greater height and moreover such an application cannot be refused if the proposed occupation is satisfactory and arrangements can be made and maintained, in the building, for the lessening, so far as is reasonably practicable, of danger from fire.

By Section 26 the Council have acquired, for the first time, a right to prescribe a standard of stability in public buildings. Sub-Section (1) maintains substantially the original clauses giving the District Surveyor control over the construction in these buildings, but Sub-Section (2)(a) provides – 'The Council may from time to time prescribe standards of stability and fire protection in relation to the construction of public buildings, etc.' No standards have yet been prescribed by the Council and the entire responsibility for the approval of the construction of public buildings rests upon the District Surveyor. Section 27 stipulates that in the conversion of a building to a public building the provisions of the Building Acts and bylaws shall apply to the conversion etc. as though it were the construction of a public building. Further that a building shall be deemed to be so converted if the purposes for which it is to be used are changed to the purposes of a public building whether structural alterations are involved or not.

Part IV – (Sections 29 to 32 inclusive). Special and Temporary Buildings and Structures; the clauses apply to any building or structure not constructed generally or substantially in conformity with the rules of Part III or any bylaws made in pursuance of the L.B. Acts.

The licensing of buildings or structures not exceeding 200 sq.ft. in area and seven feet six inches in height; certain stands and other structures wholly or mainly of wood; hoardings and similar erections is left to the Metropolitan Borough Council. An important variation is contained in Section 30 (6) in respect of these structures for the erection etc. is left thereby to the supervision of the Borough Councils and notice therefore can no longer be claimed by the District Surveyor. The operation of this part of the Act has been considerably affected by the London Government Act 1963 (q.v.) under which delegated powers were given by the Council to the newly-created London Borough Councils to deal with somewhat larger structures, also by the Council delegating to District Surveyors authority to issue Consents for certain types of structure e.g. conservatories, flue pipes etc.

Part V – Sections 33 to 43 inclusive. Means of Escape in Case of Fire: many alterations are contained in this part of the Act from the old provisions. Section 34 reads 'Every new public building which is constructed to be used or is used in whole or in part as a church, chapel or other place of worship, hall, meeting-room, school, classroom, concert-room, dancing-room or other place of assembly and every other new building ..... shall be provided in accordance with plans approved by the Council with all such means of escape therefrom in case of fire as in the circumstances of the case can be reasonably required.' Limitation on the Council's powers in respect of certain buildings mentioned are contained in the clauses following. It will be noticed that all types of buildings irrespective of the occupation, are now brought under control, whereas the old regulations were restricted to buildings occupied or inhabited by at least twenty persons.

Section 35 deals with protection against fire in certain old buildings. The original regulations on buildings occupied etc. by twenty persons are maintained, but the provisions now cover practically all buildings except a dwellinghouse tenanted by not more than one family. The regulations extend to buildings exceeding two storeys in height with any storey at a greater height than twenty feet which is let in flats or tenements; or is used as an inn, hotel, nursing home etc.; or is a restaurant, shop, store or warehouse which has sleeping accommodation above the ground storey. A place of assembly having a superficial area of not less than five hundred square feet is also included with other items subject to certain limitations.

Section 36 deals with precautions to be taken etc. in connection with projecting shops and Section 37 contains important additions to the old regulations respecting fire escapes to the main roof. The conditions are now applicable to all old buildings, except those coming under Section 35 and dwellinghouses used as such by not more than ten persons; provided the building has a storey at a greater height than twenty feet. Succeeding sections cover storage of materials liable to cause fire and explosion.

Part VI (Sections 44 to 59 inclusive). Rights etc. of Building and Adjoining Owners. The clauses have been rewritten and rearranged to cover modern practice. The original regulations (L.B. Act 1930 Part IX) are incorporated with little change, but a point is made of protecting an adjoining owner from encroachments on his land by special foundations by a clause which follows the appropriate sections – 'Nothing in this section shall authorise the building owner to place special foundations on land of the adjoining owner without his previous consent in writing.' One month's notice is necessary to the adjoining owner in respect of work to be carried out under these clauses which also applies when an owner wishes to build from a lower level than the foundations of an adjoining building within ten feet. Under the 1930 Act, which contained clauses on the ten foot limit only, two months' notice was required.

Part VII (Sections 60 to 70 inclusive). Dangerous and Neglected Structures. The Council were still empowered to require a survey of a reported dangerous structure to be made by any competent surveyor and an added clause gave them authority to pay an independent Surveyor such remuneration as they thought fit. Section 61 (4) contained an important addition which gave the Superintending Architect, the District Surveyor or any officer authorised by the Council the necessary authority to take such steps as may be necessary to remove immediate danger and steps so taken and any expenses incurred were for the purposes of this part of the Act to be deemed to have been taken and incurred by the Council. The operative clauses of the 1930 Act were reenacted with little change.

The administration of this Part of the Act was transferred to the Borough Councils on 1st January 1960 under the London County Council (General Powers) Act, 1958 but District Surveyors continue to certify whether buildings are dangerous or not and continue to provide a round-the-clock emergency service.

Part IX (Sections 73 to 96 inclusive). Superintending Architect, District Surveyors and Fees. The clauses have been altered to meet the additional control acquired by the Council over the administration of the Acts. Section 73 refers specifically to the Superintending Architect and the text has been changed to legalise an irregularity of long standing so that the person appointed can be called upon to – 'Perform such duties as the Council direct.' The Superintending Architect can now be directed to act as Architect to the Council. Other important alterations include – 'The Council may pay such salary to and attach such terms and conditions to the holding of office by a District Surveyor as they think fit. Any person appointed to the office of District Surveyor – (i) shall be by virtue of that appointment an officer of the Council; (ii) shall hold the office during the pleasure of the Council; (iii) shall in addition to discharging the functions of a District Surveyor under the said Acts and bylaws perform such other duties as may be assigned to him by the Council.' Clauses on the appointment and duties of the District Surveyor follow with special reference to the rights and privileges of existing Surveyors holding office before the passing of the Act. Particulars are included of examining boards. Members of the Board shall be appointed by the Council to hold the office for three years. They shall include persons nominated for the purpose by the Council, the R.I.B.A. and other professional bodies. The Board shall conduct in London, as and when required by the Council, examinations in proficiency to perform the duties of District Surveyor. Every examination paper shall be approved by the Board and a copy of every such paper shall be forwarded to the Council within seven days of the holding of the examination.

Section 86 provides that – 'Save as otherwise expressly provided in the L.B. Acts where in those Acts or in any bylaws made in pursuance of those Acts it is provided that any matter or thing shall be or any work shall be carried out to the satisfaction or subject to the approval of or shall be certified by the District Surveyor the builder or owner concerned if dissatisfied with any decision or requirement of a District Surveyor made under the said Acts or bylaws (other than in the case of any provision that any work shall be carried out to the satisfaction of the District Surveyor in a proper and workmanlike manner) may apply to the Council to determine the question.'[1] The words in parenthesis and underlined are important as they remove from this appeal the bylaws made under the 1935 Act. The builder can further appeal against the Council's decisions under this Section to the Tribunal of Appeal except in any case in which in the opinion of the Council the matter thing or work is likely to affect the stability or the protection in case of fire of the building or structure.

Part X. (Sections 97 to 100 inclusive). Bylaws. Powers are given to the Council to make bylaws in respect of lifts, hoists and escalators in buildings, where not already covered by other Acts; the installation of gas meters in buildings, the provision of eyelets to window frames to facilitate the use of safety belts for persons working outside windows; also in respect of steps leading to buildings; (no such bylaws have yet been made) for prohibition or regulations in connection with buildings or parts thereof used as bazaars, exhibitions etc. where a substantial number of persons, above the normal number, may be present at certain times as the result of special attractions. Bylaws can also be made, to be administered by the local authorities, in respect of the spacing of railings separating the curtilage of a building from a street; for the prohibition or regulation of spikes or broken glass etc., on any fence, or the attachment of barbed wire to the blinds of (shop) windows. The authority of the Council to make bylaws under Section 4 of the 1935 Act is extended to cover a specification of fire tests in buildings, the subdivision of buildings into cells to retard the spread of fire; the classification of buildings in relation to their resistance to the action of fire and a certification in respect thereof by the District Surveyor. Provisions are also included by which any such bylaws may replace Sections 20 to 21 (limitation to cubical extent and uniting of buildings), Section 99 gives the Council power to regulate the amount of fees which may be chargeable in respect of the services of the District Surveyor under any bylaws made in pursuance of the Acts.

Part XI. (Sections 101 to 126 inclusive). Legal Proceedings. By Section 109 the constitution of the Tribunal of Appeal is changed. A panel of six persons is to be formed in place of the four members under the 1930 Act. The two additional persons are to be appointed, one by the Institution of Structural Engineers and the other by the London Master Builders' Association. It is further enacted that the person to be nominated by the Secretary of State shall be a barrister or a solicitor and that he shall preside at all meetings of the Tribunal. Representatives nominated are to serve for three years, in lieu of five years under the old Act. The panel of six are to elect one of their number who is to select, for each appeal, two members from the panel and these two persons together with the member appointed by the Secretary of State are to constitute the Tribunal of Appeal. Any party to an appeal, on depositing the requisite sum of money, may require additional members of the panel to serve on the Tribunal. The Lord Chancellor has the right to remove for inability or misbehaviour any member of the panel. The Tribunal are to sit at County Hall, where a register of their decisions, which is to be open to inspection by the public, is to be retained.

Part XII Section 127 restricted the size of timber stacks and other flammable material. It has now been replaced by Sections 15 to 25 of the G.L.C. (General Powers) Act 1968. Section 131 restricted projections from buildings. It has been replaced by sections of the Highways Act 1959.

Section 135 reads – 'Every addition to or alteration of a building and every other work made or done for any purpose in or upon a building or structure (except necessary

---

1. Any application must be made within seven days of the Surveyor's decision appealed against. The applicant must supply the District Surveyor with copies of the application and of any documents and particulars accompanying same. Applications are to be considered and determined by a Committee appointed by the Council. A decision of the District Surveyor shall not be reversed or amended unless he has been given an opportunity, if he so desires, of being heard by the Committee.

repair not affecting the stability or construction of the building or structure or any part of the building or structure) shall be subject to the provisions of the L.B. Acts and of any bylaws made in pursuance of those Acts.' The words in parenthesis replace those in the 1930 Act which read 'except that of necessary repair not affecting the construction of any external wall'. Section 136 has reference to the extent to which a building must be demolished before the reconstruction can be considered to constitute a new building and the terms are much altered from the old provisions.

Section 139 contains important clauses for it provides that buildings shall not be converted so that any part will not comply with the Acts and bylaws and the term 'converted' includes a change of user whether or not involving any structural alterations.

Section 142 (2) (a) gives power of entry to the Superintending Architect, the District Surveyor or any authorised officer of the Council, on the production of a duly authenticated document, to enter at all reasonable times to inspect and examine any land, premises, building, structure or work to which the provisions of the Acts or bylaws apply. Under this section the District Surveyor has been provided for the first time with a 'warrant to inspect'.[1] There is an interesting proviso in this section to the effect that any person disclosing a trade secret, etc., not in performance of his duty, obtained by him on admittance to a factory or workplace is liable to a fine of £100 or imprisonment for three months.

Section 148 deals with offences against the Act and the penalties provided vary from £1 per day for failure to comply with any requirement for which no specific fine is mentioned to the sum of £100, with a daily penalty of £5, for the unauthorised setting-out etc. of any street.

Section 149. Application to Act. Exemptions from Parts III and IV (Construction of Buildings and Temporary Buildings etc.) The list of exempted buildings under the 1930 Act is maintained and doubtful points in connection therewith clarified. The electric light providers, coming within the Electricity (Supply) Acts, 1882 to 1936, have now a similar exemption to that previously given to the gas companies. Immunity from the Act in respect of construction does not apply to walls, party structures, forming part of any building not in itself exempt.

Isolated buildings not exceeding thirty square feet in area etc., and distant five feet at least from buildings and streets remain outside the constructional provisions as allowed in the 1930 Act, but the similar larger buildings previously provided for now come within two reduced limits, both of which cannot exceed ten feet in height; one class may extend to two squares in area if separated by ten feet at least from other buildings or streets and the other class may cover up to eight squares of ground if not less than fifteen feet from any building, etc.

Party fence walls, allowed up to seven feet in height under the old Act, now come within the new Act when over six feet in height and the provisions are extended to cover boundary walls.

Section 150 refers to buildings to which the provisions of Part V (Means of Escape in Case of Fire) are not applicable.

Section 151 comprises Crown Exemptions which are as hitherto but they now extend to cover His Majesty's Duchy of Lancaster.

---

1. By 142 (4) the Superintending Architect, a District Surveyor or an authorised officer entering any premises may be accompanied by necessary assistants or workmen. The clauses under the old Acts gave a right of entry only to the District Surveyor, and no such right could be claimed by him for any assistant in his employ. In 1931 a builder raised this question with the Council and objected to a District Surveyor's assistant visiting works he had in progress. There was no legal reply to the objection.

Schedules: three only are included with the Act. An additional item under the first schedule refers to fees payable to the Council for the checking of accounts, etc. on work done by their contractors on dangerous structures following the default of the owners. The second schedule has been largely repealed by subsequent General Powers Acts and the fees payable to the Council are now based entirely on the cost of the work in accordance with a schedule in the Greater London Council (General Powers) Act 1965.

CHAPTER XVIII

The Second World War

It became increasingly evident from 1937, that war with Germany was coming. Precautions against air raids were gradually made, including the erection of A.R.P. shelters.

Between January and April 1939, several letters were written by the Association mentioning the services District Surveyors could offer; one letter being addressed to Sir John Anderson, who had intimated in the House that a survey of basements would be made with a view to their use as air raid shelters. A reply received from the Home Office did not help materially and nothing definite was known before May when an extensive Memorandum dated 9th May 1939, arrived from the Council containing proposals, agreed in principle, by the Joint Committee on Air Raid Precautions of the Council, City Corporation and Metropolitan Boroughs' Standing Joint Committee. Under the scheme therein set out the Council were, in conjunction with the Home Office, to co-operate with the City and Boroughs in the formation of a rescue, shoring and demolition service. The local organisation and control of this was to come under the City and Borough Engineers, who would call on District Surveyors, operating from their own offices, for assistance and advice. The personnel of heavy and light rescue parties, the training thereof, equipment, group control and incidental matters were all included in this Memorandum.

On or about July 4th 1939 a further communication, together with a copy of a joint report by the Clerk of the Council and the Architect came containing the information that the Lord Privy Seal had decided to transfer the responsibility for the proposed rescue service from the Borough Councils to the London County Council. Particulars were given of arrangements with the London Master Builders' Association and the Building Trades Operatives by which the B.T.O. were to obtain men who would form the parties of the Rescue Service and the L.M.B.A. would apply to firms for foremen who would train the men in shoring and demolition. The operations in each Borough were to be controlled, either by the Borough Engineer and in the city by the City Engineer, or by a Senior Technical Officer appointed by the Council.

On 19th July a deputation from the Association attended a conference at County Hall at the request of the Clerk, Sir George Gater, who informed them that the Borough Councils' Standing Joint Committee were unable to agree to the Borough Engineers being responsible for the proposed Rescue, Shoring and Demolition Service, as they would have other duties on roads, sewers, etc. Sir George suggested that the District Surveyors should take over the work and he required to know whether they would assist the Council and step into the breach. At a special general meeting on 24th July the members volunteered without exception, to accept responsibility for the service, the assumption being that they would be given complete control. The members present at that meeting certainly did not realise how their control would be hedged around, hampered, and tied down by many other authorities commencing with Regional Command and extending through Group Officers, Town Clerk Controllers, County Hall Officials to Depot Superintendents and many other persons having some interest or connection with the Service or with matters analagous thereto; neither did they appreciate that at the end of the year, when they became officials of the Council under the 1939 Act, that their volunteer status would be subject to question. The city did not come into the scheme, the control remaining with the City Engineer, and one or two of the Boroughs, for a time at least, were also outside the arrangements.

War with Germany commenced on 3rd September 1939, about ten days after the District Surveyors had taken over the rescue service. In these few days they made desperate efforts to unravel a muddle of the first magnitude. The Local Authorities at certain Town Halls proved anything but helpful; equipment which the Boroughs were supposed to have received for the service, in many cases, did not exist or could not be found. The scheme by which the London Master Builders' Association and the Building Trades Operatives were to supply the personnel simply did not function and on 1st September instructions were issued by the Council for recruiting to be commenced at the Town Halls. Posters were exhibited asking for recruits for the service of Rescue Shoring and Demolition and there was no lack of response. Men of all descriptions rolled up for enlistment, a great proportion of whom had no trade other than that of a casual labourer; usually, without the slightest justification, they described themselves as carpenters or builders. Actual tradesmen were conspicuous by their absence. The Hoxton race gang found its way into the Shoreditch service and some of them did good work, but many others in various districts gave much trouble before being finally weeded out.

The position became almost hopeless and at a meeting on 7th September certain members thought that the Association should withdraw from the scheme, but fortunately other advice prevailed and finally all agreed to carry on. In the President's words – 'the District Surveyors had got to muddle through and the Council had also to set up a fresh organisation.' There can be little doubt, however, that if heavy raids had followed in the first weeks of the war then the service would have collapsed and the armed forces would have taken over. The first Air Raid warning in London was sounded at 11.25 a.m. Sunday 3rd September 1939, the day war was declared, when an unidentified plane approached the south coast. In one East End Borough a panic resulted and numerous persons tried to rush the Town Hall – after which entrance could only be obtained, on the presentation of credentials, by a small side door. Bombing did not commence until a year later. In many cases rudimentary equipment such as hammers, crowbars, pickaxes and shovels had to be purchased from the local ironmongers and there then remained the question of transport, which simply did not exist. When lorries were available they came of the type more often under repair in the garage than in action on the roads. Depots, mainly at L.C.C. Schools, the scholars from which had been evacuated, had to be organised, arrangements made for the men to receive a midday meal and numerous other matters incidental to a service being inaugurated for the first time in our history.

The Civil Defence Act, 1939, and the Defence Regulations

The above measures had come into force; two sections – 25 and 50 – of the Regulations were to have special significance for District Surveyors. Section 25 became interpreted to include the pulling down of premises and parts dangerous to the public using streets and subsequently, when the section came into use, the provisions were also held to cover danger to users of adjoining premises. The prohibition of entry to dangerous premises and Police Notices also came under this section and all District Surveyors were in due course, made responsible for all necessary acts being taken under this regulation. Section 50 covered the clearance of debris and sites; special arrangements were necessary before this section could be put into operation.

Under the Civil Defence Act the Local Authorities could requisition buildings or parts of them for public air raid shelters. Later surface shelters were erected in streets, forming formidable obstacles to traffic. Factories and commercial buildings had to be provided with shelters to the satisfaction of the Factory Inspectors and Local Authorities. Bulkheads giving access to and from basements arose on pavements together with masses of sandbags while blast walls added to the general inconvenience of the pedestrian groping his way along the footways in the blackout. Later when bombing commenced, enclosures to buildings in wood covered with tarred felt or other water proofing materials were passed as protection against the weather, while acres of roofs were formed or dealt with similarly. Later still fire watchers' posts constructed in all manners of ways sprung up on all important buildings. In short, for some six years London enjoyed an almost complete holiday from the provisions of the Building Acts which had not been so flagrantly violated for many a year.

The Rescue, Shoring and Demolition Service and the bombing of London

By the end of 1939 the Rescue Service had taken shape and summarised briefly it worked as follows: Wardens posts were established throughout the Boroughs and wardens working in reliefs were responsible for their streets or small areas. The posts had direct telephonic communication with the Control Rooms, situated generally in the Town Halls where the Town Clerks acted as Controllers. Ambulance Depots, with first aid parties were also connected by telephone to the Control Rooms and so were the depots of the heavy and light rescue parties, necessary for the removal of debris or for digging out, or for tunnelling under or for erection of temporary shoring or for any other arduous work which might be required for the rescue of trapped persons. The wardens were responsible for the original call for help and were expected to give some idea of the damage and possible casualties as well as the situation of the incident. On these messages Control acted, the Controller and the Rescue Officer, or their deputies, ordering the requisite parties, by telephone or messengers, to leave their depots for the incident. In the case of a number of incidents in one Borough the Controller could call for additional help from other Boroughs through his Group Controller. The final control rested with three Regional Commissioners, Sir Edward Gowers (Senior Regional Commissioner), Admiral Sir Edward Evans (Evans of the Broke) and Alderman Charles Key. Regional Headquarters was situated at the Geological Museum, Exhibition Road, South Kensington.

Frequent practices in answering imaginary calls were held; the time taken in the arrival of the various parties at the supposed incident being recorded carefully. Other training in rescuing persons from upper storeys, in first aid matters and anti-gas measures were all well organised and the services could be said to be ready for emergencies at the commencement of 1940. Friendly games varying from darts to cricket matches were arranged among the rescue parties of the various Boroughs and a competition followed for the honour of being recognised as the most efficient team. The final of this contest, between the service for Potters Bar and that of the Borough of Battersea was decided in June 1940 on the site of the old Crystal Palace. The prize went to the Potters Bar team, but the award came in for a great deal of criticism as each of the teams failed in one of the two rescue tests set for the competition and they both took advantage of the artificial circumstances in a way they could not have done had a wood framed structure been the imperforate wall it was supposed to represent.

The winter and spring of 1940 passed uneventfully, but stormy days were ahead. The Rescue Service provided continuous trouble and rumours were current of a proposed cut in the number of officers in charge. With summer came the fall of France and the evacuation of our Army from Dunkirk. Although the war was obviously drawing nearer to our shores economy measures were operating, and District Surveyors were being pressed for a reduction of their staffs in the Service. Certain smaller Boroughs were to be combined under one control by which one District Surveyor would be relieved of his duties and these instructions gave rise to anxious discussions at the meetings. During the following vital days the battle in the air for Britain was fought out. On 8th August, the Luftwaffe in massed formation was thrown against British convoys in the Channel and on 12th August the attacks were extended to the fighter aerodromes in the southern counties. In ten days the Germans lost nearly seven hundred planes and a lull in the fighting for five days followed. On 24th August the battle recommenced and the second phase lasted until 5th September and cost the Luftwaffe between five hundred and six hundred aircraft. On Saturday 7th September, a bright clear sunny day, the sirens sounded in London and a mass attack commenced on the docks. Dog fights occurred over London and the enemy lost over a hundred planes, but extensive fires were caused in dockland and during the night heavy bombing followed in the area. It was a night of horror for the firemen and the personnel of the Rescue Service; the civilian casualties amounted to some three hundred killed and thirteen hundred injured. The raids continued through the first half of September and reached a maximum on the fifteenth when five hundred planes attacked the capital. The enemy lost nearly two hundred of these planes, but many buildings were destroyed or damaged. Daylight attacks continued until October 5th and there were many raids by night. The minor troubles, including the staffing of the Rescue, Shoring and Demolition Service were forgotten now action had commenced; the fight was on, and the men responded in every way to the call. This book is not the medium for a discussion on incidents, shelters or the work that went on nightly by the rescue service. Time will doubtless produce the right author and the right book but he will need the genius of Edgar Allen Poe to describe faithfully the weird atmosphere and strange unrealities of the scenes. Those lorries filled with grim helmetted men rushing through the blackness of the night, the appalling din of anti-aircraft guns and the crashing noise of bombs; the indescribable mess at the incidents, piles of debris covered with a fog of dust and dirt through which the figures, by the light of flares or perhaps a blazing gas-main or a burning building, could be seen passing dimly, were reminiscent of pictures from Dante's Inferno. Daylight only brought a sense of devastation and desolation with a curious impression that buildings after all consisted merely of broken timbers, bricks and rubbish.

The autumn raids on London in 1940 brought some incidents, which viewed perhaps proportionately over the whole area of the county were insignificant, but which separately were terrible and ghastly. The use of schools and similar extensive buildings for public shelters, in which considerable numbers of persons gathered, constituted a great risk, for a direct hit or a near miss produced a direful calamity. The narrow street shelters, provided later, of 14" reinforced walls covered with a slab of concrete proved as effective in keeping down casualties as anything. The stations of the Underground Railways had to be opened as shelters, although they were originally not sanctioned for this purpose, but at least three incidents, with great loss of life, occurred at these places of refuge.

Some persons were strangely unlucky – several being killed on pavements when adjoining buildings were hit while others had miraculous escapes from death. A book could be written on this subject but one example must suffice. A block of Guinness Trust Buildings received a direct hit and a woman came down from an upper storey, surrounded by a mass of brickwork, concrete and steel joists, and yet she was found lying incapable of movement but practically unhurt in a small cavity under a terrific mass of debris.

District Surveyors and the raids

The first consideration of the District Surveyor in districts where he acted as the Rescue Officer had, of course, to be the rescue of trapped persons and the recovery of the dead. His next task – and this applied to all District Surveyors except those in the city – was the examination of premises, the closing of streets where necessary, and the serving of notices, through the Police, prohibiting entry to dangerous buildings. At times this last mentioned procedure had to wait until dangerous structures had been demolished to enable main streets to be opened for traffic. The actual clearance of debris lying in the streets came under the Borough Engineers. Finally a stream of persons seeking permits to enter burnt or damaged premises to retrieve their goods, safes or valuables, had to be satisfied. After a heavy raid this last item presented something of a nightmare. Actually the Town Clerk or Controllers were responsible for giving authority to persons who had established their rights to remove goods from blitzed buildings but they would often not do so until the District Surveyor had certified that safe entry could be obtained thereto. At times specific buildings were not easy to identify especially in the congested areas adjoining the city. After the great fire raid on 29th December 1940, many streets in boroughs adjoining the city resembled ways only piled with debris skirted with skeleton walls of burnt out buildings from which all signs and numbers had disappeared. When reasonable entry could be obtained the persons interested were told generally that they entered at their own risk. Relatively few safes passed through the great fire without their contents being reduced to ashes.

The great fire of London, 1940

The autumn attacks of 1940 culminated in the great fire raid on the city on 29th December. Thus 274 years had passed since the catastrophe of 1666, but this time there was no doubt as to the cause. The enemy tried deliberately to destroy the city entirely by fire and he might have succeeded but during the night the weather deteriorated and flying became difficult. A considerable area north of St. Pauls was devastated. The cathedral escaped, but practically the whole of the soft goods trade of the city including adjoining areas in Holborn, Finsbury and Shoreditch, went up in flames. Other trades suffered also: the well-known lane of Paternoster Row, the home of books both sacred and secular, could not be saved and millions of books were lost. On the night of the great conflagration newspapers could, by the light of the fires, be read easily in the suburbs.

Large stone fronted blocks of buildings caught in the conflagration presented a sorry spectacle after the fire; the stone in most cases disintegrated badly under the intense heat. Some streets were blocked hopelessly with masses of stone from heavy cornices and like projections, while in others the wood blocks of the roadway burned steadily for hours. Steel-framed buildings stood up to the ordeal well; the concrete and pot-floors in most cases did not collapse unless masonry had fallen thereon. Although in many buildings the floors remained unbroken the fires succeeded in sweeping the storeys clean of everything combustible. In one large six storey building the ashes left by the fire laid two feet thick over all the floors and not a vestige remained of anything that would burn. The reason why the flames passed from floor to floor so easily in certain cases, did not seem apparent; probably they belched out of the windows and licked up the fronts and so gained access that way, but again the incendiaries came from above so the fires started generally on the upper floors and there were many instances where the lower storeys remained untouched. A satisfactory explanation does not appear evident in those cases where high-grade fire-resisting buildings, on fairly wide streets, succumbed so readily to the flames. The result demonstrated clearly the effect of fire unchecked on such buildings. The National Fire Service had to deal with a situation quite beyond their control. The level of the Thames was abnormally low and the pumps delivering water became choked with mud, while broken water mains added a further difficulty. The lack of water rendered the efforts of the Service hopeless and some evidence of their onerous work remained in many lengths of partly burnt hose-pipes left lying in and over the debris littering the streets. In the city the fires passed, with little difficulty, across the narrow thoroughfares to ignite buildings opposite. The lanes were widened following the fires of 1666 and the buildings erected were restricted in height but subsequent to the Act of 1774 new buildings had been constructed to an unlimited height and consequently the old precautions taken to reduce the risk of spread of fire no longer obtained.

London by night in the Blitz

The morning after

The control of the Rescue and Demolition Service in the city remained with the City Engineer as originally proposed, and clearance commenced immediately, the Army providing the labour; streets wanted for traffic were cleared of debris without delay, while dangerous walls in convenient positions were brought down by explosives. The Boroughs adjoining the city obtained relatively little help from military sources and there the first consideration had to be given to high, unsafe walls, bordering main thoroughfares. The District Surveyors in these circumstances could call on special contractors and in most cases the high tottering fronts came down by the use of ropes and winches, or by ropes attached to lorries. The fall of a high facade on to the roadway used by trolley buses resulted invariably in the breaking of the overhead wires and a delay in the omnibus service. The Transport Board afforded excellent co-operation and they executed the necessary repairs with remarkable alacrity.

The fire of 29th December 1940 did not, by any means, complete the destruction in the city, for further devastation occurred in the raids in April and on 10th May 1941, while flying bombs and at least one rocket in 1945 added their quota to the damage.

Record of war damage in the City of London

The Area of buildings in the City of London destroyed by enemy action was 102 acres approx. (exclusive of thoroughfares).

The number of buildings destroyed or so damaged that demolition followed was 2,884 approx. Other buildings seriously damaged – 400 approx. Of these buildings it may be noted that of forty-nine Protestant Churches holding services in the city, twenty-eight were more or less damaged severely and of these, three were beyond repair, but in no case can it be said that not a vestige of the original church remains. All the others suffered slight damage. Of five buildings accommodating other religious sects two were demolished and two partially destroyed, one only remains intact.

The following Churches designed by or connected with Christopher Wren were damaged severely:

Christ Church, St. Andrew, St. Andrew by the Wardrobe, St. Augustine, St. Bride, St. Dunstan-in-the-East, St. Lawrence Jewry, St. Mary Aldermary, St. Mary-le-Bow, St. Mary-the-Virgin, St. Michael Paternoster Royal, St. Mildred (totally destroyed), St. Nicholas Cole Abbey, St. Stephens, Coleman Street (almost totally destroyed), St. Swithin, St. Vedast. Other churches with which Wren was connected in various ways received lesser damage.

Thirteen City Halls were so seriously affected, either by direct enemy action or by the necessary removal of dangerous parts that they could be counted as practically demolished. Seven other, City Halls were badly damaged, and the remains of two or three had ultimately to be demolished.

Other historical or well-known buildings destroyed or damaged included:

The Guildhall, St. Bartholomew's Hospital, the Gateway, Bart's Close, Trinity House, P.L.A. Building, The General Post Office, Smithfield Market, The Coal Exchange, The Corn Exchange, and several railway stations.

The approximate number of casualties were – killed 340, injured (detained in hospital) 873, slightly injured 1,210.

A comparison between the particulars of the destruction caused in the city by the great fire of 1666 as given previously with the statement set out above, indicates that Germany could not equal, in many attempts, on the present brick enclosed buildings the amount of devastation which resulted in 1666 from a fire which originated in a baker's shop. The lesson of that fire had not been lost and from that date onwards the main regulations of the Building Acts have been directed towards the obtaining of fire-proof buildings and in the future efforts in this direction are not likely to be abated.

The raids cease

The great air attack of 10th May 1941 cost the Germans thirty-three planes, but the casualties, which included two Mayors (one being the Mayor of Westminster) were heavy, and many buildings were destroyed. This raid proved to be the last on the capital for some considerable time. The enemy had driven through Yugoslavia and Greece to retrieve the prestige of Italy and the ill-fated attack on Russia which commenced on 22nd June 1941, was now about to be launched. It can be said that the respite came just in time to relieve the hard pressed Londoners, who were now left to patch up their homes, where possible, and clear up the mess with little labour available for the task. The winter of 1941 will be remembered in history as a time of 'sweat, blood, and tears', the words of Britain's indomitable Prime Minister, Winston Churchill. Countless thousands not only in the capital, but in other cities too, sat huddled together in cellars or shelters through nights of terror while persistent cold weather and the inconvenience of the black-out added to their misery. The British black-out began at 7.47 p.m. on the night of September 1st 1939. It ended 1,145 days later on July 15th 1945. It was by general consent one of the cruellest, most confining burdens of the war. It was certainly the most controversial.

The War Debris Survey and Disposal Service

A passing reference has been made to Group Controllers and the Regional Commissioners, and it should be recorded that the authority of the Commissioners extended over what is known as Greater London. This area was divided into nine divisions or groups, each containing a number of Boroughs. Groups functioned to distribute the services of the Boroughs within its control, in the event of any one or more of its Boroughs being unable to cope with incidents arising from a heavy raid thereon. Each of the groups within the County of London had originally an officer in charge sent from County Hall, but after the formation of the War Debris Survey and Disposal Service in October 1940 the Groups came under the control of District Surveyors.

By the end of September 1940, piles of debris had accumulated in many of the London Boroughs and protests were coming from the general public on the inconvenience and the depressing effects. The local authorities were unable to deal effectively with the situation and the necessity for a central body to direct operations became evident. It was under these circumstances that Sir Warren Fisher became Special Commissioner for the London Civil Defence Region and at his request the Council organised the War Debris Survey and Disposal Service with the Deputy Architect, Mr. J.H. Foreshaw, as Director. Five District Surveyors: Messrs. Kennard, Greig, Hall, McDowall and Whittaker were appointed with the title of Group Surveyor and Rescue Officer. Apart from their control at the Group Centres over the Rescue Service the five Surveyors had the responsibility of delegating the labour at their disposal for demolition and clearance purposes to any of the Boroughs within their Group as the necessity for urgent action arose and they had many other duties besides.

The responsibility within the County of deciding on the buildings to be demolished and the extent of the clearance fell upon the District Surveyor for the respective districts while the Borough Engineers could settle the priority in which sites were to be cleared.

Operations commenced on 14th October, 1940, the demolition contractors having to rely for the bulk of their labour on army units provided by the Pioneer Corps. The soldiers did good work and some 6,000 were employed when their efforts reached its maximum. The dual control by the army and demolition firms was not, at times, too satisfactory; an example being afforded by an incident in Finsbury for which neither party would accept the responsibility. Clearance commenced on a devastated area and a terrace of houses, not scheduled for demolition, was cleared of furniture – the goods and chattels of various owners being thoroughly mixed together and strewn over the roadway. A steady rain then commenced to fall and the rising tempers of all concerned did not improve an unfortunate situation. By the end of the year a considerable civilian labour force had been recruited and after the great fire raid on 29th December, the City Corporation claimed most of the military help available. By April 1941 the soldiers had departed, but some 4,100 sites had been cleared with their assistance.

Of the many dumps of materials which arose in consequence of the clearance the most interesting occupied a site of about one acre in Hyde Park, where fittings from radiators and baths to parts of lifts and articles such as safes, typewriters and numerous other miscellaneous items could be purchased by the general public. Many persons availed themselves of the opportunity to obtain useful commodities and the dump remained a centre of attraction until it was closed down in the autumn of 1941.

The air raids over Greater London in the nine months ending May 1941, were concentrated principally on the central Boroughs in the County of London, the East End, and the Thames-side areas downstream from Westminster. The expectation in the possible loss of life was not, fortunately, realised, but the extent of damage to buildings, roads etc. exceeded that anticipated. Buildings actually demolished by bombs or destroyed by fire were relatively few compared with the number affected in one way or another. Houses with displaced roofs, cracked walls, fallen ceilings and windows and doors blown out formed a large proportion of the buildings damaged; one estimate places the number of habitations with these defects at over a million, but this figure must be taken with reserve. The fact is that the effects of blast extended over large areas and in many districts few buildings could be said to have come through undamaged.

With the arrival of a fleet of new lorries the War Debris Service reached its peak by July 1941, when 66 contractors with 24,000 operatives were engaged in the clearance. The Government had called for a drive for steel scrap and Group Surveyors concentrated on the collection of this material – some thousands of tons being collected each week. At that time hardcore proved to be the "Cinderella" of the Service for little use could be found for the vast amount awaiting disposal; basements of demolished properties were filled in and large quantities were dumped at Becontree and at Hackney Marshes where eventually the banks of the river Lea were raised some four feet and three hundred acres of land reclaimed for recreational purposes. Later, after the entry of America into the war, hardcore became of vital importance and the whole labour force had to be employed on its collection and delivery – millions of tons being required to form the basis of the miles of runways necessary to serve the great airforce then in course of preparation. Another use for which the broken stones, bricks and dust of London's buildings served was the partial filling in of the East India Dock to form a firm bed over the mud bottom. On this foundation those remarkable structures were built termed "Mulberries", i.e. floating concrete breakwaters used to protect the craft of the invasion forces landing in France. During the autumn of 1943 all available transport was in use in the carting of hardcore for military and airforce purposes and the delivery reached the peak figure of 40,000 tons per week.

Of the millions of bricks cleaned and stacked, large numbers were used in the formation of static water tanks to serve as reserve water supplies for fire-fighting; for the erection of protective walls to open basements next streets, and for the purpose of repairs to housing and other properties.

When occasions arose, contractors, their men and plant, were transferred to areas outside the county to deal with incidents in Greater London and in such cases the work of clearance came under the charge of the respective Group concerned. The organisation built up by the War Debris Survey also proved valuable to the Ministry of Home Security when large scale demolition and clearance became necessary in the provinces. Units were sent out to assist in the clearance of the cities of Coventry, Canterbury, Bath, Plymouth and Portsmouth.

The writer is indebted to the Council for much of the information given above and the following figures are from the same source –

Metals collected – all kinds	340,000 tons
Timber	145,000 "
Debris	4,200,000 "
Hardcore	7,500,000 "
Bricks – cleaned and stacked	140,000,000
Slates and tiles	2,750,000
Total tonnage of all cartage	14,000,000 tons

The figures are, of necessity, approximate only, but they give some idea of the immensity of the task of clearing and salvaging the blitzed buildings of London. Nothing has been said of the special salvage involved in certain cases such as the food stores at the docks, of valuable plant and historical treasures, all of which work came within the Service.

A Group Surveyor, Mr. G.M. Hall stayed at Coventry for five months from March to July inclusive in 1942, and during this time he had charge of six hundred and fifty men. About one half of this labour force came from London – the billeting being arranged in emergency camps. In this clearance, under Mr. Hall's supervision, some 3,000 tons of iron and steel were recovered, while hardcore to the extent of approximately one quarter of a million tons was carted, much being absorbed by aerodromes situated within thirty miles radius of the city.

A further Group Surveyor, Mr. E.D. McDowall, also acted in a similar capacity at Portsmouth, and at the end of May 1942 he accompanied a special contingent from the mobile squads to Canterbury after that town had sustained a concentrated air attack. The mobile squads were developed during 1941 from the Rescue Service, under an arrangement termed "Inter Regional Reinforcements", with a view to rapid service in any area requiring special relief following a saturation raid.

Mr. Hall spent five weeks, mainly during March 1945, in the city of Antwerp at a period when the Germans were continually directing flying bombs against the city. He went out largely in an advisory capacity, taking with him one hundred debris lorries and three mobile cranes. The object of the visit was to organise a Belgian labour service, based on the London service, which would function to speed up clearance so that movement was not impeded on the Army's vital lines of communication which then passed through Antwerp.

The War Debris Service dispensed largely with the need for special contractors as gangs working on clearance in any Borough could be transferred at a moment's notice to deal with dangerous buildings as incidents occurred in their own or neighbouring Boroughs.

The work of demolition and clearance varied considerably, some buildings presenting little difficulty, an instance being the printing works of Messrs. Waterlow, Finsbury Market. This building occupied an island site, comprised several storeys and covered an area of approximately 25,000 square feet. A description given to the writer by a witness of its destruction stated: 'that the building became a sheet of flames and burnt like a gigantic torch.' The clearance proved a simple matter and many tons of metal type were recovered from the debris, but others were not so amenable. The printing works of Messrs. De la Rue of Bunhill Row had a solidly built tower supporting an iron tank holding some twenty thousand gallons of water, while similar tanks existed on other parts of the building – all the water from which disappeared with very little effect, apparently, on the fire. The premises covered an area of 20,000 square feet; certain of the floors were of concrete carrying numerous large Wharfdale printing presses, all of which proved unsalvageable. The demolition of the tower, the breaking up and clearing of the presses, and the removal of the many thousands of tons of building materials occupied gangs of men for upwards of twelve months. Of the difficulties encountered in dealing with high walls on congested sites, much could be written, and it can be truly said that never were there so many hundreds of thousands of tons of materials demolished and moved with so little loss of life, but several narrow escapes could be mentioned – one the writer can vouch for concerned a portion of a wall of a high building, which for some curious reason in the demolition became projected across the roof of lower premises and then crashed through a window beyond, the bricks falling upon a chair just previously vacated by a solicitor; the gentleman was not amused.

Following a raid the buildings involved were classified and listed tentatively under different categories commencing with those demolished and ending generally with an extensive list of those affected by blast and described as slightly damaged. Category C provided cases most difficult to deal with as being listed as – 'seriously damaged but capable of later repair' – they were left vacant, dilapidated and generally without roof coverings. Subsequently these properties, particularly the older types of dwellings, deteriorated rapidly under the influence of the weather and destruction caused by youths of the neighbourhood. Walls were undermined, floors and staircases removed and buildings rendered dangerous through this unauthorised interference; so the clearance, which commenced with buildings actually destroyed, had to be extended as time passed to include many dwellings which could have been saved had the labour, materials and police supervision been available.

The flying bombs and lastly the rockets, added their quota of destruction during 1944 and the early months of 1945, and the work of demolition and clearance continued with gradually decreasing labour until the autumn of 1948.

The work of District Surveyors, 1941–1944

The lull in the raids following May 1941, gave District Surveyors an opportunity to catch up with much work unavoidably delayed. With the call for Group Surveyors, a few retirements – the vacancies being unfilled – and the delegation of two members to County Hall, the districts were decidedly shorthanded. Most Surveyors were working two districts or taking on additional rescue duties; in 1943 one Surveyor reported that he had been acting as deputy Surveyor in five districts at once, in addition to his group work.

Maps were required showing by appropriate colours those buildings destroyed, damaged beyond repair, or beyond immediate repair, and those more or less only slightly affected. Programmes of clearance had to be arranged with some regard to the susceptibilities of the local residents and with due consideration to the salvage of materials. Other matters included reports on damaged historical buildings; particulars in connection with sites for water storage (static water tanks required for possible further fire fighting) and a constant flood of enquiries as to the safety of buildings. The procedure under the Dangerous Structure Clauses of the Building Act could not, with fairness, be applied to buildings damaged by enemy action as in no sense could owners be held responsible for the condition of the building. The District Surveyors had to act under Section 25 of the Defence Regulations, as previously described, and later, when the use of special contractors was withdrawn, by obtaining the removal of the danger through the Rescue Service Squads or the War Debris Clearance Gangs.

The Rescue Service called for much attention from the Officers in Charge; the wisdom of Solomon and the patience of Job were qualifications necessary to deal with the situations arising in the Service. Discipline could not be enforced and although proposals were made for a system of fines they could not be imposed lawfully. This little army of men were on a voluntary basis without the military code of punishments and every credit should be given to those in charge who managed such a system. The squads varied considerably from Borough to Borough, some were prepared to work and worked well on clearance jobs while others made every excuse to avoid working at all and they would and could make an insignificant job of work last indefinitely. It must be remembered that the

A.R.P. Service had no precedent and a satisfactory code was lacking. Many men in the heavy Rescue Squads considered that they could not be legally called upon to pull down ruinous buildings and that trade union rates of pay should accompany such work and, moreover, they were probably strictly correct in this view. Efforts were made to keep the men employed but the results were variable and often disappointing. In 1942 the service was regraded; the light and heavy parties being more or less amalgamated. Many of the younger men had been drafted into the Army and the strength of the personnel became much reduced.

The final raids 1944–1945

Bombing recommenced on a modified scale in the early months of 1944 when the raiders found a perfected defence that proved effective in keeping most of them away from the central areas, but casualties and damage resulted mainly in the western districts.

The great D-Day offensive, so eagerly awaited by all, came on 6th June 1944, when the allied forces landed in Normandy. The German reply to the succesful invasion was the launching against Southern England of their most vaunted secret weapon, which proved to be a jet-driven robot bomb carrying a ton of explosive in its head. Those who were in London on the night when the main attack by this V.1 bomb developed will long remember the buildings shaking and vibrating under the furious barrage that roared throughout the night from the anti-aircraft batteries and the rain of metal which fell from the bursting shells. This proved to be a grand finale on the part of the aircraft defence for little could be gained by bringing the bombs down when they were already over London. The guns were moved silently away together with the barrage balloons towards the south coast where the V.1 missiles were subsequently shot down in droves. Of 8,000 flying bombs sent against Britain some 2,300 reached the London area where they caused many casualties and considerable damage to property, mainly in the southern districts. The attacks continued for some months until the sites from which they were released were overrun by the allied armies.

The Civil Defence Department of the Home Office have given the following particulars, the figures being the nearest available.

	Casualties killed	Seriously injured
London Regional Area	29,890	50,507
County of London (included in above)	19,415	35,716

Damage to buildings – London Regional Area

Totally demolished	Damaged beyond repair	Seriously damaged but repairable	Damaged but habitable & repairable	Slightly damaged
73,073	43,410	161,643	126,281	1,399,241
County of London (included in above)				
52,267	17,171	66,660	55,878	517,552

Number of incidents in the County of London 20,102 (all types of bombs).

Awards etc. in County of London: George Crosses = 2
George Medals = 41
British Empire Medals = 67
Commendations = 54

A comparison of the casualties and damage given above with those suffered in the 1914-1918 war (page 102), when the incidents amounted to 922, the killed 524, injured 1,264, gives some indication of the progress in the science of destruction over a quarter of a century. The aeroplane was largely evolved in the first world war; the second has produced the atom bomb, the outcome of which appears to envisage the possible absolute destruction of cities, communities and nations.

The last effort to wreak destruction on the capital came with secret weapon V.2 – a twelve ton robot-propelled projectile having a range of two hundred miles and carrying two thousand pounds of explosive. The first of these fell on Chiswick on the 8th September 1944. The rockets approached without warning and 1,050 reached Britain, killing 2,754 people and seriously injuring 6,523. The rockets continued to fall until the end of March 1945, when the sites in Holland, from which they were discharged, were captured.

Both the rescue and clearance services had much to do in dealing with the incidents resulting from these new devastating weapons of warfare. For days and nights, for weeks on end, the work of rescue and clearance went on, with the personnel and officers in charge, particularly those for the southern districts, working without respite or question in the struggle to master what they knew to be the last desperate effort of a defeated enemy. Many of the flying-bombs fell in Greater London outside the county, and at times the Rescue Service and District Surveyors went into action to assist the hard pressed local services in their areas.

The North German Command surrendered to Field Marshall Montgomery on the 4th May 1945, and three days later the German General Staff capitulated to General Eisenhower.

At the beginning of the war all the District Surveyors volunteered to accept responsibility for the Rescue, Shoring and Demolition Service.

The members, in taking over the R.S.D. Service, did so without monetary reward of any kind, and in fact in many cases they incurred financial losses in being unable to devote the necessary time to clearing up old outstanding Building Act cases. They did not become salaried officials of the Council until January 1940, when five additional appointments were made; the new Surveyors being required to take over the R.S.D. Services in their districts.

Decorations were conferred on the following five members:

W.G. Whincop	M.B.E.	Awarded	1943
T.R.L. Gibson	M.B.E.	"	1945
C. Kennard	O.B.E.	"	1945
A.L. Handley	O.B.E.	"	1946
D.J. Clarke	M.B.E.	"	1946

The Rescue, Shoring and Demolition Service was disbanded finally on June 30th 1945, but many of its personnel had discharged themselves before that date and thus concluded that most dramatic and remarkable episode in the annals of the Association.

Building Act matters over the war years

Throughout the summer months of 1940 builders were busy with the erection of public air raid shelters and those required in connection with commercial buildings, after which building work practically closed down. The City Corporation engaged the two District Surveyors within their area to pass the plans and to supervise the erection of the many shelters necessary to protect the workers and citizens of the city.

After May 1941 the Boroughs became much occupied in the repairs of damaged dwellings for they were responsible in the first instance for the rehousing of homeless people. The work fell roughly into two categories – first aid repairs, and reinstatement. The position varied considerably in different Boroughs; in the East End the majority opinion being that old dilapidated and out-of-date houses should not be rebuilt, largely as the time had come when they should be replaced with new, while in the West End the policy of rebuilding wherever possible seemed most in favour. Many Borough Engineers were pleased to cooperate with the District Surveyors and to have their advice on the extent of rebuilding required, but in some cases differences of opinion arose as to who was to determine the question and as to what could be legitimately classed as war damage, and what could not be so classed.

Subsequently officers of the War Damage Commission, seeking information on the pre-war condition of premises on which claims for compensation had been made, frequently consulted the District Surveyor whose local knowledge was often of great assistance.

Many meetings were held at County Hall on the urgent questions arising on this subject of repairs to bomb-damaged dwellings. The Council finally decided that Building Act fees should not be charged on work carried out by contractors working under the Borough Councils. This decision complicated matters for in some districts the Boroughs demanded from the owners a proportion of the cost of the works necessary to render properties fit for habitation; their contention being that the defects in certain cases were also due partly to old age and neglect and the condition of the buildings could not be attributed altogether to enemy action. In these cases fees on the amount contributed by the owner could be charged. The position could be described only as confused and unsatisfactory. A word might be said here on the Ministry of Works as this body organised in the last stages of the bombing an efficient supply of labour recruited from all over the British Isles, and good work, if at times rough and ready, was executed by these men. The Ministry came into prominence early in the war for in October 1940 an order came into force by which any building operation to premises rated in one assessment could not exceed the value of £500 in one year; the conservation of vital materials being the reason for the order. In April 1941 the amount became reduced to £100, and in October 1944 the figure in London came down to the absurd limit of £10. The Ministry could grant licences for greater expenditure, but a strong case had to be presented before a concession could be obtained. Firms employed in the war effort could apply through the various Government Departments which controlled their supplies of raw materials, and the District Surveyor had then to decide in these cases the extent of repairs necessary before the decision was taken to repair or alternatively to leave the premises derelict and remove the works elsewhere. Food stores and works engaged on aircraft production were dealt with as priority cases, but the ordinary trading citizen could find little assistance anywhere. Perhaps the most distasteful task that fell to the lot of the District Surveyor in these distressful times was the necessity of having to inform an occupier – who possibly had spent many years of his life in building up a business, that he must vacate his unsafe, damaged premises. Probably he had nowhere to go and should he be able to obtain other accommodation his stock, if lost, could not be replaced. Relatively few works could be put in hand, other than those to dwellings, by the Borough Councils, without the support of the District Surveyor. An application to the Ministry for a licence would invariably require his backing in the way of a letter explaining the urgency or necessity for the work. Possibly the defect concerned an unsafe roof or a bulged wall or some other matter that involved a small part only of the building in question. Even small items often called for support for in most cases the £100 limit for the year had been reached and an application became necessary to cover the small additional cost. This correspondence added to the tasks of the District Surveyor's clerical staff which eventually became nearly non-existent and which generally did not extend to more than one clerk to two districts.

The London Plan

During 1942 the Architect's Department of the Council under Mr. J.H. Forshaw, together with numerous town planning experts which included Professor Patrick Abercrombie, were actively engaged in the production of a plan for the redevelopment of London. An exhibition was held at County Hall during the summer of 1943 and a book was published termed "The London Plan". By the end of 1945 all members had received a copy of "The London Plan" with instructions that they should study the book and refer builders and owners to the proposals set out therein.

Town Planning Acts and Orders

The Town and Country Planning (General Interim Development) Order 1933 followed the T.P. Act of 1932 and between 1942 and 1946 further Town Planning Acts and Orders became law. The new legislation restricted the development of all land in England and Wales with special provisions in respect of areas devastated through the war. The Town and Country Planning (Interim Development) Act amended and extended the Act of 1932 and in the following year an Act was passed which contained far-reaching provisions on the acquisition of land by Local Authorities. This Town and Country Planning Act 1944 conferred on Local Planning Authorities power to purchase land compulsorily under a simpler and more expeditious procedure – for the redevelopment of 'areas of extensive war damage' ('blitzed' areas) and areas of obsolete development and bad lay-out ('blighted' areas); and for the development of new areas ('overspill' areas) to accommodate displaced population, industry, etc.

Town Planning (General Interim Development) Orders were issued by the Ministry of Town Planning in 1945 and 1946. These Orders concerned 'Permitted Development, Powers to exclude certain Development, Provisions re applications by persons desiring to develop land, etc.' Under the last mentioned Order an application for the rebuilding, restoration or replacement of any building, not involving an increase in the cubic content, which had sustained war damage was not to be refused by the Interim Development Authority unless questions arose on lines of frontage or amenities of surrounding properties.

Association matters over the war years

Variations had become necessary in the Articles of the Association to meet the altered circumstances arising from the fact that members were now officials of the Council and the necessary amendments were duly arranged and settled at a special meeting in March 1940. The principal change concerned Article 4 by which members were to be District Surveyors appointed or deemed to have been appointed under sections 75 and 78 of L.B. Acts (Amendment) Act, 1939. Membership was limited to actual District Surveyors whereas under the original text 'Deputy and Assistant District Surveyors could be admitted.'

At the June meeting 1941, the Council's proposals for the District Surveyors' Examination Board were announced. The Board would consist of seventeen persons: representatives of the Council (5) including (2) District Surveyors, Royal Institute of British Architects (4), Chartered Surveyors' Institution (2), Institution of Civil Engineers (2), Institution of Structural Engineers (2), Incorporated Association of Architects and Surveyors (1), Faculty of Architects and Surveyors (1).

The centenary of the Association

January 1945 brings the recorded life of the District Surveyors' Association to its centenary and to celebrate the occasion a Sub-Committee received instructions in 1944 to examine old records, prepare a brief history and to put forward suggestions for a centenary celebration, but nothing was done before February 1945 when the Sub-Committee, being re-elected, proceeded to hold meetings with a view to settling arrangements for an official function.

A luncheon was held on Thursday, 31st May, 1945, in the Vintners' Hall in the City of London. The guests included four Ministers of the Crown – the Home Secretary, the Minister of Town and Country Planning, the Minister of Health and the Minister of Works.

Other visitors included the Leader of the Council and the deputy Chairman, two Parliamentary Secretaries, the senior Regional Commissioner, Chairman of the War Damage Commission, Chairman of the Metropolitan Water Board, Dean of St. Pauls, Mayors of Westminster, St. Marylebone and Holborn, the Presidents of the six allied professional bodies, the Clerk, the Architect, the Engineer and the Solicitor of the Council, while the Boroughs were represented by twelve Town Clerks and seventeen Borough Surveyors.

In all, one hundred and forty six members and guests were present at the function including twelve former members and forty six official guests. Lord Latham, Leader of the Council, proposed "The District Surveyors' Association" and mentioned many facts and figures in connection with the Rescue and Debris Disposal Services. The Rt. Hon. H. Morrison also spoke and both speakers recorded their appreciation of the work of the District Surveyors in connection with those services; an aspect made much of being the fact that the work had been carried out with little or no public criticism, a sure criterion that it had been done with efficiency and without undue irritation to the community.

St. Paul's-among-the-office-blocks

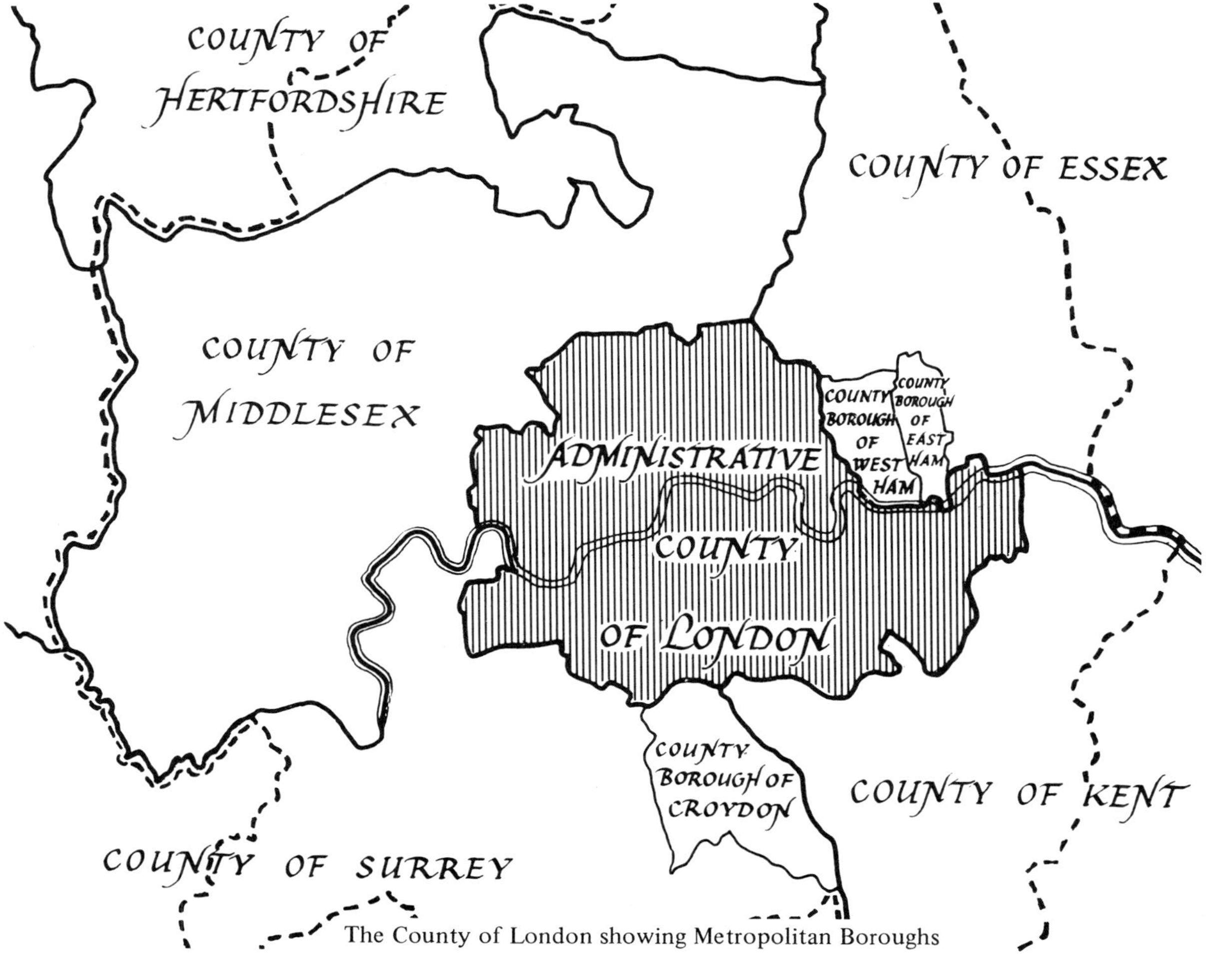

The County of London showing Metropolitan Boroughs

Greater London and the London Boroughs

ADDENDUM 1

Prosperity and rebuilding after the second world war. Changes in districts. Articles of the Association revised. The Town and Country Planning Act 1947. Years 1947–1954

In writing this Chapter, in 1954, it is heartening to record a steady progress in recovery since the war and an increasing prosperity. Two events which contributed to this record prosperity were 'The Festival of Britain' in 1951 and the Coronation of Queen Elizabeth II in 1953.

The Festival recorded the one hundred years of scientific progress since the great Exhibition of 1851 of which there is a note on page 68. A cleared site on the south side of the Thames adjoining County Hall was selected for the Festival Exhibition. 'The Royal Festival Hall' was built as a permanent development. River launches plied from the Exhibition to a 'Fun Fair' at Battersea Park where illuminations and flowers made a memorable scene.

1954 had seen the last of wartime rationing and there is now freedom in buying where and what you will. The necessity for building licences came to an end after being in operation, in varying degrees, since the 20th October 1940. The first efforts to provide homes for the homeless began about 1944 when the Government took over certain cleared sites and erected the Uni-Secco type of bungalow, the cladding of which consisted of inner and outer sheets of asbestos with a filling between of cement wood wool. Surveyors had no responsibilities for these erections.

It is a far cry from those little homes to the blocks of flats up to twelve storeys in height, complete with lifts, community centres and laundry equipment which are now a feature of the London landscape.

New ways and changing methods of building continue and the old wooden scaffold poles with their cord or wire lashings and the wood putlogs are now things of the past. The metal tubular scaffold with its adjustable cramps has come to stay. The labourer no longer carries bricks up ladders by the hod; they now go up by a hoist, or on smaller jobs by basket and tackle. The wooden wheelbarrows of yesterday are now of metal with pneumatic tyres. Cement and aggregate today, on important contracts, are mixed by batching, i.e. by weight. Concrete from mixers goes on similar works to its final position by way of pipe lines and compressed air. The labourer rarely uses the sledge-hammer and wedge for the modern pneumatic chisel chugs its way through old foundations and the jumping rammer compresses loose surfaces. The digging of large trenches and the clearing of considerable areas by hand is no longer a paying proposition. Cranes with drag-lines and shovels scoop up the soil, debris and the multiplicity of rubbish which goes to the making up of London's sites and place it all into waiting lorries.

With the passing of old methods a word of remembrance and tribute should be recorded to that sturdy independent character, the British navvy. With his corderoy suit, tied in at the knees, his clay pipe and dish of food carried in a red cloth, he had become an institution of this country. His legs were his transport, not the present ubiquitous bus, and he walked miles to and from his work. His tools seemed to be a part of the man whether working on the roads or in the bowels of the earth. Unfortunately he is seldom met with on building work today and his successor has, for the most part, little of the stamina, resource and reliability of that pioneer who had to rely mainly on his muscle, pick and shovel to cope with the arduous work of moving the earth.

District Surveyors and their districts. Twenty-eight District Surveyors for the county of London. Years 1947–1954

During these years of reconstruction the Council have pursued their aim steadily of reducing the number of Districts and bringing District Surveyors into line with the general principles governing senior officers at County Hall. It must not be thought, however, that the Council had no supporters among District Surveyors in their scheme for some of the more active members were clearly in favour of having a District consisting of a large area with numerous assistants and the Borough Surveyor was often quoted in that respect. The fact is that these members could see little prospect of material advancement and consequent increase in salary unless they could obtain this control.

The effect has been that in these larger Districts the District Surveyor must conduct his business through his assistants in the way it is done at County Hall. An Architect visiting County Hall to discuss questions relative to his work seldom sees the head of a department and a similar procedure now applies in the more important Districts. This loss of personal contact between the building public and the District Surveyor is unfortunate for it was the essence of the old system. Moreover, an assistant must look always to the letter of the law, for he cannot take upon himself that responsibility of extending the meaning of the Acts or Bylaws to meet the exigences of the case. It is obviously impossible for the District Surveyors of the principal Districts to see every caller at their offices. It would seem fortunate that the Council have no control over the Doctors of the Metropolis, or their system might lead to the majority of patients seeing only nurses while the Doctor remained a legendary figure in the background. The trouble comes about by grading: an official of the Council of a senior grade controls, by virtue or rank, numerous assistants to whom he is expected to distribute the work of his department. This spreading out of responsibility was not the intention of the old Acts and it is still difficult to see how a District Surveyor can legitimately delegate his responsibility to various grades of assistants.

With the retirement of three District Surveyors in 1954 the Council have achieved their aim of one District Surveyor to each of the Metropolitan Boroughs, except for Stoke Newington which is included with Hackney, and one District Surveyor to each of the cities of London and Westminster. The control of building in London is thus in the hands of twenty-eight Surveyors.

In 1946 when the Council announced their purpose, there were forty-three Districts and thirty-one District Surveyors including five appointments made in 1940. There were also three acting Surveyors. These forty-three Districts have been reduced to twenty-eight, graded as follows:-

Grade I plus	(five districts) – City of London, Kensington, St. Marylebone, Wandsworth, City of Westminster
Grade I	(nine districts) – Camberwell, Hackney with Stoke Newington (combined), Islington, Lambeth, Lewisham, St. Pancras, Southwark, Stepney, Woolwich.
Grade II	(eight districts) – Bermondsey, Finsbury, Fulham, Greenwich, Hammersmith, Holborn, Paddington, Poplar.
Grade III	(six districts) – Battersea, Bethnal Green, Chelsea, Deptford, Hampstead, Shoreditch.

Each of the above grades carries its appropriate salary, and the principle extends to assistants, the highest grade being that held by those who have passed the qualifying examination and who are appointed as Assistant District Surveyors.

Association matters. The Articles are revised. Years 1947–1954

The Minutes of the Association over these years are full of references to negotiations with the Council on questions of staffing, salaries and motor car allowances. Although the Association is not always in agreement with the usage of the Council which functions at times in an inexorable, purposeless way, the relations between the Association and the Council have continued to be peaceful and the negotiations mentioned above can be said to have ended with satisfaction to the majority of all concerned. On one occasion, however, the action of the Association was criticised by the Council for when the Bylaws, which came into operation in 1953, were being given public notice in the press, prior to becoming law, the Association registered objections with the Minister. This effrontery did not please the Council and questions were raised as to what right these officers had in so acting against the Council. Actually the matter was of little consequence as the Minister referred the objections back to the Council when adjustments were made.

An increasingly difficult question in the district offices is the coping with the piles of calculations for framed or calculated brick buildings which are being received daily. The Council have been helpful in allowing the work of checking to be given to Consultants outside the offices, but it is not always easy to find Engineers willing to undertake this work at the rates of pay allowed by the Council. In the case of unconventional designs, such as shell roofs, the Council have agreed to rates being paid up to one guinea and a half per hour.

New legislation

In 1947 questions arose on the effect of enactments passed during and immediately after the war on the Building Acts and Bylaws. The wave of nationalisation produced by the Labour Government after 1945 included the Transport, Gas and Electric Light Companies, but little change resulted in Building Act control.

An Education Act passed in 1944 repealed the provisions of Section 166 of the Education Act of 1921 by which school buildings were exempted from the provisions of the Building Acts and Bylaws. The new Act by Section 63 allows for exemption only by order of the Minister, who, it is understood, will use this authority very sparingly. Under Section 149(e) of the London Building Act (Amendment) Act 1939 public buildings belonging to the London County Council are exempt from Parts III and IV of the Act, but by definition a school does not come within the category of a public building unless it exceeds 250,000 cubic feet. It follows that the Council's schools, including controlled schools, under this cube will, unless the Minister decides otherwise, be again subject to the constructional clauses of the Acts and Bylaws. Also that aided or independent schools will not be exempted whatever the cubical contents may be.

The National Health Service Act 1946

This revolutionary Act affected the lives of the whole community and hospitals supported previously by voluntary gifts became a charge on the health contributions. The control was transferred, except in the case of certain special hospitals, to the Minister of Health and Regional Hospital Boards. The buildings and lands were brought under the Town and Country Planning Act 1947 and given the "Crown Exemptions" provided for under Section 151 of the London Building Acts (Amendment) Act 1939. The District Surveyor has lost his authority over these public buildings, but not over the dental and medical schools, for by Section 8 of the Act, buildings so used are not exempt.

Nationalised industries

The Transport Act 1947, The Electricity Act 1947, and The Gas Act 1948. The Council's Solicitor's opinion on these measures is the same in all cases. It is that the newly constituted authorities will be entitled only to claim the same exemptions from the provisions of the

London Building Acts as previously enjoyed by the transferred undertakings. Crown exemptions do not apply to any properties of the Area Boards.

In 1948 a perfectly useless piece of legislation, so far as building in London was concerned, came into operation. Section 13(4) of the Statistics of Trade Act 1947 required every builder on the completion of any work for which a Building Notice was required under the London Building Acts (Amendment) Act 1939 to give to the District Surveyor a notice in writing thereof. Forms were printed for that purpose setting out particulars of the work, new building, addition or alteration and requiring a return of the estimated cost of the work (as stated on Building Notice). The estimated cost of a work is often widely different from the ultimate cost so the purpose of the declaration is difficult to appreciate. Piles of these completed forms accumulated in the District Offices to remain there unclaimed and unwanted. The collection of these forms went on until 1953 when, on the combined protests of the District Surveyors and the London Master Builders, the required returns were dropped and permission given for the destruction of the documents.

Town and Country Planning Act, 1947

The screw of Town and Country Planning turned much tighter by the passing of the Act of 1947. This Act which came into force on 1st July 1948 replaced the 1946 (General Interim Development) Order mentioned on page 131. The Act provided definitely for control over development. It allowed for payment to a landowner if the value of his land had been reduced and called for payment to the State by a development charge where land is developed. The effect of the Act was to freeze the value of land so that an owner on selling can receive only a sum based on the land when sold. A sum of three hundred million pounds was set aside for compensation and claims thereon had to be settled by the 30th June 1953. The distribution of this fund was stopped by an Act of 1953. The Act of 1954 completed the changes in law and provided for compensation under various conditions such as Compulsory Purchase or on the refusal of conditional grant of planning permission.

Consent or refusals were all couched in terms of Permission or Refusal to develop. Appeals had to be lodged with the Minister of Town and Country Planning within one month of an adverse decision. A development charge was not payable for an enlargement of a property provided the increase did not exceed one-tenth of the original building or one thousand seven hundred and fifty cubic feet, whichever was the greater, but planning permission was still necessary. It was also required for any alteration of the external appearance of a property and it even extended to the making of a new entrance or the alteration of an existing entrance from a roadway.

Under this Act coverage of sites and the regulation of the heights of buildings with their use was most definitely controlled. Consent for the change of user, even for a part only of a building, must be obtained.

The Act required the Minister to make regulations controlling the display of advertisements and they were duly issued and came into operation on 1st August 1948.

There were certain exceptions, such as advertisements displayed on vehicles. No development charge was payable on any form of advertisement. The Council delegated their control over advertisements at the end of 1948 to the Borough Councils, but without prejudice to their rights with regard to lines of frontages, buildings with excess cube, buildings coming within the Petroleum Acts and Public buildings. The above outline of this most important Planning Act is all that can be attempted in these notes. It may be added that the Act controlled the land and all that was thereon or thereunder. Its ramifications extended from historical buildings and ancient monuments to trees and woodlands.

So far as the District Surveyor in London is concerned he is still merely a reporting agent. In 1951 the Council issued Warrants to District Surveyors under Section 103 of the Act. The Warrant gives authority to enter upon land and to carry out any survey under

Parts II and III of the Act. Parts IV and VIII are also mentioned in connection with compensation under the Act. The District Surveyor now holds two Warrants the other being under Section 142, London Building Acts (Amendment) Act 1939. (see page 116). He is supplied with copies of the Local Planning Authority's permission or refusals to develop and he is expected to report on the completion of the work and to give particulars of deviations or failure to observe any conditions imposed. The most operative consents concern the lay-out of building schemes, the heights and facades of buildings for which control there is ample justification. The inclusion of items, however, such as a requirement to use boot lintols and the omission or demand for sash bars to windows are petty interferences which architects rightly resent and moreover it is extremely doubtful whether such conditions can be enforced legally. The writer has yet to hear of proceedings being taken on failure to comply with minor items of a consent to develop.

The New Constructional Bylaws 1952

New constructional Bylaws made in pursuance of the London Building Acts 1930-1939 became law on 1st January 1953.

These Bylaws contained major changes and made frequent references to British Standard Specifications and on structural matters. The timber Bylaws were incorporated and a schedule of permissible defects in timber was included. One innovation was the classification of buildings into different required periods of fire resistance according to their floor area, cubic capacity and type of use. Schedules of fire resistance were given for different types of walls, floors, steel and reinforced concrete construction, stairs, glazing and doors. Thus buildings could be designed economically to meet the expected fire risk.

Of the District Surveyors who assisted with the framing of these Bylaws mention should be made of Mr. A.L. Handley, Mr. G.M. Hall and Mr. D.D.J. Clarke for their work in collaboration with the County Hall staff. These members spent many hours of their time in a praiseworthy effort to produce a statutory instrument that would be practical and lead to sound construction while keeping in view the fundamental reasons for the Bylaws, namely the prevention and the spread of fire.

The London Building Acts 1930 and 139. Amendments

The London County Council (General Powers) Act 1954 contained important amendments to the above Acts.

This General Powers Act enacts that a building (not being a school or chapel) shall not be erected or subsequently increased to a height exceeding one hundred feet without the consent of the Council. These provisions take the place of Section 51 sub-section (1) of the 1930 Act which limited the height to eighty feet. It does not affect Section 20(i) and (ii) of the Amendment Act of 1939 by which the height is still limited to eighty feet if the area of the building exceeds ten thousand square feet.

This new permitted height of one hundred feet is to be measured independently of towers, turrets and architectural features or water tanks and lift rooms, provided these erections do not exceed ten feet in height and do not extend to more than five per cent of the area of the roof of the building.

Section 6 of this General Powers Act alters sub-section (3) of Section 30 of the London Building Act (Amendment) Act 1939 so that the temporary structures referred to, which come by size under the Borough Councils, can now be used, with a County Council consent, for the storage of inflammable materials or for human habitation. The prohibition as to uniting is also removed.

Historical events. Years 1947–1954

King George VI, who came to the throne on the abdication of his brother, King Edward VIII in 1936, died, after a long illness and a severe operation, on the 7th February 1952. He had endeared himself to his people by the trials he had shared with them over the war years. His broadcasts on Christmas Day were listened to with deep interest both at home and overseas. He was a truly democratic king and his death left a void in the heart of the nation. His mother, Queen Mary, died in March 1953.

Coronation of Queen Elizabeth II

Queen Elizabeth II was crowned on Tuesday the 2nd June 1953, and there was great rejoicing in the Metropolis. Many years have passed since England had a young and beautiful Queen in the person of Queen Victoria, who ascended the throne in 1837 at the age of eighteen, and the people in 1953 were ready to show their loyalty and pleasure in once again having a youthful Queen to reign over them. History was made when the ceremony in Westminster Abbey was televised and thousands were able to follow the ancient and impressive service in all the splendour and glory of mediaeval heraldry on the television screen in their own homes. Once again the stands on which thousands of people stood to view the procession and demonstrate their loyalty to the Queen and her husband, the Duke of Edinburgh, were surveyed and passed by a District Surveyor and his staff, and no accident resulted. The only sad event to be recorded was the grey sky and rain which, nevertheless, failed to stop the enthusiasm of the crowds lining the route. The young people were not to be cheated of their great day and with the news issued on Coronation Day of the conquest of Mount Everest, they rightly took upon themselves the title of the new Elizabethans.

At the end of 1949 two old esteemed members retired: Mr. F.W.C. Barker and Mr. T.S. Hosking. Mr. Barker had at times been a stormy petrel of the Association and he claimed the unique record of having never missed a meeting of the Association during his term of office which extended to over twenty-three years. He once told the writer that he was a cockney at heart, and he certainly loved the City of London and all its pageantry. He rejoiced in being a liveryman and he is now at the age of seventy-one the Dangerous Structure Surveyor of the City. Mr. Barker in conjunction with Mr. W.G. Perkins inaugurated the ladies evening in 1929, and for many years he had virtual control of that function.

Three existing District Surveyors, all appointed in 1926, retired in 1954: Mr. R.H. Chanter and Mr. W.G. Whincop in February, and Mr. H.E. Watkinson in August. Mr. Chanter will be remembered for a book he wrote on the Building Acts and Bylaws entitled 'London Building Law'. The book was published in 1946 and it proved to be very popular. Although he supported the Association he rarely attended the meetings for he had a dislike of speaking and of entering into the debates.

Mr. H.E. Watkinson in contrast to Mr. Chanter was rarely absent from the meetings. Appointed to the district of St. Pancras North in 1926 he retained that district until he retired and in 1946 he showed his independence by refusing the Council's invitation to take over the whole of the Borough at a meagre increase in salary. In so doing he was supporting the Association's efforts to obtain adequate remuneration for much increased responsibility. He stood by the Association on all occasions and for many years he represented the Association on the British Standards Committee. It was due to his efforts that the Index on the Acts and 1938 Bylaws was produced. (He reopened his private practice on retirement and has continued to the present day – 1972).

ADDENDUM 2

The story continued, London transformed, new legislation, association affairs. Years 1954–1972

The continued demand for copies of this book, some from far-off countries, led the Association to ask the present writer to revise it and add this addendum bringing the story of the Regulation of Building in London up-to-date.

The greatest change to occur in London's history for nearly a hundred years since its creation as a County came with the London Government Act, 1963. On the first day of April 1965 in one stroke County boundaries which had held for centuries were swept away; the whole of Middlesex and parts of Essex, Surrey and Kent were subsumed by the new County of Greater London. At the same time the old Borough boundaries were altered so as to form larger units with approximate populations of 200,000 each.

The 28 Metropolitan Boroughs in Inner London were variously amalgamated to form 12 new London Boroughs which, with the City and the 19 new London Boroughs in outer London, combined to form one of the largest local authorities in the world.

In spite of the sweeping changes made at that time in the welfare services, the Fire Brigade, the administration of the schools and the alterations in planning control no changes were made in the District Surveyor system of building control. The boundaries of their districts remained unaltered and the historic names of the old Metropolitan boroughs are now kept alive officially only in this way. The retention of the old district boundaries assisted District Surveyors to maintain their personal interest and responsibility for all jobs of consequence in their districts, a difficult task were districts to have been made much larger. However well the London Building Act works and no matter how much support and approbation it receives from builders, engineers and architects used to its operation it is inevitably regarded as a relict in the context of the larger area covered by the Building Regulations. It is accepted that eventually there should be a unified system of building control throughout the whole of England and Wales. Strenuous efforts are being made by panels of District Surveyors and Ministry officials dealing separately with corresponding Parts of the Bylaws and Building Regulations, to combine them into a National Building Code.

The White Paper on the reform of Local Government outside London, which was issued in February, 1971, stated that Building Regulation should be in the hands of the County Councils, not the Borough and District Councils which were then dealing with it. This followed the recommendations of the Association and most of the professional Institutions and was a vindication of the retention of the London system in the hands of the County Council.

However, the Bill that was placed before Parliament late in 1971 proposed that the major part of the work of building control should be done by District Councils and it appears that this change was made for political reasons, not out of concern for efficient building control. Strong opposition has been voiced to this Bill and it seems wrong that the smooth-running organisation of the building control departments of major cities such as Manchester, Birmingham, Liverpool and Sheffield should be fragmented. It is hoped that the Bill will be amended to provide for integrated building control, possibly on the London pattern, in all the major conurbations. The apparent anomaly of the existence of a different system of regulation in Inner London from that in the remainder of England and Wales has now subsisted for many years. The advantages that accrue to this concentrated urban environment from the more intensive and meticulous system could equally well be enjoyed by other such urban areas. The extra cost of setting up and maintaining such a system could be met by a similar method of collection of fees on each job supervised. The rise in the status of building regulation officers would not be achieved however, without proper training and without recognised essential qualifications in this science, both of which are sadly lacking today in this Country.

London's transformation

As London has been transformed geographically so has it been transformed visually. For centuries its skyline had retained its mediaeval character with the sharp fingers of spires and steeples thrusting above the flat and smoky townscape. Now the smoke has gone, the public buildings look sharp and unfamiliar with newly washed faces and above all, above the steeples, above St. Paul's, rise the great tower blocks. These monuments to the 20th century rise year by year ever taller. First the Vickers Tower with sides of shining glass and stainless steel nearly 380 feet high then in rapid succession the Post Office tower of 600 feet and the 'umbrella' blocks with floors suspended from the perimeter of a cantilevered cap at more than 400 feet above ground level. Now a start has been made on a building nearly twice the height of St. Paul's for which the long-used and faithful 'London Clay' will not be adequate as a foundation.

Yet another part of the transformation is the immense amount of traffic and the consequent draconian restrictions on parking. This has led to some District Surveyors in Central London abandoning the use of a car altogether in getting about their districts. It must be recorded with regret that the Association's Secretary had his car stolen last year, losing irreplaceable minutes of association meetings also the President's ivory gavel, presented by Mr. Grellier, happily this was well insured.

In this period also there was a major political change. The London County Council for 33 years a Socialist stronghold became strongly Conservative with the first elections after the creation of Greater London. This has brought many alterations in administration; the creation of the office of Director General of the Council, a post first filled by Mr. A.W. Peterson; the taking over of the London Transport Executive and the appointment of its new Chairman, Sir Richard Way, and the reshaping of Council Departments. Newly formed ones include the Departments of 'Architecture and Civic Design', 'Public Health Engineering', 'Mechanical and Electrical Engineering' and 'Planning and Transportation' also the 'Inner London Education Authority'.

The offices of Superintending Architect and Architect to the Council are still combined; since the departures of Sir Robert Matthew in 1953 and of Dr. Martin in 1956 these offices were held by Sir Hubert Bennett, who received his Knighthood in the 1970 New Years Honours list. He retired in January 1971 and was replaced by Sir Roger Walters, who was previously in the Ministry the Environment.

New bylaws

The rapid advances in techniques of building construction, the advent of new materials and new methods of heating buildings necessitated a constant review of the building bylaws and drafting panels, on which many District Surveyors served, were constantly at work. It proved to be impossible to get Ministerial approval to the proposed bylaws on the height of rooms, so Part XI of the 1952 bylaws was allowed to remain in force (except for the bylaw dealing with roof coverings) and the remainder were repealed. It was for this reason that the new bylaws appeared in two parts, The London Building (Constructional) Bylaws No. 1 1964, which replaced the old bylaws Parts I to X (and to which was added a new part dealing with oil fired heating installations) and the London Building (Constructional) Bylaws No. 2 1964 which replaced the bylaw in Part XI of the 1952 Bylaws which had dealt with roof coverings. The somewhat unsatisfactory position that then arose of having three sets of bylaws was ameliorated by the publication of all three in one volume (Publication No. 156 price 5/3d). The trend in the new bylaws was to come into step with British Standards and Codes of Practice; quoting standards it was possible to shorten some Parts. This applied particularly in Part 8 (structural steelwork) where BSS 449 and its addendum were adopted entirely and, although Part 9 (Reinforced Concrete) was freshly worded throughout, it was similar in content to the Code of Practice (114) for reinforced concrete. The section of Part 7 (walls) dealing with the design of walls and piers by calculation was also similar to the Code of Practice (111) for load bearing walls. As Codes of Practice were not mandatory in wording it was considered that it was not possible to enforce these at law, however, Part 10, which dealt with construction in timber was hardly altered from the pre-war timber bylaws and was not in keeping with modern timber engineering so the Council now freely waives these bylaws, and allows timber to be designed in accordance with the Code of Practice 112. The new Part 13 dealt with oil-fired heating equipment in great detail and, although it was gradually found that there were some weaknesses and anomalies in the drafting, it preserved a good balance between safety and economy and allowed exemptions in the case of small installations. This Part of the Bylaws has been used as a guide outside Inner London, there being no comparable regulations elsewhere in this country.

Following reports of the brittle fracture of structural steel in the King's Bridge in Melbourne, Australia, and the discovery of the same phenomenon in a building under erection in the City, a new Bylaw was introduced in 1967. This enabled District Surveyors to require impact-testing of tension members in structural steelwork which are to be welded and which may be exposed to low temperatures or which are otherwise vulnerable to this type of failure.

Further Bylaws came into force in 1970 dealing with wind loading and with the overloading of buildings due to explosion and other similar causes. They provided for parts of buildings of 5 or more storeys to be designed to withstand "accidental" loading very considerably higher than anything previously envisaged; or alternatively such buildings had to be designed to bridge over damaged areas and not to collapse progressively.

A detailed explanatory memorandum was prepared by members of the Association in conjunction with the Council's Structural Engineer and this was recognised by the construction industry generally as a most useful guide.

It is inevitable that there must always be a large volume of applications for waivers or modifications of bylaws whatever their form or however they are drafted. Once it became clear which bylaw modifications were the most frequently sought, authority was given to the District Surveyors to issue many of these on behalf of the Council. This system, which resulted in a great saving of time and administrative expense, was extended to cover the issue of Consents under Sections of the London Building Acts (e.g. for temporary structures used as conservatories and external flue pipes and ducts.) The following is a list of modifications and Consents which District Surveyors can issue.

London Building Act 1930

Section 54	Raising of buildings

London Building Acts (Amendment) Act 1939

Section 17	Openings in party walls
Section 18	Position of bay windows
Section 21	Uniting of buildings, doors of special construction, roller shutters in lieu of solid steel doors

Section 30	Temporary conservatories, projecting shelters, flue pipes and ducts.
Section 37	Omission of roof escape.
Section 132	Restoration of Listed buildings.
Section 134	Retention of sub-standard fire separations between parts of buildings in different occupation.
1952 Bylaws	
11.02	Timber porches, landings and steps.
11.03	Permanent ventilation (reduction from 20 sq.in. to 3 sq.in. and its omission in offices)
	Reduced ceiling heights in habitable rooms.
1964 Bylaws	
4.02 } 4.07	Lightweight aggregates for reinforced concrete.
4.07	Aerated reinforced concrete floor and roof units.
4.08	Star shaped high tensile reinforcement.
4.08	Use of reinforcement to BSS 785 (1967) and BSS 1144 (1967)
4.12	Wood particle blocks
7.08	4″ walls between garages and stores
8.02	Galvanised steel lintels
9.03/.04/.05/ } .07/.09/.18	Lightweight aggregates for reinforced concrete
9.04 } 9.07	Star shaped high tensile reinforcement
9.14	Shear reinforcement in beams
9.20	Use of prestressed concrete
10.01/.02/.03/.04/ } .05/.06/.08/.09	Design of structural timber as CP112 (1967)
11.01	Glass in party walls between porches
11.03 } 11.12	Retention of sub-standard floors, stairs and separations
11.07	Use of steel fire curtains instead of solid steel dampers
12.03	Flue pipes of asbestos within 6′ of appliance
	Flue pipes through separate rooms
12.12	Hearths of reduced size
13.02	Application of BSS 799 Part II 1964
13.04	Omission of threshold and floor treatment
13.05	Reduction of ventilation requirement for small boilers
13.06	Use of room containing oil burning appliance for other purposes
13.08	Single 2-hour fire door instead of double for oil storage rooms

New General Powers Act

The London County Council (General Powers) Act 1954 clarified the position regarding temporary structures united to permanent buildings and extended from 1 month to 2 months the time limit for the Council's consideration of means of escape proposals.

The London County Council (General Powers) Act 1955 made revisions to the scale of fees and repealed the prohibitions on sky signs and flags.

The London County Council (General Powers) Act 1956 required fresh building notice to be given where work has been suspended for more than 3 months.

The London County Council (General Powers) Act 1958 authorised the Council to transfer to the Borough Councils the administration of dangerous structures and some Planning functions.

The London County Council (General Powers) Act 1959 dealt with the storage of containers at Covent Garden and gave the Boroughs power to deal with moveable dwellings, to make requirements for refuse storage and for the provision of lavatories at places of entertainment.

The Greater London Council (General Powers) Act 1965 required an estimate of the cost of work to be given on all building notices and altered the basis of fees for services given by District Surveyors – these were now to be based only on the cost of work done, regardless of the cubical extent of the building. (In these days of searching enquiry on the justification of professional scales of fees it is worthy of note that, for checking the design and calculations, for supervising the erection of the building at all stages and for checking all the relevant consents the fee payable on this Scale approximates to 0.15% of the cost of the structural work or, say, .05% of the total cost of the erection of the building). The fees chargeable are £3 on the first £100 of the cost of the work supervised plus 75p per £100 thereafter up to a cost of £1,000 then at the rate of 25p per £100 up to a cost of £5,000 and 15p per £100 thereafter.

The Greater London Council (General Powers) Act 1966 extended the Council's powers to deal with places of entertainment and it introduced penalties for allowing excavations within 30 feet of highways to collapse if the use of the highway has to be restricted and for any accident on construction or repair or demolition work resulting in a risk of injury to persons. In these cases the owner is held liable unless he can prove others responsible.

The Greater London Council (General Powers) Act, 1968 repealed Section 127 of the London Building Acts (Amendment) Act, 1939 – (storage of timber and other inflammable materials) – and Sections 15 to 25 of this Act were substituted for it. These strengthened the Council's powers to deal with bulk storage of such materials and appointed the London Fire Brigade to administer them. It also dealt with "night cafes" i.e. places of refreshment open after 11 p.m. and enabled the Council to require improved escape and fire-fighting precautions.

To clarify the present legislative position a list of the current London Building Acts and Bylaws follows:–

1. **Bylaws** made in 1914 under powers conferred by the London Building Act 1894 (Section 164) regulating lamps, signs and other structures overhanging the public way (not in force in the City of London).
2. **London Building Act 1930.** Repealed except for Parts 1 (definitions), V (open spaces about buildings and heights of buildings), XI (Dangerous and noxious businesses), and XII (Dwelling houses on low-lying land).
3. **Bylaws** (Drainage) made in 1934 under powers conferred by the Metropolis Management Acts of 1855 and 1899, Administered by Public Health Officers of the Borough Councils.
4. **London Building Act (Amendment) Act 1935.** This gives the County Council the power to make Bylaws, to modify or waive them and to attach conditions to such waivers.
5. **London Building Acts (Amendment) Act 1939.** The main Act today. Part VIII (skysigns) has been repealed, also Sections 127 (stacks of flammable material), 128 and 129 (Highways), 130 and 131 (Projections over streets).
6. **The London Building (Constructional) Bylaws 1952.** Repealed except for Bylaws 11.02 (Projections from buildings), 11.03 (Height, lighting and ventilation of offices and habitable rooms) and 11.04 (Floors over passages).
7. **The London Building (Constructional) Amending Bylaws No. 1 1964** (The main Bylaws).
8. **The London Building (Constructional) Amending Bylaws No. 2 1964** (Roof coverings).

9. **London Building (Constructional) Amending Bylaws 1966.** This replaced Bylaw 2.05 of (7) above and deals with the problem of "brittle fracture" in steel.
10. **London Building (Constructional) Amending Bylaws 1970.** This replaces Bylaw 2.06 of (7) above and deals with increased wind loading and strengthening buildings against accidental failure.

No account of this period, however brief, could exclude reference to Ronan Point. The partial collapse of this block of flats in the Borough of Newham in Outer London following a gas explosion in May 1968 and the subsequent Tribunal's report led to the greatest flood of publicity and technical argument, both on the emotional and factual levels, ever to attend a structural failure.

Similarly-designed blocks had been erected in several parts of Inner London but District Surveyors had obtained stronger connections between the precast floors and walls. The requirements of the London Bylaws concerning wind loading on buildings, based upon an assumed wind speed of 54 m.p.h., had for some time seemed inadequate to the members of the Association and their concern was found to be justified by the publication later in 1968 of reports by the Building Research Station suggesting that much higher wind speeds should be catered for.

Recommendations by the tribunal, by the Minister and by the Institution of Structural Engineers led to strengthening work against explosion and higher wind loading being carried out on blocks of flats all over the country and, in 1970, to the issue of amended Building Regulations and an amended London Bylaw.

The effects of the incident have been strongly marked in the field of planning where, under pressure from public opinion, many schemes for high-rise flats have been altered to houses and low-rise flats.

In the period before the publication of the new Bylaw District Surveyors were frequently called upon by engineers and developers to advise upon the design of future buildings amidst a maze of conflicting recommendations from all quarters.

Building Regulations 1965

In place of the multiplicity of bylaws adopted by the 1400 different local authorities in England and Wales, uniformity was imposed by the Public Health Act 1961. The field which could be covered was, however, limited to that authorised by the Public Health Act of 1936. Waivers of the important Regulations in Parts D and E dealing with structural safety and fire precautions could only be given by the Minister. The local authority could give others and, where they refused to do so, an appeal could be made against their decision to the Minister. The procedure for making waiver applications was slower and more complex than that under the London Building Acts and the expense of advertising such applications in the Press was a deterrent. Seven Amendments have now been made to the Building Regulations relaxing some of the original requirements and permitting local authorities to grant waivers in additional cases. Possibly the chief advantages possessed by the Building Regulations over the London Bylaws are that they deal with thermal and sound insulation and they include the drainage regulations in the same document. They are at a disadvantage, however, in not dealing with oil-fired installations or with means of escape in case of fire and they are over-complicated in dealing with unprotected areas (i.e. windows and thin sheet enclosures) and with the access of natural light to windows.

Contact is maintained between the Ministry officials responsible for the regulations and District Surveyors by the appointment of a District Surveyor to the Building Regulations Advisory Committee set up by the Minister to advise him on the operation of the Regulations and the amendments which are made from time to time.

Other new legislation affecting building in London follows in alphabetical order.

Clean Air Act, 1956

This piece of simple legislation has had a profound effect upon the customs, appearance and economics of the country generally and particularly of the towns.

The 1952 Bylaws were amended to prevent the installation in any new London building of all fires or cooking appliances except those properly designed to use gas, electricity, coke or anthracite.

Existing appliances which produced smoke were progressively banned as Smoke Control Orders were made by Local Authorities under this Act. As these Orders were made Grants were paid to occupiers who installed approved heating appliances and District Surveyors were inundated with the work of supervising thousands of these operations.

Fire Precautions Act 1971

This Act, which came into operation on 20th March 1972, widens the variety of buildings for which an approved means of escape must be provided. It takes precedence over Section 35 of the London Building Acts (Amendment) Act, 1939; it can require the occupier or the owner or the 'manager' of the premises to make application for a Fire Certificate and to give full plans of the premises concerned. A certificate can restrict the use to which a building can be put, can require structural alterations to be made, fire fighting training to be given to personnel and it can limit the number of persons allowed into a building.

The first category of buildings to be dealt with after 1st June 1972 is hotels and boarding houses (with more than six boarders). By this date every such establishment must either possess a Fire Certificate or must have applied for one. At later dates, yet to be announced, other categories of buildings, such as flats, will be dealt with similarly.

In Greater London the Fire Authority administering this Act is the Greater London Council and it is likely that the work will be shared between the Fire Brigade Department and the Building Regulations Division of the Department of Architecture and Civic Design.

Gaming Act 1968

The Greater London Council, as the Fire Authority for Greater London, may make requirements under the Gaming Act on any premises used for gaming e.g. Bingo Clubs and Casinos.

These can deal with means of escape in case of fire, the flammability of surfaces of walls etc. and the safety of electrical installations.

Gas Regulations

These regulations, made under the London Gas Undertakings (Regulations) Act 1939, came into force in 1955; where they overlapped the requirements of bylaws in Part 12 of the London Building (Constructional) Bylaws No. 1 1964 they took precedence. It was the duty of the Gas Boards to see that they were complied with as regards the gas equipment but all structural matters arising continued to be dealt with by District Surveyors.

Highways Act 1959

When this Act first came into force it did not apply to the then County of London but, with the passing of the London Government Act 1963 and the repeal of Parts 2 and 3 of the London Building Act 1930, it became applicable to the old London County Council area (now referred to as the "Inner London" part of Greater London).

All matters concerning building lines and projections from buildings are now dealt with by the "Highway Authority". (London Borough Councils in the case of lesser roads and the Greater London Council in the case of "Metropolitan Roads".) Metropolitan roads are shown on a map approved by the Minister of Transport and are main traffic routes in and out of London.

Although District Surveyors still give advice upon building lines they no longer have the duty of certifying plans for the re-erection of buildings less than the prescribed distance from the centre of highways. In effect the control of frontages has now largely passed into the hands of the Town Planning Departments of the Authorities concerned.

The Highways Act introduces a siting restriction new to London, Section 75 prevents the erection or bringing-forward of a building or an addition to the building beyond the line of the front main wall of the building on either side. This prevents an owner building up to the general line of buildings if one of the adjoining buildings is sited behind the line (unless he obtains the consent of the Highway Authority).

Housing Acts

Several Housing Acts were passed in this period but only one Section affected the work of District Surveyors, Section 16 of the 1961 Act. This dealt with means of escape in case of fire from houses in multiple occupation and brought under control some buildings which could not be dealt with under Section 35 of the London Building Acts (Amendment) Act, 1939. Local Authorities were empowered to serve Notices on persons having control of such houses requiring them to carry out work to improve the sanitary condition and/or means of escape. Should the work not be done the Authority could enter the premises and carry out the work at the owner's expense. A Code of Practice for means of escape in case of fire was drawn up by the Greater London Council and the London Boroughs agreed to observe this in making requirements. (Publication 88) Work done under this Act is not supervised by the District Surveyor except in the cases where structural alterations are involved. Where requirements can be made under both the Housing Act and the London Building Act it is usual to use the Housing Act as the powers in this Act are wider. In most Boroughs the details of work to be done are drawn up by the Public Health Inspectors.

Offices, Shops and Railway Premises Act 1963

This Act deals with amenities and means of escape in case of fire in the premises named and requires **certified** means of escape to be provided in very similar cases to those listed in Section 34 of the London Building Acts (Amendment) Act, 1939. It did, however, also require **all** offices, shops etc. to have an "adequate" means of escape for employees and anyone else on the premises. This greatly increased the volume of means of escape checking work for District Surveyors who became "Inspectors" under the Act and led to the formation of a special section in the Architect's Department of the Council for the formulation of requirements based on a Code of Practice issued by the Council.

Post Office Act 1969

Under this Act the Post Office ceased to be a Government Department and became a Public Authority not enjoying any exemption under the London Building Acts. All new building work commenced after 1st April 1970 became subject to the jurisdiction of District Surveyors.

Temporary structures

One of the changes wrought by the delegation agreement of 1965 (made under powers given to the G.L.C. in the London Government Act 1963) was that the London Borough Councils were authorised to act on behalf of the County Council in giving Consents for structures up to 500 sq.feet in area and up to 10 feet in height. This tended to increase the work of District Surveyors, who were made responsible for the structural stability of such structures, a task previously carried out by the Structural Engineering Division of the Council.

Thermal Insulation of Industrial Buildings Act 1957

The effect of this Act and of the Regulations made under it in 1958 was to require all industrial buildings or additions to them to have a high standard of roof insulation (u = 0.3) unless the building was to be an unheated one or was a boiler house or building with waste process heat. Further, the insulation had to have a low rate of flame spread (Class 1 to BSS 476) unless it was protected and could not enhance the risk of fire starting or spreading. District Surveyors had the duty placed on them of ensuring that the roofs of such buildings or additions complied with these Regulations. An application for the approval of the insulation of any new roof of an industrial building has to be made to the Council, alternatively an application may be made for formal exemption.

Town and Country Planning Acts

New acts appeared in 1953, '54 and '59, these were concerned mainly with the questions of 'betterment' and compensation and they were, with the earlier acts of 1944 and 1947 consolidated in the Act of 1962. In 1959, under the London County Council (General Powers) Act 1958 a delegation agreement was made between the County Council and the then Metropolitan Borough Councils for the transfer of some Town Planning and Building Act functions including the administration of dangerous structures work. The major part of Town Planning and Building Act work remained with the County Council, however, until the passing of the London Government Act 1963. This effectively transferred the vast majority of planning control work to the Boroughs. Applications for major developments e.g. areas of comprehensive redevelopment, new rail, bus or air terminals and new universities and large concert halls continued to be dealt with by the County Council. In some other cases where the Boroughs wished to give approval they had to refer the case to the County Council for a direction e.g. shops over 250,000 square feet, buildings over 150 feet in height, industrial buildings of more than 5,000 square feet or offices more than 2,500 square feet, development within 220 feet of a metropolitan road or within 110 feet of a railway station or within the Green Belt, also alterations to buildings of architectural or historic interest and any other development involving a departure from the London Development Plan.

The highly controversial Control of Office and Industrial Development Act, 1965 sought to divert developers and the building industry away from the lucrative creation of office and industrial buildings in London and other prosperous areas. These could not be built to a greater extent than 3,000 and 5,000 sq. feet respectively without a Certificate from the Board of Trade and there was no machinery for appeal against a refusal nor was there any compensation for a refusal. The Civic Amenities Act 1967 strengthened the powers of local authorities regarding buildings of architectural or historic interest, the improper removal of protected trees and the depositing of refuse and derelict cars. The creation of conservation areas under this act enabled whole streets and districts to be preserved and improved.

The Town and Country Planning Act 1968 placed a time limit of 5 years on the validity of all permissions issued before the Act without time limits. These would therefore expire in 1973. It placed a similar limit on all new Permissions of 5 years from the date of issue. The Minister was empowered to appoint any person to decide appeals (e.g. the Inspector at the hearing) Local authorities were empowered to serve "Building Preservation Orders" (on unlisted buildings of architectural or historic interest) with immediate effect and without the approval of the Minister. District Surveyors continued to play an important part in planning control in reporting to the Planning Authority, generally the London Borough Council, any development carried out without Permission or contrary to conditions attached to permissions. This service, given to the Borough councils since they took over as Planning Authorities from the Council, was vital for planning record purposes as the District Surveyor was the only authority to whom Notice must be given for all alterations or changes of use of buildings.

Association affairs

One of the most important functions of the Association is the traditional Question Time at 5.0 p.m. when matters of interpretation of the Building Acts or By-laws are discussed, also the technical merits of new forms of construction or new materials.

The results of these discussions were readily made available to all members by issuing them in loose-leaf form since January 1966 and these 'Recorded Questions' now form a valuable reference to decisions taken over a wide variety of matters.

At a reception held at the Savoy Hotel in November 1967 the Association celebrated the tercentenary of the first appointment of Statutory Surveyors which followed upon the Great Fire of 1666.

More than a hundred and thirty distinguished guests attended, including representatives of the Government, of the City and other local authorities and of all the Professional Institutions and the Press. A specially printed and illustrated history of London District Surveyors was presented to each guest and there was a display of historical documents relating to the Building Act of 1667. The expenses of the event were met by the District Surveyors personally and not by the Association.

One of the most outstanding examples of service to the Association was noted in 1968 by the presentation of a silver salver to Mr. J. Dufton to mark their appreciation of his 6 years work as Secretary during a period when there were many important negotiations in progress.

Sir Hubert Bennett, as Superintending Architect, attended a meeting of the Association in 1970. It was pointed out by the President that this was his second visit and that no other Superintending Architect had previously been to a meeting of the Association. Sir Hubert spoke of the future of building control in London and congratulated the District Surveyors present on the fact that, although they dealt with thousands of jobs annually, the number of disputes or appeals that reached him concerning their decisions was infinitesimal.

He made a farewell visit to the January 1971 meeting of the Association when he was presented with a silver salver to mark the cordial relationship which had existed since his appointment in 1965. His successor, Sir Roger Walters, made a formal visit to a meeting of the Association within a few months of taking office and showed great interest in all matters affecting members' work and problems.

Their chief concern was the lack of sufficient numbers of qualified and experienced assistants, without which they felt that it was impossible to maintain adequate supervision of the increasing volume and complexity of building operations.

They appreciated that the necessary extra staff could not be obtained without an increased financial allocation from the Rates or an increase in the scale of fees chargeable under the London Building Acts.

The former method being ruled out by the Council's stringent 'ceiling' on Building Regulation costs, Members pressed for an alteration in the fee scales on this and subsequent occasions.

The fees charged at present on average-size new buildings are only about 1/6th of one per cent of the cost of the structural work and this pays for nearly half of the cost of the District Surveying Service. That owners and developers are willing to pay the small extra sum concerned to obtain high quality independent supervision of structural work on their buildings is evident from the studies that have been made on building control systems abroad where, in many countries, fees of about one per cent of the cost of structural work are normal.

The graph in Chapter VII has been brought up to date to show the fees collected by District Surveyors for services performed under the London Building Act. By the time of publication of this book these fees will be well in excess of £400,000 per annum.

The cost of the Council's entire Building Regulation Division dealing with the London Building Acts, including Middlesex House staff as well as District Surveyors has risen from £860,000 p.a. in 1965 to about £1,400,000 p.a. today. Of this the cost of District Surveyors offices and staff etc. is approximately £860,000.

District Surveyors and their Districts 1954–1970

The numbers of Districts remained constant at 28 in spite of the major upheaval of the London Government Act of 1963 and the advocacy for the amalgamation of Districts to Borough size.

When the new London Boroughs were formed some anomalies were created – part of the district of Wandsworth came into the new Borough of Lambeth and the small part of Woolwich which lay north of the Thames was given up to the Borough of Newham.

There were two changes of grading; Battersea previously a 'grade III' district became 'grade II' and Lambeth, previously a 'grade I' district became 'grade I plus' on taking over from Wandsworth District the areas of Streatham and part of Clapham.

The number of Assistant District Surveyors was increased from 17 to 22 with the creation of the higher rank of Senior Assistant District Surveyor. The Assistant District Surveyors formed their own association in 1963 and have since met frequently, giving assistance and support on many occasions to the District Surveyors' Association.

Acknowledgements are made to the following:–

The Making of London. London (1837–1897). Sir Laurence Gomme.
Annals of S. Paul's Cathedral. Henry Hart Milman, D.D.
Mediaeval London, Sir Walter Besant.
The Growth of Stuart London. Norman G. Brett James.
London Life in the XVIII Century. M. Dorothy George.
The Rebuilding of London after the Great Fire. T.F. Reddaway
London, the Unique City. Steen-Eiler Rasmussen.
Historical Account of the Worshipful Company of Carpenters. Edward Basil Jupp.
A History of England. Cyril E. Robinson.
Century of Science, 1840–1940. F. Sherwood Taylor.
The Government and Misgovernment of London. William A. Robson
The Sanitary Evolution of London. Henry Jephson.
History of the London County Council 1889–1939. Sir Gwilym Gibbon and Reginald W. Bell.
The London Building Acts. Bernard Dicksee.
The War in Pictures (Second Year). Odhams Press Limited.
London Building Law. H.C. Chanter
The Building Regulations. Kennard & Dufton (Butterworth)

The Guildhall Library and the Members' Library of the GLC are thanked for supplying some of the illustrations.

The views expressed in this book are those of the writers and not necessarily those of the Greater London Council.

APPENDIX

Key to Appendix

	Page
Incomes of District Surveyors under the Building Act of 1844	151
District Surveyors appointed by the Lord Mayor and Aldermen within the City and by the Justices of the Peace outside the City under the Act of 1774 – (1774 to Sept. 1844)	152
District Surveyors appointed by the Lord Mayor and Aldermen within the City and by the Justices of the Peace outside the City under the act of 1844 – (1844-1856) ...	153
District Surveyors appointed by The Metropolitan Board of Works under the Act of 1855 – (during the years of 1856-1889)	154
District Surveyors appointed by the London County Council – (1890-1939)	155
District Surveyors appointed by the London County Council as Officers of the Council – (1939-1964)	156
District Surveyors appointed by the Greater London Council as Officials of the Council after 1964	157
Officers of Association from New Constitution in 1884	157

Incomes of District Surveyors under the Building Act of 1844

The returns of works surveyed, as made by the Surveyors under the Act of 1844, were filed and bound into volumes at the Office of Metropolitan Buildings, 6 Adelphi Terrace, Strand. It did not appear to be the practice then to compile annual abstracts giving yearly incomes so this information is not available. In the Spring of 1853, however, Lord Robert Grosvenor moved a motion in the House of Commons for a return to the House of the amount of fees received yearly for each of the districts in Middlesex. The information required was for five years commencing with 1848, and a volume numbered 306 containing a record of this return is kept with the monthly returns mentioned above in the Record Room at County Hall. The average income for each of these districts is given in the Table below.

Average incomes over the five years 1848 to 1853

Surveyor	District	Amount
J.B. Redman	Tower Liberty	£ 44
E.C. Hakewell	Covent Garden	84
W. Lovell	Stoke Newington	86
S. Angell	Saffron Hill	90
G. Legg	Holborn	108
C.H. Hill	Spitalfields	127
H. Flower	St. George in the East	162
R.C. Carpenter	St. Luke, Old Street	179
J.H. Taylor	Tottenham	183
A. Moseley	Fulham	189
R. Parkinson	Hornsey	212
C. Mayhew	St. James, Hanover Square	240
G. Pownall	St. Giles, Bloomsbury	246

Average incomes over the five years 1848 to 1853 (cont.)

Surveyor	District	Amount
R. Sibley	Clerkenwell	£264
W. Grellier, d. Jan. 1852		
H. Oliver, appt. 1852	Whitechapel	281
H.E. Kendall	St. Martin and Soho	289
J. Blythe	Bromley	299
E. Woodthorpe	Limehouse	300
H.E. Kendall Jnr.	Hampstead	365
J. Howell	St. Margaret and St. John	394
J.H. White	St. Marylebone, North	394
J. Jennings	St. Marylebone, South	394
J.C. Christopher	Hammersmith	416
J.H.Good, Jnr.	Bow and Poplar	452
E.N. Clifton	Bethnal Green	490
J. Davies	Mile End, Old Town	505
T.L. Donaldson	Kensington South	532
S. Beachcroft	Chelsea	568
C. Beachcroft	Kensington North	706
E.M.Foxall	St. George, Hanover Square	757
G. Gutch, ...	Paddington	807
T.H. Wyatt	Hackney	843
R. Warton	Shoreditch and Folgate	881
H. Baker	St. Pancras	1403
G. Edwards d. 1853	Islington and St. Sepulchre	1482

(The amounts are given to the nearest pound)

District Surveyors appointed by the Lord Mayor and Aldermen within the City and by the Justices of the Peace outside the City under the Act of 1774
1774 to Sept. 1844
(This list may not be complete)

Name of Surveyor	Appointed	Died or Retired	Name of Surveyor	Appointed	Died or Retired
Acton, S.	1806		Dade	-+	- +
Angell, S.	1831	1854 r	Davies, J.	1839	1865 d
Baker, H.	1825		Delight, E.	+	
Baker, J.		1878 d	Donaldson, J.	1809	
Beachcroft, S.	1825	1861 d	Drake	+	
Beazley, C.	+		Edwards, G.	1802	1853 d
Bunning, B.J.	1832		Flower, H.J.	1836	
Carpenter, R.C.	1837	1855 d	Foxhall, E.M.	1827	1858 r
Chapman	– +		Gibson	+	
Cliften, E.N.	1844	1861 r	Goff	†	
Cockerell, S.P.	+		Goff, M.	1817	
Cook	+		Golden	+	
Cotes	+		Goldicutt, J.	1828	
Craig, C.A.	+1774		Good, J.H.Jnr.	1838	1878 r
Croshaw	+		Grellier, W.	1838	1852 d
Crunden	+1774		Gutch, G.	1825	1874 d

District Surveyor appointed by the Lord Mayor and Aldermen within the City and by the Justices of the Peace outside the City under the Act of 1774
1774 to Sept. 1844 (cont.)

Name of Surveyor	Appointed	Died or Retired	Name of Surveyor	Appointed	Died or Retired
Hakewell, E.C.	1843	1867 r	Redman, J.B.	+1843	
Hele	+		Reynolds	– +	
Hesketh, R.	1842	1880 d	Robinson	+	
Hill, C.H.			Rogers	+	
Jagger	– +		Rogers, W.	1833	1858 d
Jupp, W.	1800		Roper, D.R.		
Kendall, H.E.			Roper, D.Jnr.	1826	1875 r
Kinnard, W.	1807		Scott, G.	+	
Legg, G.	1844	1882 d	Sibley, G.	1829	
Mason	†		Sibley, R.L.	1829	1849 d
Matthews, C.J.	1832		Smith, G.	1810	
Mayhew, J.G.	1823		Stevens, J.	1843	1857 d
Meredith	†		Stokes	– +	
Maymott	+		Stow, W.C.	1834	1859 d
Maymott, W.G. Jnr.	†1793		Tyrell, C.	1828	
Middleton	+		Ward	+	
Montague, A.W.	1808		Warton, M. (Wharton)	1802	1846 r
Montague, J.	1821		Warton, M. Jnr.	1825	
Oldham, E.			White, J.A.	1807	1851 d
Pilkington, R.W.	+1785		Wilmot	+	
Plumridge, Jnr.	†		Woodthorpe, E.	1839	1887 d
Porter, G.	1824		Wright	+	
Pownall, G.	1840	1855 r	Wyatt, T.H.	1832	1861 r
Powsey	+				

+ These Surveyors are mentioned in an edition of the 1774 Act printed at Cambridge in 1791. They were holding office in that year and those marked in addition - died or retired between 1791 and 1796 their places being taken by those marked † whose names appear in an edition of the Cambridge Book published in 1796. In both years 1791 and 1796 twenty-seven Surveyors were acting.

District Surveyors appointed by the Lord Mayor and Aldermen within the City and by the Justices of the Peace outside the City under the act of 1844
1844–1856

Name of Surveyor	Appointed	Died or Retired	Name of Surveyor	Appointed	Died or Retired
Aitchison, G.	1844.	1861 d	Beachcroft, C.	1844	1866 d
Allen, G.	1844	1847 d	Blyth, J.	1844	1874 r
Badger, C.R.	1844	1863 r	Brown, R.P.	1844	1872 d
Bartholomew, A.	1844		Christopher, J.C.	1844	1854 d

District Surveyors appointed by the Lord Mayor and Aldermen within the City and by the Justices of the Peace outside the City under the act of 1844
1844–1856 (cont.)

Name of Surveyor	Appointed	Died or Retired	Name of Surveyor	Appointed	Died or Retired
Collis, J.	1844	1886 d	Moseley, A.	1844	1898 r
Donaldson, T.L.	1844	1885 d	Moseley, J.	1853	1880 d
Fowler, C.	1855	1892 r	Mullins, J.	1844	1880 d
Garland, R.	1854	1863 d	Oliver, H.	1852	1891 d
Godwin, G.	1853	1874 r	Porter, F.W.	1854	1901 d
Hammon, J.H.	1853	1892 d	Parkinson, R.	1845	1885 d
Hiscocks, A.J.	1844	1881 d	Sibley, R.L.	1849	1882 d
Howell, J.	1848	1866 d	Snooke, W.	1847	1883 d
I'Anson, E.	1844	1888 d	Taylor, J.H.	1844	1867 d
Jennings, J.	1851	1889 d	Turner, J.	1855	1890 d
Kendal, H.E. Jnr.	1844	1885 d	Wharton, R.	1846	1871 r
			Whichcord, J.	1855	1885 d
Lovell, W.	1844	1874 d	White, J.A.	1851	1858 r
Martyr, R.S.	1844	1854 d	Young, J.	1853	1877 d
Mayhew, C.	1845	1861 r			

District Surveyors appointed by The Metropolitan Board of Works under the Act of 1855 during the years of 1856–1889

Name of Surveyor	Appointed	Died or Retired	Name of Surveyor	Appointed	Died or Retired
Ashbridge, A.	1885	1918 r	Clarkson, S.F.	1886	1910 r
Aitchison, G.	1861	1910 d	Coats, W.	1867	1885 r
Badger, C.J. (deputy)	1863		Collins, H.H.	1877	1905 d
			Conder, A.	1882	1915 r
Bannister-Fletcher, F.	1875	1899 d	Dale, D.R.	1880	1907 r
			Dru-Drury, E.	1870	1916 r
Barnes-Williams, G.	1856	1887 d	Edmeston, J.S.	1887	1887 d
			Elkington, G.	1884	1902 r
Barnes-Williams, T.	1880	1900 r	Field, H.	1862	1879 d
			Foulsham, C.	1874	1904 d
Barnet, J.	1858	1866 r	Gould, C.A.	1875	1879 d
Batterbury, T.	1887	1922 d	Grellier, W.	1888	1931 r
Bell, R.	1867		Grose, V.J.	1878	1912 r
Billing, J.	1857	1862 d	Gundry, H.	1874	1900 d
Blashill, T.	1876	1887 r	Hammond, F.	1880	1919 d
Bovill, A.	1878	1893 r	Hansom, H.J.	1867	1901 r
Caritt, E.	1882	1908 d	Hart, H.	1867	1903 d
Cheston, H.	1888	1917 r	Hardcastle, W.J.	1888	1925 r
Clarkson, J.	1878	1915 r	Hayward, C.F.	1871	1905 d

District Surveyors appointed by The Metropolitan Board of Works under the Act of 1855 during the years of 1856–1889 (cont.)

Name of Surveyor	Appointed	Died or Retired	Name of Surveyor	Appointed	Died or Retired
Hewitt, E.R.	1882	1915 d	Payne, A.	1880	1914 r
Hunter, P.	1884	1916 r	Peebles, A.	1867	1887 r
James, R.C.	1876	1876 d	Plumbe, R.	1874	1901 r
Jarvis, H.	1859	1891 r	Power, E.	1869	1908 r
Jennings, N.E.	1867	1874 r	Quilter, J.S.	1880	1907 d
Johnson, J.	1861	1875 r	Roger-Smith, T.	1875	1903 d
Kerr, R.	1862	1904 d	Smallpiece, W.	1888	1896 d
Knightly, T.E.	1863	1904 r	Spiers, W.L.	1887	1904 r
Lansdown, G.	1863	1893 r	Stenning, A.R.	1883	1896 r
Large, W.A.	1882	1907 d	Stevens, J.H.	1862	1876 d
Lees, W.H.	1885	1906 r	Stock, H.W.	1888	1906 d
Legg, G.	1861	1903 r	Street, E.	1885	1918 r
Legg, H.S.	1865	1906 d	Tabberer, B.	1870	1910 d
Long, C.A.	1867	1875	Tanner, A.W.	1883	1920 r
Lovegrove, H.	1887	1920 r	Tolley, J.	1867	1902 d
McDonnel, G.	1880	1905 r	Walker, R.	1875	1896 r
McLachlan, H.	1886	1906 r	Wallen, F.	1878	1915 r
Markham, S.S.	1863	1896 r	Watson, T.H.	1875	1913 d
Marsland, E.	1885	1925 r	Williams, A.	1876	1903 r
Mathews, J.D.	1874	1915 r	Willis, T.W.	1879	1914 d
Meeson, F.R.	1875	1904 r	Wood, S.	1856	1886 d
Mundy, T.E.	1886	1918 r	Woodthorpe, E.	1888	1906 d
Nash, E.	1856	1884 d	Woodward, J.A.J.	1874	1900 d
Notley, R.P.	1875	1903 d			
Parsons, H.	1858	1902 d			

District Surveyors appointed by The London County Council 1890–1939

Name of Surveyor	Appointed	Died or Retired	Name of Surveyor	Appointed	Died or Retired
Barker, F.W.C.	1926	1949 r	Dicksee, B.J.	1893	1926 r
Black, P.J.	1911	1945 r	Dovaston, J.	1926	1951 r
Bromley, H.T.	1911	1937 r	Elton, P.I.	1914	1942 r
Chanter, H.R.	1926	1954 r	Elsey-Smith, R.	1907	1926 r
Coggin, C.T.	1902	1926 r	Fillary, A.A.	1907	1940 r
Crow, A.	1891	1926 r	Fisher, E.J.	1930	1960 r
Cubitt, H.	1926	1945 r	Ford, L.R.	1903	1927 r
Davidge, W.R.	1907	1920 r	Gibson, T.R.L. (M.B.E.)	1930	1957 r
Daubney, C.A.	1911	1925 d	Glasson, A.H.W.	1902	1926 r
Dean, R.R.S.	1934	1964 r			

District Surveyors appointed by The London County Council 1890–1939 (cont.)

Name of Surveyor	Appointed	Died or Retired	Name of Surveyor	Appointed	Died or Retired
Goodchild, J.	1890	1918 r	Morrice, A.G.	1911	1935 r
Greig, B.	1911	1943 r	Mundell, J.E.	1915	1933 r
Griffiths, R.C.	1933	1969 r	Padget, J.I.	1935	1959 r
Hall, G.M.	+1932	1966 r	Pearson, F.G.	1928	1958 r
Hamilton, F.W.	1898	1921 r	Perkins, W.G.	1903	1934 r
Handley, A.L.			Pratt, D.W.	1933	1939
(O.B.E.)	1930	1962 r	Rogers, W.H.	1922	1944 r
Hansom, R.D.	1902	1921 d	Scott, F.P.	1934	1964 r
Hills, O.C.	1902	1930 r	Shiner, L.A.D.	1925	1951 r
Hosking, T.S.	1927	1949 r	Stokes, A.P.	1909	1933 r
Kennard, C.			Surrey, C.W.	1907	1934 r
(O.B.E.)	1927	1961 r	Tarver, E.J.	1890	
Kerr, H.N.	1907	1933 r	Tinslay, T.P.	1926	1947 r
King, R.H.	1934	1962 r	Todd, J.	1907	1930 d
Knight, E.W.	1914	1927 r	Tolley, G.	1907	1940 r
Knight, J.A.G.	1903	1925 d	Verstage,		
Knowles, C.C.	1925	1955 r	A.H.	1911	1940 r
Lane, A.	+1930	1948 d	Walker, I.D.	1934	1966 r
Lees, E.W.	1907	1934 r	Watkinson		
Legge, H.A.	1907	1932 r	H.E.	1926	1954 r
Ling, R.B.	1930	1940 r	Watson, F.P.	1925	1951 r
McDowall, E.D.	1934	1963 r	Whincop, W.G.		
Mayhew, A.E.	1927	1950 r	(M.B.E.)	1926	1954 r
Mayhew, R.H.J.	1911	1939 r	Whyte, D.	1933	1966 r
Mennie, F.E.	1926	1942 d	Woodward,		
Meston, A.C.	1926	1947 r	A.L.	1926	1943 r
Monier-Williams,			Young, E.A.	1911	1930 r
S.F.	1898	1926 r	Young, H.H.	1922	1939 d

+ Mr. Hall appointed Assistant District Surveyor 1930
† Mr. Lane appointed Assistant District Surveyor 1929

District Surveyors appointed by the London County Council as officers of the Council 1939–1964

Name of Surveyor	Appointed	Died or Retired	Name of Surveyor	Appointed	Died or Retired
Back, N.E.	1947		Clarke,		
Bettany, G.A.	1962		D.D.J.	1940	1970 r
Bowers, G.S.	1952	1966 r	Dean, P.T.	1940	1967 r
Boxall, C.A.	1957		Dixon, P.S.	1940	1948 d
Burcham, D.G.	1963		Dufton, J.	1955	
Campbell, E.L.	1964	1969 r	Eves, L.R.	1958	

District Surveyors appointed by the London County Council as officers of the Council 1939–1964 (cont.)

Name of Surveyor	Appointed	Died or Retired	Name of Surveyor	Appointed	Died or Retired
Featherstone, E.P.	1947	1967 r	Nunn, S.J.	1947	
Felgate, F.L.	1947	1972 r	Pitt, P.H.	1964	
Fogden, D.G.	1962		Puddy, G.H.	1959	
Goulden, G.L.	1950	1954 r	Silber, R.M.	1951	
Jones, D.S.	1948	1970 r	Skrimshire, S. G.	1940	1961 d
Kitchen, E.P.H.	1951		Stainton-James, L. C.	1961	1972 r
Lenton, R.T.	1954		Thurlow, R. C.	1961	
			Timms, R. G.	1960	
			Whittaker, J. H.	1940	1969 r

District Surveyors appointed by the Greater London Council as officials of the Council after 1964

Name of Surveyor	Appointed	Died or Retired	Name of Surveyor	Appointed	Died or Retired
Black, W.A.	1966		Martin, R.F.	1969	
Branigan, C.A.	1966		Newby, R.W.	1966	
Jenkinson, A.R.	1969		Parker, D.J.	1969	
Lawrence, S.T.	1966		Shiner, L.T.D.	1970	
Lewis, W.S.	1970		Whitmore, F.W.	1967	
			Williams, A.J.	1967	

Officers of Association from New Constitution in 1884

Year	President	Vice-President	Treasurer	Secretary
1884–5	Edmund Woodthorpe	H.Parsons	C.Fowler	B.Tabberer
1886–7	Henry Parsons	C.Fowler	R.Walker	"
1888–9	Charles Fowler	C.F.Hayward	"	"
1890	Charles Foster Hayward	T.R.Smith	"	"
1891	"	"	J.D.Mathews	"
1892–3	Prof. Thomas Roger Smith	J.D.Mathews	H.H.Collins	"
1894–5	Joseph Douglas Mathews	H.H.Collins	A.Payne	"
1896–7	Hymen Henry Collins	H.Gundry	"	"
1898–9	Horace Gundry	B.Tabbererq	"	F.Wallen
1900–1	Benjamin Tabberer	A.Williams	"	"
1902	Alfred Williams	A.Payne	H.Lovegrove	"
1903–4	Alexander Payne	T.H.Watson	F.Wallen	H.Lovegrove
1905	Thomas Henry Watson	E.D.Drury	"	"
1906	Edward Dru Drury	F.Wallen	J.Clarkson	"

Officers of Association from New Constitution in 1884 (cont.)

Year	President	Vice-President	Treasurer	Secretary
1907	Frederick Wallen	H.Lovegrove	J.Clarkson	B.J.Dicksee
1908	Henry Lovegrove	J.Clarkson	W.Grellier	”
1909	John Clarkson	W.H.Hardcastle	”	”
1910	Wilfred John Hardcastle	A.Conder	”	”
1911	”	J.Goodchild	”	”
1912	Alfred Condor	”	”	”
1913	”	E.Marsland	”	”
1914	Ellis Marsland	W.Grellier	H.A.Legge	”
1915	William Grellier	B.J.Dicksee	”	O.C.Hills
1916	Josiah Goodchild	”	”	”
1917	Bernard John Dicksee	H.Cheston	”	”
1918	”	A.Crow	”	”
1919–20	Arthur Crow	O.C.Hills	”	W.G.Perkins
1921	Osborn Cluse Hills	H.N.Kerr	”	P.J.Black
1922–23	Henry N.Kerr	L.R.Ford	G.Tolley	”
1924	Lawton Robert Ford	C.T.Coggin	”	”
1925	Albert Anthony Fillary	”	”	”
1926–28	”	G.Tolley	A.G.Morrice	”
1929–30	George Tolley	W.G.Perkins	”	”
1931–32	Percy John Black	B.Greig	”	J.Dovaston
1933	William George Perkins	”	W.H.Rogers	”
1934–35	Baxter Greig	P.I.Elton	”	”
1936	Percie Ion Elton	H.H.Young	”	”
1937	Percy John Black	”	”	”
1938–40	”	J.Dovaston	”	C.Kennard
1941	John Dovaston	W.H.Rogers	L.A.D.Shiner	”
1942	”	”	”	D.Whyte
1943	William Herbert Rogers	L.A.D.Shiner	T.P.Tinslay	”
1944	Horace William Cubitt	”	”	”
1945	Lawrence Alexander David Shiner	T.P.Tinslay	A.E.Mayhew	”
1946	Thomas Percival Tinslay	H.E.Watkinson	”	”
1947	Harold Edward Watkinson	F.P.Watson	”	”
1948	Frederick Percy Watson	C.Kennard	E.D.McDowall	”
1949	Cecil Kennard	C.C.Knowles	”	”
1950	Clifford Cyril Knowles	T.L.R.Gibson	”	”
1951	Thomas Reuben Leonard Gibson	D.Whyte	”	R.C.Griffiths
1952	David Whyte	A.L.Handley	”	”
1953	Arthur Lonsdale Handley	F.G.Pearson	”	”
1954	Frederick George Pearson	F.P.Scott	”	”
1955	F.P.Scott	E.D.McDowell	C.Kennard	”
1956	E.D.McDowell	G.M.Hall	”	”

Officers of Association from New Constitution in 1884 (cont.)

Year	President	Vice-President	Treasurer	Secretary
1957	C.Kennard	A.L.Handley	D.D.J.Clarke	R.C.Griffiths
1958	,,	,,	,,	,,
1959	R.C.Griffiths	D.D.J.Clarke	E.P.Featherstone	E.P.H.Kitchen
1960	G.M.Hall	P.T.Dean	,,	,,
1961	D.D.J.Clarke	,,	,,	,,
1962	P.T.Dean	S.J.Nunn	,,	J.Dufton
1963	S.J.Nunn	E.P.Featherstone	J.H.Whittaker	,,
1964	E.P.Featherstone	J.H.Whittaker	E.P.Kitchen	,,
1965	J.H.Whittaker	N.Back	,,	,,
1966	N.E.Back	E.P.H.Kitchen	R.C.Griffiths	,,
1967	E.P.H.Kitchen	R.M.Silber	,,	,,
1968	R.M.Silber	J.Dufton	,,	R.T.Lenton
1969	J.Dufton	L.R.Eves	R.C.Thurlow	,,
1970	L.R.Eves	R.T.Lenton	,,	J.Dufton
1971	R.T.Lenton	C.A.Boxall	,,	D.G.Burcham

INDEX

Page
Act – Building of 1562 12
Act – Building of 1589 14
Act – Building of 1592 14
Act – Building of 1563 15
Act – Building of 1667 30
Act – Building of 1707 37
Act – Building of 1724 37
Act – Building of 1760 38
Act – Building of 1764 39
Act – Building of 1765 40,41
Act – Building of 1767 (City) 41
Act – Building of 1770 (bricks) 42
Act – Building of 1771 (St.Botolph, Aldgate) 42
Act – Building of 1772 49
Act – Building of 1774 49
Act – Building of 1844 60
Act – Building of 1855 75
Act – Building of 1878 82
Act – Building of 1882 83
Act – Building of 1894 93
Act – Building of 1905 97
Act – Building of 1909 99
Act – Building of 1930 111
Act – Building of 1935 112
Act – Building of 1939 112
Addendum I 1947-1954 133
Addendum II 1954-1972 139
Advertisement Regulations 1948 136
Air Raids – description 121,122
Air Raid Precautions 1915-1918 101
Air Raid Precautions 1939 118
Air Raids - first in Second World War 119
Air Raid Shelters 119,121
Aldermen in 1100 7
Alfred the Great 3
Ancient lights 6
Antwerp - debris clearance 126
Appeals to Council against D.S. 114
Appeals to Petty Sessions against D.S. 99
Appeals to Tribunal 97
Apprentices (1667) 33
Arbitration - Official Referees (1844) 63
Arbitration by Surveyors 34
Architects - not professionals 30
Armies - (16th Century) 16
Assize of Buildings 6

Balconies (1661) 26
Barbon Dr. Nicholas 35
Bazalgette, Sir Joseph 86
Besant - Sir Walter 7
Bitumastic roof covering (1810) 56
Black Death 10
Boadicea 3
Bomb damage 1915-1918 102
Bombing of London 1915-1918 101
Bombing of London 1940 121,122
Borough boundaries altered 1963 139
Borough Councils formed 1899 95
Borough Councils complaints re D.S. 100
Brest–summers - to be of oak 32
Brest–summers - height of 33

Page
Bricks - for jambs, heads and sills 20
Bricks - length for wall thicknesses 20
Bricks - London City of 19
Bricks - making of (17th Century) 21
Bricks - making of (1770) 42
Bricks - price of (17th Century) 21
Bricks - quality of (1891) 90
Bricks - standard size (17th Century) 21
British Standards Institute 108,109
British Standards– in Bylaws 137
Brittle fracture (1967) 141
Building Act Case (1302) 9
Building Bylaws (1937) 112
Building Bylaws (1952) 137
Building Bylaws (1964) 140,141
Building Classification (1667) 31
Building Classification (1774) 49
Building Classification (1844) 63
Building Control outside Inner London 139
Building licences 14,20,22,24
Building lines (1821) 58
Building lines (1855) 74,78
Building lines (Case in 1864) 79
Building lines (1878) 82
Building lines (Certification 1890) 88
Building lines (1894) 93
Building lines (1964) 145
Building Notices (1667) 32
Building Notices (1774) 52
Building Notices (1844) 61
Building Notices (1855) 76
Building Notices (1965) 143
Building Regulations 1965, The 144
Building Regulation in London, cost of 149
Building Trades Operatives in Rescue
Service 119
Buildings - Prefabricated (1598) 15
Burial grounds (16th Century) 16
Bylaws (12th Century) 4,6,7,20
Bylaws (1857) on streets 77
Bylaws (1878) 82
Bylaws (1882) concrete buildings 83
Bylaws (1891) 90
Bylaws (1915) lamps and signs 102
powers to make 112
Bylaws (1964) 140

Calculations - checking of 135
Canute, King 4
Carpenters 9
Carpenters Company 24,33
Carpenters - Sworn Masters 44
Canton 11
Cellars (Henry III's reign) 7
Cellars shape of (1619) 20
Cellars, banned 20
Certification - building lines 88,91
Certification - open spaces 91
Changes in use of buildings (1620) 20
Charles I Proclamation (1625) 20
Charles I Ordinance (1630) 22
Charles II Proclamation (1661) 26

Page

Charles II - in Great Fire 28
Charles II Proclamation (1666) 29
Charles II Act of 1667 30
Charles II - Surrender of City Charter 35
Cheapside - Tournament in 9
Cheapside - Market in 27
Chimneys (12th Century) 7
Chimneys (15th Century) 10
Chimneys and Sweeps (18th & 19th Centuries) 55
Cholera outbreaks (1855) 71
Churches (13th & 14th Centuries) 9
Churches and Chapels exempt 24
City Chamberlain (1667) 32
City Companies (17th Century) 46
City Rebuilding (1667) 34
City Treasury (1667) 32
City Viewers 43,44,45
City Wall 27
Civic Amenities Act 1967 147
Civic Defence Act 1939 119
Civil Defence - Statistics 128
Civil War 23,27
Classification after war damage 127
Clean Air Act (1956) 145
Cleansing - Streets in City (1764-1770) 41
Cleansing - Footpaths (1817) 57
Cleansing - Footpaths (1834) 59
Coal Tax (1667) 33
Collapse of buildings (1845) 65
Collapse of buildings (1835-1857) 79
Collapse of buildings (1875) 82
Commissioners for Buildings 19,20,22,24
Commissioners of Paving (1855) 73
Commissioners of Police (1855) 76,78
Commissioners of Police (1882) 83
Commissioners for Rebuilding (1667) 30
Commissioners of Sewers (1760) 39
Commissioners of Sewers (1767) 41
Commissioners of Sewers (1771) 43
Commissioners of Sewers (1817) 57
Commissioners of Sewers (1834) 59
Commissioners of Sewers (1848) 69
Commissioners of Sewers (1854) 73
Commissioners of Sewers (1855) 76
Commissioners of Sewers - History of 84
Commissioners of Works and Buildings (1844) 62,65
Common Council (12th Century) 8,11
Common Council (14th Century) 10
Common Informer 43,49,71
Commonwealth, Act of 1656 24
Compensation - loss of property (1666) 29
Compensation - use of party wall (1765) 41
Completion surveys (1760) 39
Completion surveys (1774) 52
Compulsory purchase (1667) 32
Compulsory service on roads (1563) 15
Concrete Buildings - Bylaws (1882) 83
Concrete Foundations (1879) 82
Concrete casing to steelwork (1909) 99
Consent given by District Surveyors 141
Control of Office & Industry Act 1965 147
Cost of building - stone/timber (1661) 26
Cost of living (16th Century) 12
Council Schools - exemption of 135
County of London - formation of 87
County Hall - building of, 1922 103
Court cases (1863-1875) 79
Court cases, LCC schools (1909) 100
Court cases, Public House (1915) 100
Court cases, Temporary Structure (1902) 100
Court cases, Virgin soil 85
Coventry - debris clearance 126
Cromwell - fines on building 14

Page

Crow, Arthur 2
Cubical extent - limit (1844) 63
Cubical extent - limit (1855) 75
Cubical extent - limit (1890) 89
Crystal Palace (1851) 67

Damage - Air Raid - in City 123
Damp proof courses (1879) 82
Dance, George - reports by 48
Dangerous structure procedure (1724) 37
Dangerous structure procedure (1760) 39
Dangerous structure procedure (1774) 52
Dangerous structure procedure (1855) 76
Dangerous structure procedure (1869) 78
Dangerous structure procedure (1882) 83
Dangerous structure procedure (1939) 114
Dangerous structures (1835) 79
Dangerous structures in City (1848) 69
Dangerous structures, numbers of (1920) 104
Dangerous structures, report (1742) 48
Debris clearance (1940) 123,124
Delegation to Boroughs - temporary structures 113
Delegation to Boroughs - dangerous structures 114
Departments, new, of G.L.C. 140
Deputy District Surveyors (1844) 63
Deputy District Surveyors (1855) 76
Destruction of City buildings 123
Developers (17th Century) 35
Development charges (1947) 136
District Boards (1855) 71,73
District Boards, abolition of (1899) 95
District Surveyors appointed:–
- under 1774 Act 151-152
- under 1844 Act 152
- under 1855 Act 153
- by L.C.C. (1890-1939) 154-155
- as officers of L.C.C. (1939-1964) 155
- by GLC after 1964 156
- by Metropolitan Board of Works 75

District Surveyors -
conditions of appointment (1889) 87
conditions of appointment (1894) 94
conditions of appointment (1939) 114
District Surveyors, duties of (1844) 62
District Surveyors, duties during War 127
District Surveyors, duties as Group Surveyors 124
District Surveyors, duties as Rescue officers 121
District Surveyors, duties - Rescue services . 118
District Surveyors, duties - Town Planning . 137
District Surveyors Examination Board (1941) 131
District Surveyors - first so entitled (1844) . 61
District Surveyors - honours awarded 128
District Surveyors - in 1774 and 1832 54
District Surveyors - incomes inadequate (1907) 98
District Surveyors - incomes of (1848-1853) 150
District Surveyors - oaths administered (1844) 63
District Surveyors - retirements 138
District Surveyors - salaries proposed for (1889) 87
District Surveyors - salaries proposed for (1905) 97
District Surveyors - salaries proposed for (1936) 110
District Surveyors - staff and premises (1865-1889) 80
District Surveyors - under G.L.C. 139
District Surveyors - Service - cost of 148

Page
District Surveyors' Association ...65,68,78,80,81
- Amendments to 1894 Act 94
- Amendments - Articles changed (1940) 131
- Amendments - Centenary lunch (1945) 131
- Amendments - formation of 64
- Amendments - meetings at R.I.B.A. 109
- Amendments - officers since 1884 ...156-158
- Amendments - Questions 148
- Amendments - Reception (1967) 148
Districts - (1774) 54
Districts - (1890) 88
Districts - boundary changes (1965) 149
Districts - rearranged (1920) 104
Districts - regraded 134
Docks, development of (19th Century) 96
Doomsday book 4
Drains (1667) 33
Drains - Bylaws 143

Edward I 6
Edward III 6,9
Elections to District Boards (1855) 73
Elections to Metropolitan Board of Works .. 73
Elizabeth's Acts (1562) 12
Elizabeth's Acts (1589-1592) 14
Elizabeth's Acts (1563) 15
Encroachments on Highways 7
Enforcement procedure (1844) 65
Enforcement procedure (1855) 76
Enquiry into District Surveyors work
(1854) 67
Entry - powers of 116
Euston Road - formation of 39
Euston Road (1821) 57
Euston Road (1855) 74
Examination Board for Qualifying
Certificate 114
Examination by R.I.B.A. (1855) 76
Exemptions from Building Act (1589-1630) 22
Exemptions from Building Act (1939) 116
Explosion forces 121

Fees - for checking setting-out (1667) 32
Fees - monthly returns (1844) 63
Fees - monthly returns (1855) 76
Fees - scale of (1774) 52
Fees - scale of (1844) 64
Fees - scale of (1855) 71
Fees - scale of (1865-1889) 80
Fees - scale of (1965) 143
Festival of Britain (1951) 133
Fires of 961 and 1087 7
Fires of 1136 6
Fires of 1661 26
Fires of 1666 28
Fire Brigade - formation 37
Fire Brigade (1833) 78
Fire Court (1667) 33
Fire Engines (1774) 52
Fire Insurance (17th Century) 36
Fire Insurance (18th Century) 40
Fire Insurance Companies 78
Fire Precautions Act (1971) 145
Fire Precautions in mediaeval days 7
Fire resisting construction (1905) 97
Fire resisting materials (1894) 93
Fitz Ailwyn, Henry 4,6,20
Fitz Ailwyn Assize 4,7
Flats in 1400 10
Fleet, river 9
Flooding from Thames (1928) 105
Floor area - limited (1774) 50
Flying bombs - damage by 128
Folkmoots 4,7
Foundations (1667) 33

Page
Foundations, cases on "virgin soil" 85
Framed buildings(1909) 99
Freemen (14th Century) 10
Freemen (16th Century) 13
Frontage lines 9
Frontage lines (1878) 82
Fronts of buildings - perpendicular (1771). 43

Gaming Act (1968) 145
Gas Regulations (1955) 145
Glass in 1400 10
G.L.C. (General Powers) Acts 1965-1968 . 143
Gomme, Sir Lawrence 3,5
Great Fire of London (1666) 28
Great Fire of London (1940) 122
Greater London - creation of (1963) 139
Growth of London (18th Century) 53
Guildhall 11
Guildhall - destroyed 28
Guilds in 14th Century 10
Guilds in 15th Century 11
Guilds in 16th Century 13

Hackney coaches (1660) 27
Hardcore salvaged in War 125
Hearth money 29
Height of buildings (1667) 34
Height of buildings (1774) 50
Height of buildings (1844) 64
Height of buildings (1855) 76,77
Height of buildings (1890) 89
Height of buildings (1894) 93,94
Height of buildings (1939) 112
Height of buildings (1954) 137
Height of rooms (1619) 19
Height of rooms (1620) 20
Height of rooms (1855) 75
Height of rooms (1894) 94
Height of rooms (1964) 140
Henry III 5,10
Henry VII 23
Henry VIII 13
High buildings in London 140
Highways Act (1959) 145
Highways - condition of (1660) 27
Highways - work by Water Companies 40
Hoardings - around dangerous structures
(1760) 39
Hoardings - licences (1760) 40
Hooke, Robert 29,34,43,47
Hospitals - exemption of 135
Hospitals - exemption of (1656) 24
Hustings, Court of 6

Immigrants (16th Century) 12
Inspectors of Nuisances (1855) 71
Insurance - fire (17th Century) 36
Irregularity - Notices of (1844) 61
Irregularity - Notices of (1855) 76
Irregularities, survey of (1667) 34

James I - Act of 1607 18
James I - Decree of 1615 18
James I - Proclamation (1603) 18
James I - Proclamation (1619) 18
James I - Proclamation (1620) 20
James I - Proclamation (1621) 21
Jerman, Edward 29,34
Jerry building (17th Century) 35
King John 5
Oliver, John 43,47
Justices - duties of 15
Justices of the Peace -
- building restrictions 12,18
- appoint surveyors (1774) 51

	Page
Justices of the Peace	
- appoint surveyors (1844)	61
Jutting prohibited (1619)	20
Landlords, of tenements	23
Lead on roofs (12th Century)	6
Leadenhall Market	11
Leases - voided by War action (1666)	28
Licence - as ale-house (17th Century)	24
Licence - extension beyond building line (1855)	74,78
Licences - temporary structures (1939)	113
Lighting - street - in City (1767)	41
Lighting and ventilation of rooms (1894)	94
Lime	8
Lines of frontage (1894)	93
Local Government Act (1888)	86
Lodgers prohibited (1580)	14
London Boroughs created (1963)	139
London Bridge	3,6
London Bridge - exemption of buildings on	22,26,37,38
London Building Act (1894)	93
London Building Act (Ammendment) Act (1905) ,,,,,	97
London Building Act (1930)	111
London Building Act (Amendment) Act 1935	112
London Building Act (Amendment) Act 1939	112
London Building Acts and Bylaws,- list of	143
L.C.C. - formation of	87
L.C.C. - growth of	103
L.C.C. - (General Powers) Act (1890)	88,90
L.C.C. - (General Powers) Act (1909)	99
L.C.C. - (General Powers) Act (1915)	102
L.C.C. - (General Powers) Act (1920)	105
L.C.C. - (General Powers) Act (1923)	105
L.C.C. - (General Powers) Act (1926)	105
L.C.C. - (General Powers) Act (1928)	105
L.C.C. - (General Powers) Act (1954)	137
L.C.C. - (General Powers) Act (1954, '55, '56, '58, '59)	142
London Government Act (1899)	95
London Government Act (1963)	139
London Growth of (17th Century)	24
London Master Builders Assn. - Rescue Service	119
London - overcrowding (16th Century)	12,16
London - overcrowding (17th Century)	18,27
London under Danes & Saxons	4
London under Romans	3,5
Lord Mayor - to appoint District Surveyors (1774)	51
Lord Mayor - to appoint District Surveyors (1844)	61
Low-lying land	105
Magna Carta	5
Markets - street (1667)	34
Marylebone - wells	9
Masons	9
Masons as sworn Masters (14th Century)	44
Mayor - as Judge	6
Mayor - building restrictions	13
Mayor - first in London	5
May, Hugh	29
Means of escape in case of fire (1894)	93
Means of escape in case of fire (1905)	97
Means of escape in case of fire (1939)	113
Medical Officers of Health (1855)	71
Metal salvaged in war	125
Metropolitan Board of Works	73-75,86
Metropolitan Fire Act (1865)	78
Metropolitan Water Board	100

	Page
Metropolis Local Management Act (1855)	71
Metropolis Management Amendment Act (1862)	77
Metropolis Management Act (1878)	82
Metropolis Management Act (1882)	83
Michael Angelo Taylor's Act (1817)	56
Mills, Peter	29,34,43
Mithras, Temple of	5
Modifications of Bylaws by District Surveyors	141
Monument to fire of 1666	33
Naming of Streets (in City) (1767)	41
Naming of Streets (1855)	73
Naming of Streets (1882)	83
Naming of Streets (1939)	112
Nash, John	53
New buildings restricted	12,14,15,18,21,24,25
Notice, building (1667)	32
Notice, building (1774)	52
Notice, building (1844)	61
Notice, building (1855)	76
Notice, building (1965)	143
Numbering of houses (in City) (1767)	41
Numbering of houses (1855)	73
Numbering of houses (1882)	83
Numbering of houses (1939)	112
Obstructions - removal of (1771)	43
Obstructions - on highway (1817)	57
Occupation of houses - restricted (1603)	18
Officers of District Surveyors Association..	156-158
Offices, Shops and Railway Premises Act 1963	146
Official Referees	62,63,65,70,76
Oil-fired heating installations - Bylaws	141
Oliver, John	34
Open spaces around buildings (1844)	64
Open spaces around buildings (1882)	83
Open spaces around buildings (1894)	93
Overcrowding - mediaeval days	12,16,18,22
Overcrowding - 19th Century	72,93,96
Panel walls - thickness of (1909)	99
Parapets required (1707)	37
Party walls (1667)	32
Party walls (1844)	63
Party walls - openings in (1774)	50
Party walls - parapets (1774)	50
Party walls - reinforced concrete (1915)	102
Party walls - timber (1774)	50
Party walls - three feet thick	6
Paving Act (1817)	56
Paving of streets in City (1767)	41
Paving of streets in Aldgate (1771)	43
Pepys, Samuel	28
Peter Mills	43
Petty, Sir William	25,28
Pipes, rainwater (1667)	32
Plagues	13,16,18,28,60
Plantagenets	5,10
Plastering, Bylaws on (1890)	89
Population of London (16th Century)	16
Population of London (17th Century)	25,27
Population of London (1845)	60
Population of London (1855)	70
Population of London (19th Century)	96
Portsmouth - debris clearance	126
Post Office Act (1969)	146
Power of entry for builders (1765)	41
Powers of entry for District Surveyors (1939)	116
Pratt, Roger	29
Prefabricated buildings (1598)	15

Page
Prefabricated houses (1944) 133
Price of building materials (1667) 32
Price rises (16th Century) 12
Price rises (17th Century) 25
Proclamations (1580) 12
Proclamations (1603) 18
Proclamations (1619) 18
Proclamations (1620) 20
Proclamations (1621) 21
Proclamations (1625) 20
Proclamations (1661) 26
Proclamations (1666) 29
Proclamations (1667) 33
Proclamations (1671) 35
Projections - from buildings (1774) 51
Projections - limitation of - mediaeval days 8
Projections - limitation of (1667) 32
Public executions (1850, 1868) 67
Public buildings - to approval of District
Surveyors 75
Public buildings - 1939 Act 112
Punch - article on Surveyors (1890) 91
Purprestures 8

Qualifying Certificate as District Surveyor
(1844) 62
Qualifying Certificate as District Surveyor
(1855) 76
Queen Anne style 38
Queen Victoria 60

Rakers 8,27
Refuse in mediaeval days 10
Refuse in 16th and 17th Centuries 16
Registrar of Metropolitan Buildings .. 63,65,70,76
Reinforced concrete - Power to make
Bylaws (1909) 99
Reinforced concrete - Regulations (1915) ... 102
Reinstatement after fire in 1760 40
Repairs to war damaged buildings 128,130
Rescue Service - formation of 118
Rescue Service - organisation 120,127
Restoration 26
Restrictions on building work (1920) 104
Richard I 5
Roads (1563) 15,16
Robert Hooke 43,47
Rockets - damage caused by 128
Roman walls 11
Romans 3,5
Ronan Point 144
Roof coverings - mediaeval days 8,9
Roof coverings (1774) 51
Roof coverings (1810) 56
Roof escapes (1905) 97
Royal Commission on Local Government ... 105
Royal Commission on Local Government
in London (1922) 105
R.I.B.A. - District Surveyors Exam 76
R.I.B.A. - premises 80,81
Ruinous buildings - not to be repaired 20
Ruskin, John - on ruinous buildings (1835) 79

Salaries first proposed for District
Surveyors (1889) 87
Salaries of Statutory Surveyors (1667) 35
Salvaged materials in war 125
Sanitary Inspectors (1855) 72
Sanitary Inspectors (1899) 95
Scaffolding in mediaeval days 9
Scale of Fees (1744) 52
Scale of Fees (1844) 64
Scale of Fees (1855) 71
Scale of Fees (1865-1889) 80
Scale of Fees (1965) 143

Page
Scavagers 43
Second World War 119
Setting-out of party walls (1667) 32
Sewers (1667) 33
Sewers (1845) 60
Sewers Commissioners of - history of 84
Shakespeare 16
Shops - arches over 20
Shops - pilasters 20
Sign posts (1667) 33
Sky signs - prohibition (1891) 89,90
Snow clearance from streets 42
Special structures (1774) 49
Speculative building (17th Century) 36
St. Pauls 4,6,7,27,28
St. Pauls rebuilding (1667) 34
Star Chamber 14,17,18
Star Chamber - decree of 20
Star Chamber - history of 23
Statutory Surveyors - first 34
Steel framed buildings (1909) 99
Stone - buildings to be of (1615) 20
Stone - party walls to be of 6
Street cleaning (16th Century) 13
Street lighting (1415) 11
Street widening (1666) 29,30
Streets, width of (1844) 63
Streets, width of (1855) 74
Stresses for reinforced concrete (1915) 102
Stuarts, The 18
Subletting - prohibition of 14
Superintending Architects of Metropolitan
Buildings (1855) 76
Superintending Architects 148
Superstructure - under Surveyors directions
(1667) 32
Survey of London (1666) 29
Survey on completion of new building
(1760) 39
Surveyor of His Majesties Works (1661) 26
Surveyors Oath (1774) 51
Surveyors of roads (1563) 15
Surveyors Institute (1880) 80
Surveyors Institute (1889) 87

Tax on coal (1667) 33
Temporary buildings (1882) 83
Temporary buildings (1939) 113
Temporary buildings - delegation to
Boroughs 146
Thames - River in 1660 27
Theatres (16th Century) 16
Thermal Insulation of Industrial Buildings
Act 1957 147
Tiles on roofs (12th Century) 6,7
Timber - Bylaws 1937 112
Timber - framed buildings 16
Timber - near chimneys (1667) 33
Timber - prevention of in party walls (1724) 38
Timber - prevention of in party walls (1764) 39
Timber - prevention of in all walls (1765) .. 40
Timber - proximity to flues (1707) 37
Timber - scarcity of 20
Timber - sizes in 1667 Act 32
Tolls in Euston Road (1821) 58
Tower of London 4
Town and Country Planning Act, 1932 111
Town and Country Planning Act, 1944 131
Town and Country Planning Act, 1947 136
Town and Country Planning Act, 1953, '54
'59, '68 147
Town Planning - during Elizabeth I's reign 13,14
Town Planning - after 1666 fire 34
Town Planning (17th Century) 35
Town Planning (1774) 53

Page
Town Planning - District Surveyors duties (1925) 105
Town Planning - schemes (1934) 108
Town Planning - schemes (1942) 128,131
Trade on highways (1817) 57
Trades - Noisome and perilous (1667) 33
Tribunal of Appeal - constitution changed (1939) 115
Tribunal of Appeal - powers extended (1894) 94
Tribunal of Appeal - started 1890 88,89

Underground rooms (18th Century) 53
Underground rooms (1844) 64
Underground rooms (1855) 69,72
Uniting of buildings (1774) 50
Uniting of buildings (1844) 63
Uniting of buildings (1855) 75

Ventilation of rooms (1619) 19
Vestries (1855) 72
Vestries - abolition of (1899) 95

Wages - in mediaeval days 7
Wages - in time of Elizabeth I 12
Wages - (1667) 32
Waivers of Bylaws - by District Surveyors ... 141
Walbrook 9
Walls - of concrete (1882) 83
Walls - to be of brick or stone (1607) 18,21

Page
Walls - to go straight up 20
Walls,- thickness of (1619) 20
Walls - thickness of (1620) 21
Walls - thickness of (1667) 30-33
Walls - thickness of (1707) 37
Walls - thickness of (1764) 39
Walls - thickness of (1774) 49
Walls - thickness of (1844) 63
Walls - thickness of (1855) 76
War damage repairs 128,130
War debris survey and disposal service 124,125,127-129
Wardmotes 7
Wards in 1100 7
Water Pipes in mediaeval days 9
Welding (1932) 108
Westminster)..., ... 4,27
Widening of streets after 1666 30,32,34
Widths of streets (1857) 77,78
William The Conqueror 4
Winchester 4
Whittington, Mayor 11
Wind loading increased 141
Window Tax - repealed 1851 95
Windows - at time of Richard I 7
Windows (1400) 10
Windows - to be recessed (1774) 51
Windows - to be recessed (1855) 75
Wool 11
Wren, Dr. 29,30